D1736553

# The Best of Our Lives

## SHARING THE SECRETS OF A
## HEALTHY AND HAPPY RETIRED LIFE

*It's a joy a
worship the Savoir
with you.*

*Trisha & John*

# The Best of Our Lives

## SHARING THE SECRETS OF A
## HEALTHY AND HAPPY RETIRED LIFE

TRISHA AND JOHN PARKER

LANGDON STREET PRESS

Copyright © 2009 by Trisha and John Parker. All rights reserved.

Langdon Street Press
212 3rd Avenue North, Suite 290
Minneapolis, MN 55401
612.455.2293
www.langdonstreetpress.com

All rights reserved. No part of this publication may be reproduced, stored in a retrieval system, or transmitted, in any form or by any means, electronic, mechanical, photocopying, recording, or otherwise, without the written prior permission of the author.

ISBN - 978-1-934938-49-2
ISBN - 1-934938-49-1
LCCN - 2009936274

**Book sales for North America and international:**
Itasca Books, 3501 Highway 100 South, Suite 220
Minneapolis, MN 55416
Phone: 952.345.4488 (toll free 1.800.901.3480)
Fax: 952.920.0541; email to orders@itascabooks.com

Cover Design by Kristeen Wegner
Typeset by Peggy LeTrent
Cover photos by Jen Parker Photography
Edited by Sheryl Trittin

Website: thebestofourlives.com

*Printed in the United States of America*

# DEDICATION

This book is dedicated to our family and friends who have filled our lives with love and joy. We especially want to acknowledge our parents, Mary and Cecil Nystrom and Marty and Frank Parker, for being wonderful role models and instilling positive values. We also dedicate this book to our children and grandchildren, Michael, Jennifer, Lucy, Jack, and Charles Parker, David and Michelle Anne Parker, and Daniel, Michelle, and Juliette Parker. Thank you all for your love, laughter, and support.

Trisha & John

# TABLE OF CONTENTS

*May you build a ladder to the stars, and climb on*
*every rung, may you stay forever young.*
—Bob Dylan

# CHAPTER 1

# JUST THE BEGINNING
*By John*

Well, fellow boomers, we made it. Over the next few years, nearly eighty million of us will retire, and what a ride it's been. With all due respect to the greatest generation, we have survived socialism, communism, racism, sexism, rock 'n' roll, disco, hip-hop, free love, safe sex, hippies, yuppies, Gen Xers, stock market booms and crashes, assassinations, terrorist attacks, predictions of global cooling and warming, and far too many wars.

A majority of us married, some more than once, while others remained single by choice or circumstance. Many of us who had children have now become grandparents. Our generation has worked hard, played hard, and experienced all the ups and downs life could throw at us. Guess what? That was just the beginning; *The Best of Our Lives* is here now.

*The Best of Our Lives* is our philosophy of living as retired persons. We consider it a time of life when work is voluntary, being fulfilled is mandatory, sharing good fortune is its own reward, and living with passion and excitement is the order of the day. No rocking chairs just yet, thank you.

We are Trisha and John Parker, a married couple who retired early after working very hard in our respective careers. Trisha was an executive in the corporate world, and I was a college professor. As kids, we grew up in middle-class families and lived very normal lives. We met in high school and began dating a couple of years later. After a very long courtship, we married and started a family. We are blessed with three wonderful sons and have always had a very close-knit and loving family. When the boys married, our family gained three exceptional daughters. We now have four beautiful grandchildren, and like most grandparents, are looking forward to many more in the years to come.

As our sons were growing up, our family never really took vacations in the typical sense. The boys were very active in both school and summer sports. In the summer, any vacation time we had was spent following their teams. We loved every minute and would not trade those times together for anything in the world. I'm sure many of you have had similar experiences. We could never figure out how other people were paying for those expensive vacations anyway.

Life was good, but incredibly busy. With kids and work, the years just seemed to fly by. Trisha had become a workaholic, and with each promotion, her work responsibilities and schedule became more impossible. She rarely took any time off, and when she did, it was only to rest up for more work. I worried all the stress was beginning to take a toll on her health. It was at this time I began to plan on getting her away for awhile.

The boys were at a point in their lives when they were finishing school and starting careers. It seemed like the perfect time for us to go on that vacation we had never taken. I suggested we sign up for our first cruise. It took a bit of persuading, but Trisha finally agreed, and off we went. Neither of us knew it at the time, but it was to be a life-altering decision.

We later learned that some people waiting to board the ship had referred to Trisha as "the woman on her cell phone." She was constantly talking to her staff back at the office. This continued until we got to our cabin, at which point I politely threatened to throw her phone into the water. Fortunately for both of us, when the ship got out to sea, she could no longer get reception. For the next ten days, we had no telephone calls, no e-mails, no family issues, and no business or school activities. What we did have was delicious food, dancing, entertainment, socializing, new sights, and tons of fun. The bug had bitten and our lives were changed forever. We jokingly began to fantasize about living the rest of our lives more like a pleasure cruise, with less stress, more fun, and lots of adventure. Although it started as a fantasy, the more we talked about it, the more we became convinced we could make it happen.

Back home, the first question we asked was, "How soon can we retire?" Trisha has an extensive background in and a true gift for managing finances, so we put her expertise to work. She developed a financial plan that allowed us to retire a few years early. She has shared her ideas on financial planning and management for retirees in subsequent chapters.

When our retirement became a reality, we were determined to make it something very special. In the past, we had rarely looked beyond the present day's activities and responsibilities. Now, we consciously set goals and made plans. Overall, our strategy was to enjoy our personal relationship even more than before, meet and bring new people into our lives, reconnect with old friends, share our good fortune, and see new places to experience great adventures.

We didn't claim to have all the answers, but realized our retirement was becoming a wonderful work in progress, one that we discussed and modified on a daily basis. And that is an important point. We began to look forward to each day with excitement and passion, consciously planning our activities, with lots of room for spontaneity. We began living what we now call *The Best of Our Lives*. When our family or friends call us, they often begin the conversation with, "Where are you?"

Are we so different from other retired people? You can be the judge, but I'll tell you we are on to something wonderful. Even though we both enjoyed successful careers, never in our lives have we felt so fulfilled. It's exciting to wake up each morning looking forward to what the new day will bring.

When I think back, I realize that throughout our marriage, Trisha and I had never really talked much about retirement. We were always busy and never considered we might get old. Then, when the boys began to leave home, reality set in. When we finally did discuss it, we thought about many of the retired people we had known throughout our lives. It seemed several had simply stopped working when they reached retirement age. At that point, their lives stayed pretty much the same, only without the work. Quite a few remained in the same location, traveled very little, and appeared to live pretty routine lives. A number of them became babysitters for their grandchildren, some working harder than before. Still others appeared to have chosen one activity, like golf or fishing, and literally did the same thing most every day. None of these lifestyles seemed right for us.

Now let's make sure everyone understands. None of the previous remarks are criticisms of anyone. We truly believe every retired person should spend his or her retirement years as they wish. If you want to play golf every day, by all means do so. We love our grandkids and schedule plenty of time with them, often babysitting. That's what we want to do. We would never be so arrogant as to criticize someone for their choice of lifestyle.

Our choice, and the point of this book, is very simple. We do not consider retirement an end, but rather a beginning. We see it as an opportunity to redefine one's life. Remember being young and everyone asking you what you wanted to be when you grew up? Well, what do you want to be when you retire? Where do you want to live? What do you want to see and experience? You have probably worked very hard in your life, whether it was for a job, raising a family, or both. It's time to enjoy the fruits of your labor.

Trisha and I have found that retirement has given us newfound freedom and the time to explore and experience different opportunities. We seek out as many of these opportunities as possible. Along the way we have made a number of wonderful discoveries that clearly benefit our lives in retirement. We share our many discoveries in this book.

It should be noted that, for the most part, we have lived very modest lives. There have been numerous times, as with most families, we wondered how we would ever pay our bills. As a result of careful planning, we are more comfortable now, but not wealthy. To this day we are very frugal, and if a coupon cannot be used or an item is not on sale, we probably aren't going to buy it. This is an important point, because *The Best of Our Lives* is about the quality of life, not wealth or possessions. It's about living and loving passionately, fulfillment and happiness, peace and security, friendships and adventures, and living the best you can live.

At this point, you might be asking yourself about our qualifications to give retirement advice. It's a fair question. The obvious answer is that our collective education, training, careers, and experiences all lend themselves to a certain degree of expertise in each of the areas we have covered. Most of our credibility, however, comes from the fact that we really are living and doing the things we write about in this book.

Interestingly, the idea for this book did not completely originate with us, but resulted from conversations with family members and friends. We have often been asked to share our ideas on financial planning, budget traveling, relationships, and even Trisha's fitness program. After hearing the comment "You two should write a book" a few times, we began to organize our ideas. The result is *The Best of Our Lives*, in which we have combined our experiences and advice with the research and expertise of others.

As you continue to read through the information and suggestions we have presented in *The Best of Our Lives*, please keep in mind our intention has never been to provide anyone with an exact blueprint for retirement. Every retired person or couple should consider this information and use it to create a personal and unique retirement plan of their own. Do more research, be creative, and, most importantly, have a good time. From the beginning, our goal in writing this book has been to inspire readers to take charge of their retirements and make them the best times of their lives. We wish you all happiness and good fortune. Remember, this is just the beginning.

*A positive attitude may not solve all your problems, but it will annoy enough people to make it worth the effort.*
—Herm Albright

CHAPTER 2

# BE POSITIVE AND REDUCE YOUR STRESS
*By John*

Simply stated, in living *The Best of Our Lives,* Trisha and I are convinced that a key component is developing and maintaining a positive attitude. I'm sure you've heard this advice before, but do you truly strive to make it an active part of your life? In this chapter, we will examine the important role a positive attitude plays in our health and well-being, and introduce a number of principles and suggestions Trisha and I follow to manage our stress. At our age, we should all be taking advantage of the numerous benefits a positive attitude can provide.

In our research on this topic, we have found numerous studies that scientifically affirm the importance of a positive attitude, especially for those over fifty. In fact, the National Institutes of Health is currently funding nearly fifty grants for research on the effects of optimism. The evidence is so convincing, we believe it might be impossible for a person to be truly healthy, happy, or prosperous without a positive attitude. Here are some research examples:

- A fascinating seven-year investigation, conducted at the University of Texas, concluded a positive attitude may actually delay the aging process. Based on study findings, researchers theorized that emotions alter the chemical balance of the body, which results in beneficial physical changes. Subjects with positive attitudes became less frail and maintained better endurance and strength over time than those who were less positive.
- A research team from North Carolina State University examined the possible effects of positive attitude on memory performance. After analyzing the results, they concluded that "a positive attitude can promote effective functioning" (Memory and Aging in Context/Hess, T. M.). In other words, a better attitude produces a better memory.
- In a landmark investigation, the Ohio Longitudinal Study of Aging and Retirement, conducted over a twenty-year period, found that people over fifty who held a more positive attitude about aging lived longer than those with a more negative attitude. Of the almost 1,200 subjects, those with more positive attitudes lived an

average of 7.6 years longer than the other subjects (Ohio Longitudinal Study of Aging and Retirement/Atchley, R.).

A positive attitude can actually help you live longer! Heard enough? OK, let's all be positive. If you are like me, you may sometimes struggle with this suggestion. When I wake up in the morning, I'm not very social and need plenty of time before I can face the world. Then, when my day begins, I have a tendency to let little things annoy me, such as bad drivers, tardiness, loud music, barking dogs, and a host of other irritants. These are typical daily stressors, and when stress hits me, I often want to hit back. Not physically, but emotionally and sometimes verbally. Trisha once laughed hysterically when she heard me barking at a neighbor's poodle that had awakened me. I wasn't completely serious, but I was definitely stressed. How we manage our stress, whether it stems from everyday irritants or the truly traumatic events in our lives, is defined as attitude, or our predisposition to react positively, negatively, or neutrally toward people, objects, or events.

Whenever I discuss maintaining a positive attitude, I wish everyone could meet my wife Trisha. There would be no reason to elaborate further. As the story goes, if you looked up *positive attitude* in the dictionary, you would see her picture. That probably sounds like an exaggeration, but I swear to you it's true. She awakes every morning, smiles, and, in a lilting voice, says, "good morning." From that point, every situation, even ones that would make most of us crazy, is met with a genuine calm that I envy. Stressful situations are merely problems to be solved, and she goes about solving them in a very positive manner. She manages her stress very well. At night, she goes to sleep very quickly, actually in seconds, and sleeps the whole night through. I know what you're thinking, but she is too sweet to strangle.

I first became interested in the effects of stress on attitude and health as a college professor. As part of my work with students, I coauthored a book entitled *The Student Success Workbook*. In the book, I detailed all the study skills techniques and secrets I had discovered as a student and refined as a professor. In the last part of the book, I wrote a segment on stress management. One day during the writing phase of the book, I met with a friend of mine for lunch. He was a planetary geologist at the Jet Propulsion Laboratory in Pasadena, California. I showed him a rough draft of the book and noticed he was paying particular attention to the section on stress. I remember thinking he was going to laugh and tell me it was too touchy-feely. To the contrary, he related to me his difficulty in dealing with stress as a graduate student studying under the famous astronomer and astrobiologist Carl Sagan. The stress my friend experienced resulted in hospitalization and nearly cost him his academic career. He told me how pleased he was that stress management was part of my book.

Can we all agree that managing our stress and maintaining a positive attitude is essential for our emotional and physical well-being? In living *The Best of Our Lives*, Trisha and I believe it is one of the most important things we can do for ourselves. Of course, we realize that not everyone may agree with the premise that developing a positive attitude is an important goal. What about the idea that people need to let off a little steam once in a while, maybe even use intimidation tactics to get what they want?

I have known people who pride themselves on engaging in conflict just so they can assert their personalities and dominate others. For example, I rarely send food back in a restaurant unless it's clearly not what I ordered or not really to my liking. Having my meat slightly rarer or more well-done is not worth the trouble, and I assume the kitchen staff did their best. If I do send something back, I simply make a polite request of the server. It's no big deal and not really worth conflict or stress.

I'm sure you know individuals, as I do, who send back food at almost every occasion. Of course, it's not the food; it's an opportunity to assert themselves. On a recent cruise, Trisha and I had a tablemate who would always make special demands on the wait staff. If it was lobster night, he would always be sure to get a second lobster. The dessert menu was never quite right, so he would always have them make something special for him. He thought he was pretty important, but the staff and his cruise mates did not.

We all know people who use intimidation to try and dominate others. While a parent, a boss, a coach, or even a family member or friend may sometimes achieve what they desire through intimidation, the stress levels that this type of behavior produces are not advisable. It doesn't help your popularity either. A major benefit of managing your stress and developing a positive attitude is that people will like you more.

Trisha and I have discovered a number of principles we find effective in reducing stress. These principles are essential in developing and maintaining a positive attitude. Although it's impossible for a person to live completely stress-free, we are convinced that following these principles will go a long way in helping reduce your everyday stress.

## STRESS MANAGEMENT PRINCIPLES

*Surrounded by people who love life, you love it too; surrounded by people who don't, you don't.*
—Mignon McLaughlin

## SPEND YOUR TIME WITH POSITIVE PEOPLE

Spend your time with positive people, which will lower your stress, creating a more positive attitude, which will result in people liking you more. We call this the Positive People Principle of stress management. Think about the people with whom you most like to spend time. I'll bet they have positive attitudes. I will also bet the people with whom you don't enjoy spending time tend to have negative attitudes and surround themselves with constant worry, crises, and drama. Spending more of your time with positive people will do wonders for managing your stress.

I know the older I get, the more time I want to spend with people who are positive and less time with those who are not. This doesn't mean I hate the other folks, it just means I don't really have much time for negativity at this stage of my life. Actually, I've always tried to follow this principle, but along with getting older, I think one really does get wiser. There is a sense of freedom that comes with age, and perhaps we have less guilt about our choices. Hopefully, all of us become a bit more discriminating and choose to spend time with people we find enjoyable and motivational.

As an example, when the weather is warm, Trisha likes to spend time exercising in the pool. She usually meets up with "the girls" and they all chat while enjoying the water. I have noticed a phenomenon: there are typically different breakout groups among the women. Trisha is always in the group bragging about children and grandchildren, sharing recipes, or reviewing a new restaurant or movie. The conversation is quite positive in nature. There is almost always one other group; let's call these ladies the complainers. Every topic they discuss seems to involve negativity, and there appears to be a competition among them as to who has had the most troubling experience. In listening to these conversations, I even start to feel a bit depressed. Of course, in using this example, I don't mean to imply only women engage in this kind of behavior; men can be just as negative. I know more than a few grumpy old men. It seems as human beings, we develop patterns of behavior. We suggest you try very hard to socialize with those who tend to be more positive.

---

*I don't tolerate negativity in my life. I don't tolerate whiners . . .the issues of boundaries is so important, so that you don't let invasive or negative people into your life.*
—Judy Collins

---

## SPEND YOUR TIME WITH THOSE WHO DESERVE IT

Having been raised with the golden rule, I have truly tried to treat every person I've encountered throughout my life with respect. But I have also been very discriminating with whom I spend my time. Some of my family and friends have taken me to task for this, but I have never felt the need to develop even casual relationships with people with whom I don't really click. This is most often related to my perception of the other person's attitude.

I'm sure you know people, as I do, who count among their best friends those who they don't particularly like or enjoy spending time with. Still others invite obnoxious family members to functions, only to complain about them later. This is baffling to me, and becomes more curious as I grow older. I value my time and want to spend it in ways that are pleasing to me.

Is this selfish? Of course, but it's my time. At our age, the sand is running through the hourglass a little more quickly. Time is becoming a very valuable commodity, so why waste it on undeserving people?

Following this principle may also have health benefits. Dr. Lillian Glass, author of *Toxic People*, contends that the people in our lives who make us feel irritated, angry, and confused are also bad for our health. I could not agree more. Have you ever lost sleep because you were upset about something a friend, colleague, or family member said or did? Was it the first time or is there a pattern to the behavior? If the answer is "a pattern," you have a toxic person in your life. It's time for you to do something about this stressful relationship.

While some of these toxic people may be easy to deal with, others will not. There are those in your life you can simply cut loose and wish well on their cosmic journey. While this may sound a bit harsh, remember, we are dealing with a very serious issue. The toxic people who have a role in your work or family structure will be a bit more difficult, but still must be managed. The key here is to stand up for yourself, decide what is best for you, and draw up some guidelines.

As an example, in the case of a family member who makes you feel insecure, present them with your issue and respectfully describe how you want the relationship to continue. It's their choice. If a family member consistently makes you uncomfortable, tell them you will not subject yourself to that behavior and they will no longer be invited if the behavior continues. It is said misery loves company, but, after making a good effort, I suggest you bid the misery adieu.

In a personal example, some years ago, one of my grandmothers moved directly across the street from my parents. Even though I frequently visited my parents, I made the decision not to spend time with my grandmother. She was very critical and consistently negative. Most of my other relatives put up with her behavior and endured a lot of frustration and stress. I felt badly about my decision, but it was really in my best interest.

Shortly thereafter, a relative from out of town came to visit my parents with her two young children. She asked me if I wanted to go visit Grandma. I told her about my policy and she thought it was just awful. After all, she reasoned, Grandma was family. Twenty minutes later she came back across the street with her children. She was crying and asking how Grandma could say those things to her. It was sad, but very predictable.

As I mentioned previously, Trisha is an incredibly positive person. One day, early in our marriage, I picked her up from work and she looked depressed. When I questioned her, she said that she liked her job, but a number of people she worked with constantly complained about their jobs. It was starting to get to her. That evening, she began looking for a different job. Ironically, her next job was the one that opened the door for her entire career. What's that saying about one door closing and another one opening? The point is, even in the job situation, if there are people who make life intolerable for us, it's time to resolve the issue or move on. Sometimes the grass actually is greener. As retired folks, we have even more freedom to make such decisions.

Think about your circle of family and friends. Are you giving toxic people too much of your valuable time? It's not really complicated in theory, but most of us are not programmed to stand up against people who have made us feel inferior and insecure. Remember, I'm not talking about a crusade in which you are supposed to right every wrong ever committed against you. But it should be obvious if a person's behavior pattern is causing you emotional and even physical problems. Be calm and direct. As a professor, I used to ask my students faced with stressful situations, "What is the worst that can happen?" When dealing with a toxic person, the worst may be that rather than accede to your wishes, the person decides to leave your life. Be prepared for that reality, and know it's in your best interest.

---

*If you can laugh at it, you can survive it.*
—Bill Cosby

---

## SURROUND YOUR LIFE WITH HUMOR

You have probably heard the saying, "Laughter is the best medicine." We now know it's really true. A number of scientific studies have concluded that humor is very effective in managing stress. Humor has been found to:

- Relax tense muscles
- Reduce stress hormones
- Lower blood pressure
- Lower serum cortisol levels
- Speed more oxygen into the system
- Increase blood flow
- Trigger the release of endorphins (the body's natural pain killers)
- Help in weight reduction
- Boost the immune system by raising levels of infection-fighting T-cells, disease-fighting proteins called gamma interferon, and B-cells, which produce disease-destroying antibodies
- Provide a feeling of overall well-being

Quick, somebody say something funny! When I began doing the research for this book, I thought I was somewhat familiar with most of the studies on humor and wellness. I admit I was stunned by the sheer volume of scientific evidence that now supports the notion that humor is beneficial to our emotional and physical health. This wealth of evidence has even given rise to the practice of humor therapy in many places throughout the world.

You may be familiar with the late political writer and journalist Norman Cousins, who, in his extensive writings, contended there was a correlation between humor and wellness. He chronicled his battles with severe illnesses, which were fought in part by watching humorous movies and television shows. This is one of many reasons Trisha and I, now more than ever, tend to look for our entertainment in things that make us laugh.

Given the wealth of evidence on humor research, I now realize how fortunate I was to grow up in a home that thrived on humor. My father has always had a tremendous sense of humor and much of it embarrassed my mother, who is quite shy. But the humor was always good-natured and fun. I now understand it also did something much more important. It always seemed to diffuse serious and stressful situations. I learned not to take myself or the rest of life too seriously. Humor has always been a great safety valve.

I fondly remember the day trips my family would take to visit my aunt and uncle who lived about two hours away. My father and my uncle Jack were two of a kind, and before long, we would all have tears of laughter running down our faces. I thought it was normal and all families engaged in this kind of behavior. Of course, I was wrong.

As I grew older, and began to visit my friends at their homes, I could not figure out why everyone was so serious. Sometimes, I could feel the tension between the parents, or between the parents and my friends. How lucky I was to grow up in a household that treasured laughter and sought to live in a more lighthearted atmosphere. Both of my parents are still living, and to this day, Dad is still making jokes and Mom is still embarrassed. It's a principle I have learned well, and one that Trisha and I continue to implement in our daily lives.

So, the assignment here is simple. Read amusing books, watch funny television shows and movies, share jokes with friends and family, find websites that provide humorous stories and videos, and surround your life with as much humor as possible. Some might ask, "Isn't that just avoidance?" Certainly, we cannot compensate for all the stress of life's serious side, but we can attempt to balance that stress with lots of beneficial humor.

*As you begin to experience this exultation of spirit in everything that is alive, as you become intimate with it, joy will be born within you, and you will drop the terrible burdens of defensiveness, resentfulness, and hurtfulness . . .then you will become lighthearted, carefree, joyous, and free.*
—Deepak Chopra

## KEEP LIFE LIGHTHEARTED

While we cannot find humor in every situation we face, we may be able to stay positive by viewing stressful situations through a lighthearted prism. Hans Selye, author of *Stress Without Distress*, suggests we can consciously alter our perceptions of events and view them in a more lighthearted fashion. In so doing, he advises we should not view situations as being threatening or challenging, but rather view them in a way that gives us a certain degree of control.

This principle reminds me of an incident I encountered while serving overseas in the United States Air Force. Our base commander had summoned everyone in our department to his office for a stern chewing out. It was a very rare occurrence for all of us. As the colonel began to let us have it, one of the youngest people in the room leaned over and whispered, "Look at Bill; he's scared to death." Well, so was I. But after this young man's comment, I realized I was stressed because I was giving this situation too much importance. The colonel simply wanted us to do more work in less time. In the military way, he decided yelling at us would do the trick. We all knew the game, so there was really nothing to be so fearful about. The young man had the right perspective. We often give other people and situations too much control over our emotions. When you keep a lighthearted frame of mind, you stay in control.

One of my students several years ago was a delightful woman somewhat older than the rest of the class. She was married and had children. In discussing issues related to stress, she confided that her family could never get ready on time. This caused her tremendous stress and caused several family arguments. I asked her to try something for me. I suggested she make clear the time she wanted her family ready for the next event, and then sit down, relax, and see what happened. The following week, I saw her walk into class with a big smile. She told me she set the time her family should be ready, got herself ready, and then went downstairs and began to read a magazine. In just a few minutes, her entire family was ready to go. She related how foolish she felt for stressing over something that really wasn't that important.

The more I explore the benefits of humor and lightheartedness, the more aware I have become of other people and their predisposition for optimism. While this is completely unscientific, and totally anecdotal, I find individuals who seem less optimistic also appear to be more involved with books on very serious topics, dramatic movies, and heart-tugging television programs. It also seems to me these same people frequently become very involved with the most depressing news stories of the day, following every new development. As I said, this is not scientific, but it is my experience.

Now, of course, there is nothing wrong with enjoying a good drama or staying current with news events. It's simply a matter of proportion. Tipping the balance toward humorous activities and lighthearted entertainment becomes more important as we get older. I recently heard a comedian talking about grumpy-old-man syndrome. He described his father, who with each visit got grumpier. At their last meeting, upon greeting his father, the old man threatened to "beat him up."

Try to keep life in perspective by keeping it lighthearted. Don't take yourself or anything else too seriously. Don't become a grumpy old man or woman. Strive to maintain a positive attitude.

---

*Patience is the companion of wisdom.*
—Saint Augustine

---

## TAKE THE LONG VIEW

If our attitudes aren't positive, we will often feel like we are swatting at flies, reacting to each and every stressful person, comment, or situation. Has anyone ever made a comment that upset you so much you could not seem to get over it? Of course; it's happened to all of us. With time, things probably were resolved and it turned out not to be a big deal. There are many factors that create stress for us, but if we can just learn to take a little more time and take the long view, we will stay more positive and be better for it.

Let me share another personal example that is quite painful. Some time back, one of my family members decided to host a family reunion. Most of our family lived in the same state and received their invitations about the same time. One family member lived out-of-state and the invitation took a couple of extra days to be delivered. In the meantime, telephone calls were made, and the out-of-state relative heard about the reunion. Rather than give the benefit of doubt, this person fired off an angry letter and said many hurtful and irretrievable things. Of course, when the invitation arrived, postmarked on the same day as the others, it was too late. A simple apology could not mend the damage, and the relationship between the person who was in charge of the invitations and the out-of-state family member was never the same.

In a less serious example, a colleague recently told me how upset his wife had become on her birthday. As the day went along, she became more and more upset that no one had remembered her special day. Of course, when everyone jumped out and yelled "Surprise" at the party he had planned for her, she wished she had taken the long view.

Remember to take the long, more patient view when dealing with stressful comments or situations. Try not to overreact, let things unfold, and give people the benefit of the doubt. We would ask the same of them. Honestly, this is sometimes a difficult principle for me to follow, but I consciously work at it. I find the more times I am able to take the long view, the more natural it becomes. The reward is, in most instances, things really do work out, and without all the stress.

---

*So often times it happens, we all live our life in chains,*
*and we never even know we have the key.*
—The Eagles, *Already Gone*

---

## BECOME SOLUTION-ORIENTED

I mentioned earlier how Trisha deals with stressful situations when they arise. She tries to minimize emotions and goes forward looking to resolve the problem. This comes from her natural positive attitude, her business training, and having an ex-marine as her first executive mentor. He did not need to know all the "gory details," and certainly wasn't interested in how everyone felt about a particular situation. His most important concern was getting problems resolved in a timely fashion. The two of them remain in touch to this day.

The reason most people become stressed when faced with problems or decisions is they allow too many emotions into the process. The best way to make a decision or solve a problem is to follow a problem-solving or decision-making plan. This is done all the time in business, and can work quite well for us as individuals. These are the five basic steps most plans follow:

1. *Identify and define the problem or decision.* Make sure you understand the true nature and scope of the problem or decision to be made. Try to eliminate incor-

rect assumptions and downplay your personal anxieties. Seek input from others you trust.

2. **List and prioritize your criteria.** Write down the criteria you think will be beneficial in helping you decide the best solution to your problem or decision, then rank them in order of importance.

3. **Brainstorm possible solutions.** Don't stop to evaluate, just write down every possible solution or decision you can think of, even getting input from others. Get all the ideas down before you move on.

4. **Compare each of your solutions or decision possibilities to your prioritized criteria.** Having your criteria prioritized should make it easier to limit your options.

5. **Make your final decision.** Based on your criteria, make your final decision and implement it.

People not only let too many emotions into their process, they also make the mistake of looking at possible solutions or decision options as a first step. As an example, if you need to purchase a new car, you shouldn't just walk into the showroom and start looking at all the shiny cars. Go through your criteria, such as budget, mileage, and insurance costs. At this point, guided by your ranked list of criteria, you will make a better decision. Most people don't do this, and it's why so many people are driving around in expensive, uncomfortable, gas-guzzling cars. They are usually red.

---

*What seems impossible one minute becomes,*
*through faith, possible the next.*
—Norman Vincent Peale

---

## EXPLORE YOUR FAITH

While it's not the purpose of this book to discuss our religious beliefs, I would not be honest if I did not share with you that Trisha and I are both persons of faith. We are members of a church and try to live our lives according to our religious principles. It's been our experience that our faith provides us with great comfort, especially during times of extreme stress. We would never diminish the tremendous role faith plays in our lives. While we encourage everyone to explore their spirituality, it is such a personal and complex topic that we have chosen not to discuss it in detail. It would, however, make a wonderful topic for a future project.

Now, let me share some of the specific stress management suggestions Trisha and I use in our daily lives. These are suggestions that work well for us, and we invite you to try them and discover which ones work best for you. We hope they are beneficial in your effort to reduce stress and develop a positive attitude.

## Stress Management Suggestions

---

*Breathe. Let go. And remind yourself that this*
*very moment is the only one you know you have for sure.*
—Oprah Winfrey

---

## Breathe

Both as a college professor and a business consultant, I've had many years of experience advising people faced with a variety of stressful situations. These situations include job interviews, courtroom arguments, press conferences, television and radio appearances, and even testimony before the United States Congress. There is no question: the best results I've ever had for short-term stress management have come from the advice to breathe.

Yes, I do realize we all have to breathe. What I'm talking about here is breathing in a very deliberate and purposeful manner to relieve stress. The next time you encounter some type of stressful situation, take a moment and slowly inhale and exhale. Be very conscious of what you are doing and focus only on your breathing. Let your hands and arms hang loosely at your sides. You may want to close your eyes. Some people slowly count to ten as they breathe. Feel your muscles relax with each slow breath. Try it next time; it works quite effectively.

I know of one president of the United States who became very stressed when questioned by the press. His advisors feared he would lose his temper any time he was interviewed. They gave him a little card to carry in his pocket to remind him of his simple instructions. First, he was to smile when asked a question. Next, he was to breathe slowly and count silently to himself. Only then was he supposed to answer a question. It worked. He became more relaxed, appeared in complete control, did not lose his temper, and was often considered to be very thoughtful with his answers. This is an effective suggestion all of us can use to combat stressful situations we encounter in our everyday lives.

---

*I don't care if anyone else sees me, I never really feel good about*
*myself unless I've cleaned up and look good.*
—Trisha Parker

---

## Look Good, Feel Good

Trisha and I were both brought up in families in which our parents were always well groomed. Our fathers shaved every day, even on the weekends, and always dressed nicely. Not in fancy or expensive clothes, but clean and pressed clothing. Our mothers also set a good example. Both of them, in addition to maintaining a very clean and well-organized home, were always nicely groomed and well-dressed. Even toward the end of her life, when Trisha's mother lived in an assisted-care facility, she would fix her hair each day, dress nicely, and put on some makeup. It made her feel better. To this day, my mother does the same thing. Without knowing it, our parents taught us the concept of "look good, feel good." It's something we try to do every day.

I'm sure everyone understands the importance of grooming and how it communicates not only a first, but a continuing impression to others. Trisha and I believe it also communicates a strong and important message to one's self. While there isn't much scientific evidence on this topic, we can all relate to the concept of feeling better when we think we look good.

When we are at home, I've frequently witnessed Trisha work all day on one of her many projects. While others might just flop down and relax for the evening, she will take a shower, curl her hair, put on some makeup, and slip on something nice to wear. When she comes out to join me, I usually say something clever like, "Got a date?" Of course, she did it for me, but also for herself. She is truly convinced that when she looks good, it puts her in a positive mood. I think it's great because I get to spend the evening with such a beautiful, positive woman.

Let me share a couple of examples of how our appearance not only communicates to others, but to us. A few years back, I was working with a group of attorneys, helping them prepare for the courtroom. This involved both the actual preparation of arguments and the nonverbal elements of their presentations. While doing my research, I visited a number of courtrooms and then interviewed the presiding judges. During one such interview, I asked the judge if the grooming of an attorney had much importance. He spent the next several minutes lecturing me on his objectivity and flatly stated he did not even notice such things. When I asked my next question, which referenced a specific attorney, he thought for a moment and asked, "Was he the one with the long hair?" Our appearance is always communicating.

Not long after that experience, in a training seminar I was teaching, I encountered a young and exceptionally shy attorney. Yes, it surprised me too. After the seminar, he asked me for some additional one-on-one help. It turned out he was not only very timid in the courtroom, but in all aspects of his life. Step-by-step, I helped him with his courtroom presentations. As he began to gain some confidence, he wanted more. He then disclosed debilitating insecurity with his personal appearance and its negative impact on both his professional life and personal life. He shared with me that his social life was almost nonexistent. It was then I realized the full scope of his despair.

At that point, I called in my business partner and we went to work on our new project. We both felt like Professor Higgins in *My Fair Lady*. As a first step, we sent the young man to a modern hair salon. Next, we sent him off to the gym to shed a few pounds and get in shape. We then hired a professional stylist to take him shopping for a new wardrobe. With each step he took, we could see his inner confidence grow. As time went on, he began to date more and his personality became more positive and outgoing. Several weeks later, and now on his own, he stopped by our office to thank us and show off his new car. He had replaced his old boring car with a new sports car. I smile every time I think about that young man. It was an extreme makeover before its time.

It almost seems out of touch to be discussing dress and grooming at this point in our culture. During a recent ninety-minute rapid transit trip to an airport in a major U.S. city, Trisha and I were shocked by what we saw. It just happened to be during commute time, so the train cars were packed. What caught our attention was how poorly people were groomed.

Now, we are talking about professional people commuting home from work. We felt so out of place because we seemed to be among the minority of people on the train with any sense of grooming. Wrinkled clothes, messy hair, two-day growths of beards, and an overall lack of grooming seemed to be the standard. Now, we aren't so out of touch that we don't recognize style trends. We get the whole bed head and slob chic thing. But what really disturbed us was how few smiles we saw from these folks. They looked sloppy, but more importantly, they looked unhappy.

As it happens, just a few weeks ago, I reported for jury duty. It had been some time since I had been to court. I was a bit shocked. None of the male staff, with the exception of attorneys and prosecutors, wore coats and ties. Some of them actually were in tropical shirts. The female staff was also dressed very unprofessionally. Not surprisingly, this court could not have functioned more poorly. It seemed no one knew what was supposed to be done, and the attitudes seemed to be, "I don't know and I don't care." It's not a coincidence that this staff functioned in accordance with how they looked. Nothing about them looked good, and they behaved the same way.

As a side note, the topper of my recent court experience was the two gang members who, for a short while, were actually seated on the jury. They had their baseball caps on sideways, long, baggy shorts with crotches down to their ankles, vulgar tattoos, and huge chains around their necks. Fortunately, they were dismissed after it was determined they both had pending dates for their own upcoming assault trials. I wish I were kidding, but I'm not.

This is an old but favorite example of mine. In 1971, George Allen became the coach of the Washington Redskins. At that time, they were the worst football team in the sport, and had been for many years. One of the first things Allen did was create a dress code that was even enforced at practice. No torn jerseys, no shoes without a shine. During twice-daily practices, clean uniforms and shoes were to be worn for both. He believed that players played like they looked, and he made sure they looked good. You sports fans may remember that he took that formerly ragtag team to the Super Bowl.

For the most part, I think people over fifty better understand the impact of good grooming. Trisha and I hope this remains the case throughout your—and our—retirement years. We're convinced it will pay dividends, especially as it relates to developing a positive attitude.

*Take a music bath once or twice a week for a few seasons, and you*
*will find that it is to the soul what the water bath is to the body.*
—Oliver Wendell Holmes

## LET YOUR MUSIC RELAX YOU

One of the most enjoyable ways Trisha and I deal with stress is listening to music. This is something we have begun to do daily. As a matter of fact, for the last few years, I have made music CDs for both of us. I make it a project by selecting what I consider to be the perfect music for the desired mood. After selecting the music, I make personalized cases for the CDs. For example, when I make one for Trisha, after selecting the music, I find an appropriate picture of her, make up a title, and create a cover for the CD case. Recently, it made me feel great when I heard her listening to one of these CDs, entitled *Always Positive,* which has a picture of her smiling while on a tropical beach. While I'm sure you have listened to music throughout your life, the point here is to make selections carefully for the purpose of reducing your stress. Whether it's inspiring or soothing, it will accomplish the same purpose.

Some years ago, a doctor thought a food allergy was causing my muscles to cramp. He suggested I get a therapeutic massage. In retrospect, I think it was probably more than a food allergy. This was one of the most stressful times of my life. I was teaching several courses, finishing my doctorate, and launching a new consulting business, and we had recently purchased our first home and just welcomed our third child into the world. I was left alone on the massage table for a few minutes before the therapist came into the room. The music was quite soothing and I nearly fell asleep. I remember thinking how good I was feeling at that moment. My stress was already easing, and the massage had not yet begun. It occurred to me that everyone should take a few minutes each day to relax and enjoy some soothing music. It was a valuable experience that became an important life lesson.

In making your music selections, be sure to pick something to achieve the mood you want. If I'm feeling sluggish, but it's time for my walk, I might pick out music from the *Rocky* movies. There is no way I can listen to that music and not be motivated to "go the distance." I dare anyone to listen to *Gonna Fly Now* and not be inspired. Often, in the middle of the day, Trisha will draw up a warm bubble bath, pick out some soothing music, and simply relax. If she is exercising, she picks music that is upbeat and enjoyable.

Most scientists who study the effects of music agree it can be very beneficial. Interestingly, there is not a consensus as to why. Some believe it is related to the beating of our hearts and the rhythm of the music. I remember reading a textbook in college that attempted to explain human emotions. The one area the author admitted she could not explain was the human reaction to music. It is still one of the most baffling aspects of the human experience. I do know, even before learning to speak, our little grandson found ways to request specific music he enjoyed. Every culture has some form of music, so there must be something about it that is inherent and important to us as human beings. For now, it's enough to know that music relaxes us and helps us reduce our stress.

*An acquaintance that begins with a compliment*
*is sure to develop into a real friendship.*
—Oscar Wilde

## COMPLIMENT OTHERS

One of the activities Trisha and I both enjoy is to frequently compliment people, even total strangers. While we consciously look for opportunities to give people compliments, our comments are always spontaneous and sincere. It's something we have always done, but we only recently realized all the positive benefits we have received as a result.

This activity has actually become a bit of a game for us. The reason it's become a game is because I don't ever recall going somewhere with Trisha without her getting some sort of compliment. It's her hair, her shoes, her purse, always something. I once had a very elderly lady at a restaurant tell me she liked my shirt. While I have had other compliments in my life, I only admit to having that one. Each time Trisha gets another compliment, I jokingly tally up the score, with me always being stuck at one.

It's not surprising how much people enjoy getting compliments, but we are always amazed how often the same kinds of comments flow back to us. Both giving and receiving compliments gives us joy and makes us feel very positive.

I was very fortunate at one time in my life to have the late Dr. Leo Buscaglia as a colleague. Leo was a professor and author who wrote bestselling books such as *Living, Loving, and Learning* and *Born for Love*. When I knew him, in addition to his regular courses in the education department at the University of Southern California, he taught the very popular noncredit evening course Love 101. Leo not only taught the principles of being positive, love and respect, he lived them.

The first time I met Leo, he was the keynote speaker at a luncheon where I was one of the planners. I was able to assign myself to his table in order to get acquainted. He was a fascinating individual. After we finished lunch, he was introduced and began his presentation. A few moments into it, he paused, walked around the lectern, looked at a woman in the middle of the room, and said to her, "Your smile devastates me." He then returned to his prepared remarks. That was Leo. He told me later that he never wanted to observe something positive in someone without complimenting them on it. This, of course, is quite a contrast from those of us who typically see only the negative side or flaws in others. Thanks for the great lesson, Leo; it's a wonderful way to live.

I should also share with you that Trisha and I provide each other with compliments all the time. No, we're not one of those couples you hear out in public, loudly proclaiming, "Oh, I love you so much." Our comments are usually simple and honest, such as "That was a delicious dinner," or "You look great in that shirt." The comments aren't public and certainly are not routine. But as I think about it, they are frequent. We also say "I love you" frequently in a variety of ways. That, of course, could be another entire book, or even a movie. Everyone who knows us will tell you we are truly in love, even after all these years, and we are not afraid to express it.

---

*Do not lose your inward peace for anything*
*whatsoever, even if your whole world seems upset.*
—Saint Francis De Sales

---

## FIND SOME QUIET TIME

We really do value our quiet time. In this fast-paced age of cell phones, loud noises, freeways, and e-mail, it's wonderful to take a few minutes out of each day for quiet reflection and relaxation.

Some experts on stress reduction suggest we use this quiet time for meditation or self-affirmations. Both involve self-talk, which is positive and inspirational. I know many people who use these techniques and they report positive results. To be honest, my quiet time is usually spent on some relaxing activity such as walking or swimming, and I do engage in lots of positive self-talk during these times. I try to focus my thoughts on thankfulness for my good fortune of family, friends, and life in general. I also try to fully appreciate the beauty of my surroundings. While I now have more time for this sort of thing, I realize that even during some of the busiest times of my life, I have employed this suggestion.

As an example, for a number of years, I was a faculty member at Pepperdine University in Malibu, California. On one occasion, as I walked into an evening class, some of my students asked me if something was wrong. I told them I was fine and asked why they were concerned. They said they had seen me before class staring off at the ocean for some time. They assumed something might be troubling me. I smiled and thanked them for their concern. I also told them I was simply enjoying the beautiful sunset.

Let me share a secret with you. Trisha is truly like the Energizer bunny. She seemingly keeps going all day long. I once asked her, as she whisked through our living area yet one more time, "Are there other rooms in this house I don't know about?" She is able to keep that torrid pace because of her secret. She frequently takes breaks for some quiet time. I have already told you about her frequent bubble baths with soothing music in the middle of the day. She is the perfect example of someone who likes to find a peaceful place, away from distraction, and enjoy her thoughts in solitude.

At the end of the day, one of our favorite activities is to get into a nice, warm Jacuzzi (if one is available). We prefer a lower temperature than most folks because it allows us to stay in longer. For health reasons, staying in a hot Jacuzzi for more than fifteen minutes is not recommended. While we're in the Jacuzzi, we usually start out talking about lighthearted things. After a while we simply enjoy the stars and reflect. For me, the night sky not only reveals our place in the universe, but also the magnificence of life. It's something wonderful to share and is completely relaxing.

The point of this suggestion is not so much to tell you how to spend your quiet time, but simply to encourage you to find it. A warm bath, a cup of tea, or a beautiful sunset will all accomplish the same peaceful feeling. Find your quiet time: you deserve it.

---

*No news before bedtime is not only good news, it's a rule.*
—John Parker

---

## NO NEWS BEFORE BEDTIME

Some years back, I heard a psychologist suggest that watching or listening to news before bedtime can produce unnecessary stress. He asserted it had a very negative impact on sleep, and that loss of sleep could lead to an ongoing cycle of stress. I decided I would stop watching the news before bedtime. It probably won't surprise you to learn it really worked. For many years now, Trisha and I have followed a rule of no news before bedtime. Please don't tell our oldest son, who writes and produces evening news segments for a major network.

When Trisha and I do watch television or a movie, or read a book before bedtime, we try to make it something light and humorous. At the end of a tiring day, it feels so much better to share laughter than worry about whether or not they catch that carjacker. We can always catch up with everything in the morning. In the meantime, we sleep quite peacefully.

---

*We shape our dwellings, and afterwards our dwellings shape us.*
—Sir Winston Churchill

---

## CREATE A STRESS-FREE ENVIRONMENT

For some time before we retired, Trisha and I knew our home was not properly organized. We have made great progress since then. It's amazing how much stuff we had accumulated over the years. Much of it belonged to our grown children, who had not lived at home for many years. If you've ever heard the late comedian George Carlin's routine in which he makes fun of people who have too much stuff, know that he was talking about us.

Am I saying that having a house and garage full of objects we rarely or never used was causing us stress? Yes. Don't get me wrong: we have always maintained a clean and orderly home. But after we retired, we knew we didn't want to live with so much stuff around us. (To be completely honest, I should point out that, as of this date, Operation: Get Organized is not completed. But we are getting there, feeling more positive and much less stressed.)

The first order of business was to have our children go through all of their things. We asked them to take the items they wanted to keep. Of course, there were some things they did not have room to store, so we allotted a certain amount of space and asked that they label and organize everything neatly. Next, we began to sort through all of our stuff and placed everything into one of three categories: first, the items we really needed to keep; second, the things in good enough condition to be given to charity; and, third, the things we needed to throw away. If you are thinking "yard sale" at this point, that's fine. Philosophically, we prefer to give things away, but the end result is the same: less stuff. Perhaps it should be called the less stuff, less stress principle.

As this process continued, we determined the remaining items still created too much clutter, especially in the garage. Even though I'm not much of a carpenter, I built a storage shed to hold lawn equipment, gas cans, bicycles, etc. Inside the garage, I installed a number of storage cabinets for the smaller items. That still left many other things such as Christmas decorations, Halloween decorations, party supplies, and other items Trisha had stored in plastic bins. One week, while she was away helping out with the grandkids, I built an entire storage system that would hold plastic bins of varying sizes. It went from floor to ceiling, and was about 15 feet wide and 3 feet deep. I even painted it white to match the inside of the garage.

On the night she returned, which happened to be Valentine's Day, I drove her home from the airport. Now I understand not every woman is like Trisha, but given the choice between diamond earrings and a new storage system for her bins, this was a no brainer. As I pulled into the garage, she squealed, "Oh John, it's wonderful." I know it's not very romantic, but given our goal, she thought it was the perfect gift.

I must admit to you, I'm terribly claustrophobic. Clutter of any kind drives me crazy. For that reason, I've always been impressed by how model homes appear to be very spacious and uncluttered. Whenever I've walked through a model, it's always been a pleasant and relaxing experience. While I'm not an expert, I've also noticed the art work and other decorations in model homes tend to be larger objects as opposed to smaller ones. You are not going to find small figurines of dogs or unicorns in a model home. Trisha and I decided we wanted our home to be like a model.

When we purchased our current house, the one we plan to spend most of our retirement in, we decided to wait a while before decorating. Wanting to do it right, we took a long time deciding what colors to paint our rooms. After painting, we carefully planned the furnishings of each room, staging them one at a time. That doesn't mean we went out and bought the most expensive items to furnish our rooms. What we did was create a clean and simple plan. We kept the furnishings minimal so we could move about our rooms easily.

Before someone is offended, let me acknowledge the fact that we all have different likes and tastes. The point here is each person or couple should create an environment that works for them. If you have an appreciation for small objects, and they make you feel good, they should be in your home. The idea is to assess what works for you and what doesn't. Give it some thought; decide what would be your ideal stress-free environment for your retirement, and work to achieve that goal. In our case, we followed our plan to completion, and it has accomplished two very important things. One, our home is very easy to maintain because of the simple interior design, and two, it is so relaxing not having lots of clutter around. We have truly created our stress-free environment, and we love it.

---

*Sex at the age of eighty-four is a wonderful experience.*
*Especially the one in the winter.*
—Milton Berle

---

## ENJOY YOUR LOVE LIFE

Let me begin by acknowledging that not everyone reading this may have a partner, the physical ability, or, in some cases, the interest to have a love life. Given that disclaimer, let me say that sex is a very effective stress reliever. The question often arises, "At what age should a person stop having sex?" The best answer is, "When you are no longer able to engage in sexual relations, or you no longer choose to do so."

Personally, Trisha and I truly believe our newfound freedom from work has done wonders for our love life. Our relationship has never been better, and we often feel like we are on an extended second honeymoon. I will spare you the details, but they are fantastic. Many of our friends tell us they read when they go to bed, which they claim relaxes them. On a couple of occasions, friends have shared something they read in bed the night before. Trisha always gives me a sly grin, which between us says, "We didn't get much reading done last night."

As we grow older, most experts in the field say we should take more time with intimacy because our bodies may require it. They recommend more talking, more touching, and more patience with our partners. This will be discussed further in the next chapter, "Health and Fitness Over Fifty."

---

*We are all searching for the same thing: a hand to hold and heart to understand . . .*
*Keep it simple. Smile a lot. Be nice to other people . . . Life is a joy.*
—Terry Bradshaw

---

## KEEP LIFE SIMPLE

I'm sure you know the feeling. So many things on your schedule that you start to feel a little crazy. The telephone keeps ringing, the doorbell won't stop chiming, and everybody wants something. Actually, these are all good things. In retirement you should stay busy. But when it starts to tilt away from being enjoyable and becomes stressful, it's time to simplify.

Here is a personal example. I have the primary responsibility for maintaining the grounds around our house. I made a decision some time ago that as long as I'm able to do it, I'm taking care of our house and yard. I enjoy getting out there and trimming trees, cutting the lawn, fixing sprinklers, and all the other little jobs a yard requires. Some of my retired neighbors have asked why I don't just hire someone to do these things. My answer is, "Because I want to do them." But sometimes, the numbers of things that mount up make me feel stressed.

My solution is a simple to-do list. Both Trisha and I had professional careers, and our things-to-do lists always kept things on track. By keeping this list now that I'm retired, and checking things off as I go, something gets done every day. I don't get overwhelmed, and if something doesn't get done, I simply add it to tomorrow's list.

I have also mentioned this example for another reason. Someday, with any luck, I will not be able to complete all the things on my list. I've heard lots of reasons people are reluctant to give up their home or property, but when the time comes, we plan to downsize. It's something all of us should consider to help simplify our lives.

The suggestion to keep things simple can help reduce stress in many other ways. You may know people, as we do, who spend much of their free time attending numerous functions such as weddings, graduations, birthdays, and other such events. Often, these folks have told us they get a bit stressed with so many "obligations." I'm now going to make a very radical suggestion. Only attend functions you truly want to attend. Keep it simple, and only do those things you really enjoy. Of course, we all have events in our lives that are true obligations, but they don't include every single invitation you receive. Recently, I shared with a friend that I was not planning on attending a certain function. The response was, "Well, you have to go." Actually, I didn't.

I think people feel that "we got invited here, so you have to attend there" or "those folks came to this, so we have to go to that." It's all a little confusing, so simplify and repeat after me: "I only have to attend the functions I want to attend." Doesn't that feel good? Now, guys, if you are part of a couple, and your lady decides she wants to go, you're going. It also works the same way for the ladies. I say this because if you are a couple, I really do think both parties need to support each other in these decisions.

You may be asking yourself, "Didn't he say earlier to spend time with positive people?" Yes, but not if an event will cause you stress. Last year, Trisha and I invited a number of guests to one of several parties we give at our home each year. Among our invited guests were the father of one of our daughters-in-law and his wife. A few days before the party, he called me and said he really didn't like parties all that much and wondered if we minded if they did not attend. I told him absolutely not, and I appreciated his honesty. We get along very well, and have enjoyed several other family functions together.

At the root of the suggestion to keep life simple is the admonition to always let your true desires guide you. Don't worry or feel guilty about the things you don't want to do. Put your energy and attention on the really important things. It will all sort itself out and you will be far less stressed.

*If you permit your thoughts to dwell on evil, you yourself will become ugly.*
*Look only for the good in everything so you absorb the quality of beauty.*
—Paramahansa Yogananda

## LOOK FOR THE GOOD IN EVERYTHING

A couple of years ago, Trisha and I had the good fortune of taking a cruise with some friends to several islands in the Caribbean. We were so excited about the trip and had broad smiles on our faces as we reached the passenger terminal. After checking in, we were directed to walk through the covered gangway to the ship. A line had formed as passengers went through security to board. We began to hear loud voices just ahead of us. It was two couples, husbands and wives, already arguing with each other. We realize we are not perfect, and we don't expect it of anyone else. However, if you are about to begin a Caribbean adventure on a cruise ship, what in the world are you arguing about? Yes, he was supposed to put that paper in his shirt pocket, but can't we all just get along? We are noticing this kind of public behavior more and more. I'm convinced that looking for the negative has become a bad habit with some people.

After attending a recent musical performance, Trisha and I noticed how many people leaving were discussing the one "bad singer" or the one "bad dancer." When did we all become so critical? What about the rest of the cast? Weren't they terrific? The same thing seems to happen with movies, food, people—basically, everything in life. It's so easy to be negative, but so counterproductive to managing stress. Look for the good, for the beauty in everything life has to offer. When you meet someone for the first time, pick out their best feature and remember them for it. If you are fortunate enough to visit some new place in the world, savor the experience. If you have someone with whom you can share an adventure, keep them close, and let them know how much they mean to you. Look for the good; you will be better for it.

*The weak can never forgive. Forgiveness is the attribute of the strong.*
—Mahatma Gandhi

## FORGIVE

For over two decades, I coached youth baseball. I never permitted my players to argue with umpires, and I tried to set a good example for them. I was very proud of my coaching record, which included the fact I had never been thrown out of a game. One night changed all of that. During a play at second base, my player was knocked over by the runner. It was a clear violation of the rules. I called time-out, and went onto the field to talk to the umpire. He said he didn't want to hear what I had to say and told me to return to the dugout. As I turned to go back, I noticed my player had now slumped to the ground. As I went to the aid of my injured player, the umpire yelled, "You're out of the game."

Now, I may have been too prideful, but I couldn't get this injustice out of my mind. For some time I brooded over my perfect record being tarnished by such an idiot. I would go to bed and replay what had happened over and over. I asked myself, "How can I get even with him?" I prepared for the next time we met, and rehearsed the nasty things I would say to him. It was tearing me up.

A few games passed, and then it happened. As my team took the field, guess who showed up to umpire at third base? I walked very deliberately toward the third-base coaching box, and then headed straight for my "friend." When I got to him, he seemed a bit fearful of what I might say or do. I looked him in the eye and said, "The last time I saw you, you threw me out of a game for going to my injured player. I forgive you." I extended my hand, and a very relieved man smiled and shook. This not only ended my anger and stress, I had gained a new colleague. From that day on, this fellow always treated me with the utmost respect, and at one point, even apologized for his bad judgment on that troubling night.

Obviously, I have shared this personal story to illustrate a powerful stress-reliever, forgiveness. It's so easy to become angry and stressed over the behavior of others, wasting our time and energy in unproductive ways. Just recently, I found myself lying in bed, troubled by the rude actions of an acquaintance at a party we had attended. As I thought about it, I started to get stressed, but then realized it was just the way he sometimes behaves. I smiled, said to myself, "I forgive him," and then went to sleep. It was no longer an issue for me.

It should be noted that forgiving someone does not mean you must also spend time with that person or put up with his or her behavior. No, it simply means you let go of your anger and negative feelings toward that person. He or she may or may not change, but that is not your concern. Not only will forgiving someone relieve your stress, it is the right thing to do. In most religions, forgiveness is a tenet of appropriate behavior. Trisha and I truly believe this, and the practice has often given us peace and comfort.

---

*If I had my life to live over, I would not worry.*
—Edna Parker

---

## DON'T WORRY

One of my father's aunts, the wife of his uncle for whom he was named, was a wonderful woman. We all called her Aunt Eddy. She was one of the sweetest and most gracious people I have ever met. I have thought about her often while writing this chapter.

One of my fondest memories is helping her move to a care facility several years after her husband passed away. When I arrived, she was going through a box of old books, sorting the ones she wanted to give away from those she wanted to keep. One by one, she would look at each book, tell me what she wanted to do with it, and hand it to me, and I would place it into the appropriate box. When she picked up one of the old books, I noticed it was a text on learning to speak French. She paused for a very long time, handed me the book, and said, "I'll keep this one. I need to brush up." Aunt Eddy was in her late eighties at the time. What a great spirit and attitude.

One of Aunt Eddy's loves was the symphony, but she no longer had a way to attend. Trisha and I said we would be glad to take her, and she graciously purchased tickets for the season. These became wonderful evenings for us. We enjoyed both the music and the conversations with her afterwards. She was quite wise and very inspiring.

I share this memory with you because of something Aunt Eddy said on one of those nights. We were driving home after an evening of delightful music. The conversation turned a bit philosophic, and I simply asked her what she would do differently if she could live her life over. She paused only briefly, and then in a very steady voice said, "If I had my life to live over, I would not worry."

This, of course, is not a novel idea. We've all heard or read the suggestion "not to worry" countless times in our lives. But on that night, with such a gracious and thoughtful lady, her words were forever etched into my memory. I can still hear her sincere tone of voice. This was not advice given lightly, but a powerfully reflective and thoughtful response.

Honestly, I have not always been able to follow Aunt Eddy's admonition. I'm not sure any of us can. But, it is true that when I find myself beginning to worry excessively about something, I remember her wise words. They always give me guidance and comfort. Trisha and I both loved our Aunt Eddy, and we have benefitted from her wisdom.

I hope you find these principles and suggestions beneficial in reducing your stress and helpful in developing and maintaining a positive attitude. The fact is every topic we have written about in this book is intended to help you relieve stress, be positive, and live *The Best of Our Lives*.

*If I'd known I was going to live this long,*
*I'd have taken better care of my body.*
—Eubie Blake (on his 100th birthday)

CHAPTER 3

# HEALTH AND FITNESS OVER FIFTY
*By John*

As we age, Trisha and I try to stay in good mental and physical condition to live *The Best of Our Lives.* I must admit she is the more disciplined, but we both have specific goals and support each other. Health and fitness should arguably be the most important part of your retirement lifestyle plan. We recommend you set goals for yourself, and when you reach them, maintain them.

To help you set and reach your health and fitness goals, this chapter provides you with vital age-related information and specific suggestions collected from leading researchers around the world. After a brief overview of health and fitness as it relates to aging, we will look at mental fitness, physical fitness, proper nutrition, the importance of sleep, and senior sex. In addition, you will find recommendations for routine medical checkups and screening tests for persons in our age group. Along the way, I've included some of the practices Trisha and I have found to be effective in accomplishing our health and fitness goals.

**A word of caution: You should always consult with your doctor before you begin any new health or fitness program. If you have any health issues or concerns, by all means, seek medical attention.**

## OVERVIEW OF HEALTH, FITNESS, AND AGING

There is no question that as we age, health and fitness become much more important issues in our lives. For some, especially those with previously unhealthy lifestyles, these issues can seem overwhelming. The approach Trisha and I have taken is to get as much good information as possible, and deal with health and fitness issues directly. We can't pretend we're not getting older, but we can strive to be as mentally and physically fit as possible.

Certain age-related mental and physical changes are common. These changes may include hearing impairment, weakening vision, and increased probability of arthritis, hypertension, heart disease, diabetes, and osteoporosis. Additionally, we may suffer some degree of memory loss and difficulty in processing information and communicating with others. That's the bad news.

The good news is, if we work to make health and fitness an active part of our lives, we may be able to lessen the severity of these changes. Over the last several years, scientists throughout the world have made great strides in understanding the mental and physical effects of aging. These studies, including many conducted in the United States by the National Institute on Aging, have come to one common conclusion. Simply stated, extreme mental and physical decline with aging is not inevitable.

In a recent article titled "Mental Fitness," Susan Tannen, writing for the website bellydoc.com, reports on a landmark study conducted by the National Institute of Mental Health. In this study, men's cognitive skills were tested at age eighty-one, and the scores were compared with their test results obtained at ages seventy and seventy-five. She quotes the researchers as concluding, the "pattern of decline of cognitive . . . capabilities generally associated with advanced aging" was "neither extensive nor consistent." This is great news because it means if we keep our minds active and challenged, we can potentially maintain a high level of mental fitness throughout the aging process.

In another example, Miriam Nelson, a scientist at Tufts University who specializes in research on aging, quoted in an article written for evolutionhealth.com, has stated, "Biologically, we can reverse the aging process by 15 to 25 years. We can do that by becoming stronger." This, of course, is accomplished by regular exercise. Unfortunately, 85 percent of seniors do not exercise regularly, leading many to believe physical decline is a much more rapid process than it needs to be.

While there is an abundance of research to suggest the aging process can be slowed down, serious mental and physical health issues are always a possibility. Make sure you are proactive and get regular checkups. If you discover that you have a health issue, don't live in depression, fear, or pain. Seek out the best medical advice available and do everything you can to resolve it. With that said, let's get our minds and bodies in shape.

## MENTAL FITNESS

By following the suggestions in Chapter 2, "Be Positive and Reduce Your Stress," you have already started the process of achieving mental fitness through reduced stress and a positive attitude. With that information in mind, let's examine some common psychological myths often associated with older people. These myths, and the actual facts, have been provided by the American Psychological Association.

**Myth:** *Most older people are pretty much alike.*
**Fact:** *They are a very diverse age group.*

**Myth:** *They are generally alone and lonely.*
**Fact:** *Most older adults maintain close relationships with family.*

**Myth:** *They are sick, frail, and dependent on others.*

**Fact:** *Most older people are independent.*

**Myth:** *They are often cognitively impaired.*
**Fact:** *If there is decline in some Intellectual abilities, it is not severe enough to cause problems in daily living.*

**Myth:** *They are depressed.*
**Fact:** *Community dwelling older adults have lower rates of diagnosable depression than younger adults.*

**Myth:** *They become more difficult and rigid with advancing years.*
**Fact:** *Personality stays relatively consistent throughout the lifespan.*

**Myth:** *They barely cope with the inevitable declines associated with aging.*
**Fact:** *Most older people successfully adjust to the challenges of aging.*

Here is one more myth I have found many people our age still believe.

**Myth:** *If a person lives Long enough, he or she will eventually suffer some degree of Alzheimer's disease.*
**Fact:** *Based on scientific evidence, this is not true.*

A leading expert in this field, Stanford University neuroscientist Robert Sapolsky, Ph.D., quoted in an article by Katherine Greider and Jill Neimark in *Psychology Today*, has said, "Thirty-five years ago we thought Alzheimer's disease was a dramatic version of normal aging. Now we realize it's a disease with a distinct pathology. In fact, some people simply don't experience any mental decline, so we've begun to study them." This is truly encouraging news.

A review of the research on aging and mental fitness suggests a number of measures we can take to keep our minds fit. They are as follows:

- **Get regular physical exercise** – Physical exercise will provide your brain with increased blood flow and stimulate nerve growth. Many experts suggest moderate aerobic exercise, such as walking, to achieve your goal. Other experts have conducted research that found exercises that combine mental challenges with social interaction are best. A good example is dancing. The more complex the dance, the better it is for the brain. Another example is shopping in a mall with a friend. Walking provides the exercise, the friend adds the social interaction, and hunting for bargains supplies the mental challenges.

- **Socialize** – Socializing is another good way to maintain mental fitness. Talking, laughing, and discussing various topics with other people is good for your brain. In addition, research demonstrates that socializing provides the attention, affection, and belonging that are necessary for optimum brain function. If you don't have much of a social life, there are clubs and organizations for almost every interest. Seek them out and join up; it's good for you.

- **Continue your education** – For some time, researchers have known that education early in life is a positive factor for long-term mental fitness. There is now research that suggests people who continue to challenge themselves with education throughout the aging process also receive positive benefits. Reading newspapers, books, and magazines can be very helpful. I even suggest signing up for college or technical courses. As a college professor, it was always interesting to have an older person sign up for one of my classes. In every case, they were among the best students in my classes.
- **Reduce your stress** – This will positively alter the chemistry of the brain and buffer it from harmful stress hormones. For more information on reducing stress, refer to Chapter 2.
- **Increase your mental activity** – Just as physical activity helps keep the body in shape, mental activity helps keep our brains in shape. This can be accomplished by reading, writing, playing board and video games, playing musical instruments, solving puzzles, and participating in group discussions.
- **Improve your nutrition** – Research tells us there are specific foods that are better for both our mental and physical fitness. These foods will be discussed later in this chapter.
- **Vary your activities** – Many experts suggest that varying your daily routine is good for mental fitness. Change things up a bit. You don't have to take a long trip, but make plans to go see and do something completely different. Go to a new park, explore a new neighborhood, or take a different route to the grocery store. New sights, smells, and experiences can all be good for mental fitness.

The idea that we can maintain mental fitness throughout the aging process has further support. Monique LePoncin, founder of the French National Institute for Research on the Prevention of Cerebral Aging, has written a book titled *Brain Fitness*. In her book, LePoncin recommends we exercise our minds daily, just as we would exercise our bodies. Here are the mental abilities she recommends we exercise and possible exercise suggestions:

- **Perceptive abilities** – These are our abilities of sight, smell/taste, memory, hearing, and smell/touch.
  *Exercise suggestions:* For sight: after seeing someone, try to draw that person shortly afterward. Exercise the ability of smell/taste by trying to determine how many different foods you can recognize when entering a home or restaurant. When tasting food, see if you can determine the different spices being used in the recipe. For memory, each week try to remember the names of all your friends and family. For hearing, a good exercise is to try and immediately guess the voice of each caller on your telephone. And finally, for smell/touch, see if you can identify objects with your eyes closed.

- **Visuospatial abilities** – These are our abilities to make quick and accurate estimates of distances, areas, and volumes.
  *Exercise suggestions:* After entering a room, quickly try to estimate the number of people on your right and on your left. When you have returned home after visiting a new location, attempt to draw a map of the route you took. Try to guess the distance from one point to another, then step it off to see how well you did.
- **Structuralization abilities** – These are our abilities to build a logical whole from disparate elements after close observation of the elements.
  *Exercise suggestions:* Jigsaw puzzles, word games such as crossword puzzles, and number games are excellent exercises for testing and maintaining these abilities.
- **Logic abilities** – These are the abilities to reason and find an orderly sequence for disparate elements.
  *Exercise suggestions:* Card games, chess, and board games that involve strategy work well to exercise these abilities. The caution here is to make sure you don't play the same game all the time. The brain needs to have variety for best results.
- **Verbal abilities** – These are our abilities to use precise spoken or written words, which make demands on short-term and long-term memory.
  *Exercise suggestions:* After listening to a news report or reading a book, try to summarize the report or book plot, either verbally for someone else or in writing. Be as concise and precise as possible. Try to use the most accurate words and phrases possible.

In summary, LePoncin's extensive research and writings on mental fitness contend a poor memory and slow thinking are not inevitable as we age. On the contrary, she believes that if we exercise our minds, the negative effects of aging can be greatly lessened.

Are you feeling more mentally fit? OK, it may take a while. While it's unrealistic to think we can stop the mental aging process completely, the majority of evidence in this area is encouraging. Think about the older people you know. Doesn't it seem like the ones who keep their minds active and challenged maintain better mental fitness? Trisha has a relative nearly eighty years old who daily writes lengthy and thoughtful letters. During our visits with him, we detect no slow down in mental function. While this is anecdotal evidence, we genuinely believe his practice of daily letter writing is a positive factor.

## SOME THINGS WE DO

As with so many aspects of life, Trisha and I try to have fun and vary our activities to keep us mentally fit. She loves word and number games, and plays them regularly. I like trivia, and, when listening to music, try to guess the name of every singer or group I hear. This sometimes drives Trisha crazy because if she's around, I will always challenge her to take a guess. I do the same with movies and television programs. I'm always asking questions like, "What is that actress's name? Who directed this movie? Is that actor still married to that singer?" I even admit to reading all the credits after a movie or television program. Now that we spend most of our time together, Trisha is getting very good at answering trivia questions. I guess practice makes perfect.

Since we retired, we've also tried to become more creative. Trisha has launched a number of projects involving her organizational skills. Almost every type of paper or electronic record we have is organized and labeled. She has put everything paper into color-coded folders or binders which are clearly labeled and easily accessible. Receipts, brochures, instruction and owner manuals, etc. have all been carefully organized and stored. She has done the same with our electronic data, organizing it and then putting it on discs that are labeled and stored.

In addition, she is constantly getting involved with various other creative projects. These include charity projects, decorating projects such as creative window coverings, sewing fun pillow cases for our grandkids, and, my favorite, collecting her best recipes and putting them into book form for friends and family. The point here is not about the specific projects, but the fact that she is constantly exercising her mind.

In my case, I continue my habit of reading the newspaper from cover to cover to start each day. I also enjoy using the computer and have taken several courses to become more proficient. Since my retirement, I've gotten out my old guitar and I try to play every day, even making up new songs when I'm feeling especially creative. There is another goal I have been working on. Even though I studied Spanish in high school, I never learned to speak fluently. Last year I purchased a Spanish instruction book with a CD, and I try to spend a little time each day studying. It makes me feel a little smarter.

Together, Trisha and I play games like Scrabble, research different cultures and countries, and constantly discuss and plan new adventures. When we go on a travel adventure, we take dozens of photos and lots of video. Making CDs and DVDs when we return takes a lot of time, but it's an enjoyable activity. We also enjoy keeping in touch with friends and family on the internet. I've earned a bit of a reputation for my doctored photos and similar fun stuff. For several years now, Trisha and I have also been involved in a project researching issues related to aging and retirement. You may have noticed we have even written a book on the topic. We actually practice what we preach.

Throughout my life, I've always looked for role models. Let me tell you about one of my favorites. Have you heard of Forest Bird? Dr. Bird was born in 1921. He became a pilot at the age of fourteen, and was a flight instructor during World War II. He became qualified to fly almost every type of airplane and helicopter in existence, including jets. As an inventor and aero-medical scientist, he went on to invent the Bird Universal Medical Respirator, which became standard equipment in hospitals throughout the world. Later, he invented the Baby Bird, which dropped breathing-related infant mortality rates from 70 to 10 percent. He also opened the Bird Aviation and Invention Museum in Sagle, Idaho. He is my hero because to this day, he runs his business, continues to invent, and flies his collection of aircraft. Yes, he is still an FAA-qualified pilot.

While we can't all be like Dr. Bird, it is now evident we can slow down the rate of aging when it comes to mental fitness. Carefully consider the measures and exercises presented here and try to come up with some of your own. At the very least, you will be doing something very positive for your mental fitness.

## PHYSICAL FITNESS

As seniors, perhaps the most important goal we can set for ourselves is to achieve and maintain a high degree of physical fitness. For some, that might seem to be an impossible challenge. Given my family history of weight-related health issues, I truly understand such skepticism. The undeniable fact is, to live *The Best of Our Lives*, we must accept the challenge.

As seniors, we need to be realistic and specific about our definition of physical fitness. One of the websites I often consult, Seniors-Site.com, has provided this superb definition:

> Physical fitness is to the human body what fine-tuning is to an engine. It enables us to perform up to our potential. Fitness can be described as a condition that helps us look, feel, and do our best. More specifically it is: The ability to perform daily tasks vigorously and alertly, with energy left over for enjoying leisure-time activities and meeting emergency demands. It is the ability to endure, to bear up, to withstand stress, to carry on in circumstances where an unfit person could not continue, and it is a major basis for good health and well-being.

With this inspiring definition in mind, I have researched and summarized fitness goals from a variety of experts for those of us over fifty years old.

- **Increase cardiovascular fitness** – Provide your body with the ability to supply a high level of oxygen and nutrients to tissues and provide adequate removal of waste.
- **Increase muscle strength** – Provide your muscles with the ability to exert adequate force over a short period of time.
- **Increase muscle flexibility** – Provide your joints and muscles with the ability to achieve a full range of motion.
- **Increase muscle endurance** – Provide your muscles with the ability to sustain contractions or force over time.
- **Control your weight** – Achieve and maintain the proper ratio of fat to lean mass through exercise and proper nutrition.
- **Reduce heart disease risks** – Maintain a regimen of exercise and proper nutrition to lessen the risks of heart disease.
- **Control blood pressure** – Maintain a blood pressure of 130/80 or less.
- **Prevent bone loss** – Maintain adequate bone density levels through exercise and proper nutrition.
- **Develop strong immune system** – Fortify your body through exercise and proper nutrition to prevent illness and disease.

- **Control anxiety and depression** – Maintain a positive attitude through reduced stress, regular exercise, and proper nutrition.

With these physical fitness goals in mind, let me share a story I think you will find inspiring. A few years ago, I was helping one of Trisha's uncles, a man in his mid-seventies, move a small refrigerator. We took it outside to his pickup truck, and when he put the truck's tailgate down, I began to climb up to get into position to help him lift it. Before I could do so, he jumped from a standing start directly up into the back of the truck. I was amazed.

At his home later that evening, I asked him how he stayed so physically fit. He smiled and said, "Come with me." In one of the rooms of his house, he had assembled an entire workout station. It included weights, pulleys—everything one might imagine a professional athlete would use. He told me much of the equipment had come from a local community college that sold it to him when they remodeled.

As I said, this was a few years ago. This man is almost eighty now, still works as a house painter, and takes his wife out dancing every Friday and Saturday night.

I have shared this story to illustrate something Trisha and I firmly believe about physical fitness: *The human body is incredibly resilient and adaptable, even as we get older.* We believe this because we have experienced it in our own lives and observed it in the lives of so many others.

## OUR FITNESS HISTORY

If you remember, in Chapter 1, "Just the Beginning," I shared with you that before she retired, Trisha was a workaholic. That was actually an understatement, and there is more to the story. At that time in her life, she was not taking good care of herself. Obviously, her extreme dedication to career was causing tremendous stress. She didn't allow herself time for proper exercise or nutrition. She began to gain weight and her physical condition suffered. For the first time in her life, she began to lose her positive attitude. Most of her time at home was spent trying to catch up on much needed rest. Given her stress, weight, and diminished physical condition, she was miserable. Finally, being the strong-willed woman she is, she decided enough was enough. She took control of her situation, began to eat right and work out, and gradually got herself back into fantastic shape. In the process she lost nearly forty pounds. Eventually, when we retired, she continued to work hard, but this time it was to keep mentally and physically fit. At present, Trisha looks great and feels fantastic. Her positive attitude is back and she is bursting with energy and confidence.

My personal situation is somewhat different. During most of my adult life, I had been very physically active and participated in several sports, including racquetball three times a week. I coached my sons' baseball teams for over twenty years. At one point, I required elbow surgery, which ended my racquetball routine. A few years later, I needed extensive shoulder surgery. It wasn't particularly successful, and my doctor actually stopped my rehab effort to prevent further damage. This was a tremendous setback for me, and I didn't deal with it properly. I became a bit depressed that I couldn't do the things I used to do and stopped exercising almost completely. Of course, during this period of time, I gained a lot of weight and was completely out of shape. Fortunately, with Trisha setting the example, over the last several years I've gotten back on track. I now eat more carefully, have lost a considerable amount of weight, and gotten into pretty good physical condition. I'm still a work in progress, but feel much stronger and years younger. Like Trisha, I now work at my mental and physical fitness.

I hope this glimpse into our personal fitness history provides some inspiration for those of you who feel it can't be done. We are living proof that you can dramatically change your life in a positive way by getting healthy and fit.

## ESSENTIAL COMPONENTS OF PHYSICAL FITNESS

To accomplish our physical fitness goals and live *The Best of Our Lives*, Trisha and I have found there are four essential components: weight control, nutrition, exercise, and sleep. In addition, to monitor and maintain health and fitness, it is mandatory for everyone in our age group to get routine checkups and age-specific health screening tests.

### 1.  Weight control

Simply put, in the United States, one third of the entire population is overweight, and another 30% are clinically obese. Being overweight is such a problem, it is estimated over 300,000 deaths a year occur as a direct result. In addition to the deaths, being overweight is blamed for a host of other serious health problems. These include:

| | |
|---|---|
| High blood pressure | Strokes |
| Some forms of cancer | Depression |
| High cholesterol levels | Type 2 diabetes |
| Back pain | Low self-esteem |
| Heart disease | Gall stones |
| Sleep and respiratory problems | Eating disorders |

If you don't feel like reading this section, I understand. Weight control is a very personal and difficult topic. There seems to be new and conflicting information out there every day. Miracle and fad diets abound. Every magazine on the rack has the promise of some new and easy way to lose weight. Sadly, we all know these promises aren't realistic.

As with every aspect of this book, Trisha and I want to be honest with you. There are no shortcuts to weight control, at least none that don't include some very serious health risks. I want to also acknowledge that weight control is a very different experience for each individual. For example, I have a cousin who is three years older and weighs five pounds more today than the day he graduated from high school. Is he an extreme athlete? Is he a health freak that only eats birdseed? Not by a long shot. He is an "eat anything, put some more ice cream on that pie, where's my candy bar," kind of a guy. I gain weight just watching *him* eat.

Genetics play a big role in our ability to achieve and control a healthy weight. The bottom line is it will take more effort for some than for others. We must accept that fact and develop an individual plan to reach our goal. It doesn't have to be done by next week, but it needs to be done. We can start by understanding where we rank on the Body Mass Index (BMI).

**Body Mass Index**

| BMI (kg/m²) | 19 | 20 | 21 | 22 | 23 | 24 | 25 | 26 | 27 | 28 | 29 | 30 | 35 | 40 |
|---|---|---|---|---|---|---|---|---|---|---|---|---|---|---|
| Height (in.) | Weight (lb.) | | | | | | | | | | | | | |
| 58 | 91 | 96 | 100 | 105 | 110 | 115 | 119 | 124 | 129 | 134 | 138 | 143 | 167 | 191 |
| 59 | 94 | 99 | 104 | 109 | 114 | 119 | 124 | 128 | 133 | 138 | 143 | 148 | 173 | 198 |
| 60 | 97 | 102 | 107 | 112 | 118 | 123 | 128 | 133 | 138 | 143 | 148 | 153 | 179 | 204 |
| 61 | 100 | 106 | 111 | 116 | 122 | 127 | 132 | 137 | 143 | 148 | 153 | 158 | 185 | 211 |
| 62 | 104 | 109 | 115 | 120 | 126 | 131 | 136 | 142 | 147 | 153 | 158 | 164 | 191 | 218 |
| 63 | 107 | 113 | 118 | 124 | 130 | 135 | 141 | 146 | 152 | 158 | 163 | 169 | 197 | 225 |
| 64 | 110 | 116 | 122 | 128 | 134 | 140 | 145 | 151 | 157 | 163 | 169 | 174 | 204 | 232 |
| 65 | 114 | 120 | 126 | 132 | 138 | 144 | 150 | 156 | 162 | 168 | 174 | 180 | 210 | 240 |
| 66 | 118 | 124 | 130 | 136 | 142 | 148 | 155 | 161 | 167 | 173 | 179 | 186 | 216 | 247 |
| 67 | 121 | 127 | 134 | 140 | 146 | 153 | 159 | 166 | 172 | 178 | 185 | 191 | 223 | 255 |
| 68 | 125 | 131 | 138 | 144 | 151 | 158 | 164 | 171 | 177 | 184 | 190 | 197 | 230 | 262 |
| 69 | 128 | 135 | 142 | 149 | 155 | 162 | 169 | 176 | 182 | 189 | 196 | 203 | 236 | 270 |
| 70 | 132 | 139 | 146 | 153 | 160 | 167 | 174 | 181 | 188 | 195 | 202 | 207 | 243 | 278 |
| 71 | 136 | 143 | 150 | 157 | 165 | 172 | 179 | 186 | 193 | 200 | 208 | 215 | 250 | 286 |
| 72 | 140 | 147 | 154 | 162 | 169 | 177 | 184 | 191 | 199 | 206 | 213 | 221 | 258 | 294 |
| 73 | 144 | 151 | 159 | 166 | 174 | 182 | 189 | 197 | 204 | 212 | 219 | 227 | 265 | 302 |
| 74 | 148 | 155 | 163 | 171 | 179 | 186 | 194 | 202 | 210 | 218 | 225 | 233 | 272 | 311 |
| 75 | 152 | 160 | 168 | 176 | 184 | 192 | 200 | 208 | 216 | 224 | 232 | 240 | 279 | 319 |
| 76 | 156 | 164 | 172 | 180 | 189 | 197 | 205 | 213 | 221 | 230 | 238 | 246 | 287 | 328 |

Find your height in the column on the left, then go across to the right and find your weight. Look above your weight to the top row to find your BMI number.

Under 19 is Underweight          25-30 is Overweight

19 – 25 is Normal          30 or greater is Obese

## USING THE BMI

Recently, when my long-time personal physician moved his practice to another city, I had to find a new doctor. The first time this new gentleman walked into the room, I was looking at the BMI. We introduced ourselves and I said, "Doctor, I have a serious problem." He responded with concern, "What is it, Mr. Parker?" I said, "In looking at this index, I am way too short."

He thought it was very funny, if not original, but then cautioned me about the BMI. It should only be used as one indicator of a healthy weight. Body type, belly fat, and weight-related health problems are also factors to consider. So remember, the BMI is only one tool for you to use in determining your healthy weight. Consult your physician for more guidance.

Once you have determined your healthy weight goal, it's time to develop a personal plan of action to achieve it. This, of course, involves essential fitness components 2 and 3, proper nutrition and exercise. Oh, I suppose you could go out and buy some more of those "miracle" diet books or diet pills, but you already know how that will turn out. Actually, the best use of a diet book I've ever heard of comes from one of my relatives. Many years ago, and after buying every new diet book that came along, she put them all in a large bag, and every time she went up or down her stairs, she carried the bag of books. I didn't make that story up: she really did it.

### 2. Proper nutrition

It's a fact that the nutritional choices we make each day have an effect not only on our weight, but our daily and long-term health and fitness. However, just seeing the word "nutrition" may make some of you cringe. When it comes to food, it's very hard for most of us to make changes. Our likes, dislikes, and habits have been formed over many years and decades. We have to be realistic and practical, but as we age, to live *The Best of Our Lives*, we also need to be healthy and fit.

## NUTRITIONAL SUGGESTIONS

During the aging process our bodies change; therefore, our nutritional needs change. Since there is so much complex and confusing information on nutrition and aging, I have collected and summarized what most experts currently consider to be the best age-related nutritional suggestions.

- Eat a variety of foods and avoid the tendency to eat the same things over and over.
- Learn to read labels and eat foods that provide more calcium, fiber, iron, protein, vitamins A and C, and folic acid.
- Reduce calories by eating nutrient-dense foods, or foods that have the same or similar nutrients, but contain fewer calories.
- Eat smaller amounts of foods that are high in fat, sugar, and sodium.
- Avoid overcooking, which makes food soft and drab.

- Experiment with new flavors.
- Include two to four daily servings of dairy products, such as milk, yogurt, or cheese. Women should be especially careful to get enough calcium in their diets.
- Do not to eat too much protein, because doing so can potentially stress kidney function.
- Reduce fat content in your diet.
- Try to get about 60 percent of your calories from carbohydrates, especially complex carbohydrates.
- Maintain adequate fiber content by eating plenty of fruits, grains, cereals, seeds, legumes, and nuts.
- Include juices and vegetables that contain vitamin C, which helps with the absorption of iron.
- Eat foods with zinc and vitamins C and E, which may prevent the onset of age-related macular degeneration. They can be obtained in dark-colored fruits and vegetables such as oranges, cantaloupes, kale, spinach, broccoli, and peas.
- Include vitamin E, which may play a role in the prevention of Alzheimer's disease. It is plentiful in whole grains, peanuts, nuts, vegetable oils, and seeds.
- Get sufficient quantities of vitamin B12 in meat, poultry, fish, eggs, and dairy foods. Low levels of this vitamin are often associated with loss of memory and hearing.
- Monitor your appetite level, since appetites tend to lessen with age.
- Drink sufficient water, five to eight glasses per day, because it is the most important nutrient and vital to proper kidney function.

Another simple nutritional suggestion Trisha and I follow is to eat foods that are colorful. Colorful foods have been shown to be very high in nutritional value. For this reason, Trisha now tries to include as many of these foods, such as peppers, in her recipes. It's great because we are experiencing many new flavors and getting better nutrition. Next time you are shopping, pick up the most colorful fruits and veggies, and add them to your meals.

Many people struggle with their nutrition, especially the quantity of food, when they eat at restaurants. We used to feel the same way, but now we simply split and share a meal. Breakfast is very easy, because in most cases, they offer combination plates. We order one and split it up. In the situations where we don't share, we just ask for a container and take the rest home for another meal. At first, I thought I would feel a bit cheated at not getting a full portion, but honestly, I get all I want in splitting meals. Even though I'm a big guy, at this point, I don't think I could eat a full meal at most restaurants.

I feel a special obligation to comment further on the nutritional suggestion to drink sufficient water. Some time ago, I began to notice my parents were not drinking very much water. When we had meals together, I would observe they often did not even have a glass on the table. Naturally, I became concerned, especially when my father complained of being constantly tired, frequently dizzy, and having sore muscles. I fought a few battles with them trying to encourage more water consumption. I even consulted my physician and learned something very important about the aging process. As we age, we tend to gradually lose our appetites and our sense of thirst. This is why we see so many older folks eating the same foods, such as cereal, and drinking so little water. Of course, the result is poor nutrition and dehydration, which in turn causes tiredness, dizziness, sore muscles, and possible kidney damage. All of us need to be aware of our appetites and be sure we are getting the proper nutrition and sufficient water intake.

## ANTIOXIDANTS

In addition to the aforementioned nutritional suggestions, let's now learn about antioxidants. I'm sure you've heard of them, because the term is everywhere in the media and on a number of food, juice, and supplement labels. You may have asked yourself, "Why all the excitement?"

An antioxidant is anything that slows down, or in some cases stops, the process of oxidation. In the human body, many metabolic processes use oxygen, which results in the release of oxygen-containing molecules. These molecules, sometimes referred to as free radicals, are considered harmful and a negative influence on the aging process. Some people have likened this process to the way oxidation rusts the metal on an old car. For those of us interested in maintaining good health and fitness, it's important to know that a growing number of researchers and medical professionals believe free radicals play a negative role in heart disease, cancer, and other serious health problems. Simply put, antioxidants act to sop up these free radicals, thereby helping to eliminate them.

I must tell you about a good friend of mine. He is a physician and ten years my senior. Besides being one of the brightest and funniest people I know, he is also well-informed and employs excellent health and fitness practices. One of his nutritional practices is to include large quantities of antioxidant foods in his diet. In fact, he claims to be so full of antioxidants, he has instructed friends and family that should he collapse, they are to revive him and immediately "place a lighted cigarette in my mouth and rub my body with pepperoni pizza."

I told you he was funny. He's also extremely healthy, and, when traveling or socializing, is the first one up for a hike or adventure, and the last one to leave the dance floor at night. Of course, my friend's example is anecdotal, and I cannot tell you that science has 100 percent confirmed all the positive claims antioxidant proponents have made. For the last several years, Trisha and I have tried to increase our consumption of foods and beverages that are high in antioxidants. We can report our personal results appear to be positive. Does this mean you should run out and stock up? No, but I suggest you do more research, and with the counsel of your physician, discover how foods high in antioxidants might benefit you.

The following chart, prepared by the U.S. Department of Agriculture, lists the top fruits and vegetables in rank order of their Oxygen Radical Absorbance Capacity (ORAC). The top fruits range from prunes to pink grapefruit, and the top vegetables range from kale to eggplant. The research was conducted by the Agricultural Research Service's

Human Nutrition Research Center on Aging at Tufts University in Boston. (The ARS is the chief scientific agency of the USDA.) Early research results indicate that eating plenty of these high-ORAC foods may be beneficial in the battle against aging. Some research also suggests it might be best to get antioxidant benefits from food rather than supplements.

## FRUITS

| | |
|---|---|
| Prunes | Plums |
| Raisins | Oranges |
| Blueberries | Red grapes |
| Blackberries | Cherries |
| Strawberries | Kiwi fruit |
| Raspberries | Pink grapefruit |

## VEGETABLES

| | |
|---|---|
| Kale | Beets |
| Spinach | Red bell peppers |
| Brussels sprouts | Onions |
| Alfalfa sprouts | Corn |
| Broccoli flowers | Eggplant |

We should consider eating sufficient quantities of these foods high in ORAC. They taste good, and the benefits hold the potential for improved health and fitness.

### 3. Exercise

The most important advice in any discussion of aging and physical fitness can be summed up in one sentence: **Get at least thirty minutes of aerobic exercise each day.** While Trisha and I are not medical doctors or professional trainers, in living *The Best of Our Lives* we have researched and experimented with a number of exercise methods to find what works best for us. When it comes to aging and fitness, Trisha always says, "I'm going down fighting."

One thing we know works for us is to vary our forms of physical exercise, keep it fun, and be sure to get in the required thirty minutes each day. We probably get in at least one hour of aerobic exercise each day, but we never really watch the clock. We start by stretching, slowly warming up our muscles, which has become more important as we've gotten older. Flexibility is essential, and for that reason we are getting interested in yoga. It's the ultimate exercise activity joining mind and body. There are many cultures in the world that contend flexibility is the key to health. I'm beginning to think they are on to something.

Most often, we take a walk in the morning. We really enjoy walking and try to take different routes each day. There are lots of things to see, and we use the time to simply talk with each other. On other days, we go to a reasonably priced health club that offers a variety of activities. We use the treadmills, workout equipment, and swimming pool. Trisha absolutely loves water aerobics. After each class, one of her favorite activities is to hold onto a small paddleboard and kick her way across the pool. She enjoys this very much and can do it forever. I also enjoy water aerobics, but will admit how surprised I was the first time I tried it. While it looked easy, it really provided a complete workout.

While I spend most of my time walking or using exercise machines, Trisha has a number of creative and fun exercises she uses every day. One of these involves the use of a weighted hoop. Remember the hula hoop? Well, this is the same idea, only it's thicker and weighted. When she first got one about four years ago, she could only keep it going for about five minutes. Now she does it twice a day for thirty minutes each time. She listens to music, watches television, and sometimes even works her arms with small weights while "hooping." It has become part of her life. I tease her about it, but it really does work wonders. Our little grandson is fascinated by this activity and every time he sees her says, "Grandma, hoop." He wants to see her "hooping" and runs around her laughing as she does it.

Another activity Trisha enjoys is using the exercise ball. I'm sure many of you have seen these in stores or television infomercials. The balls are used for various exercises, all of which strengthen your core muscles. She varies her workouts each time, emphasizing different muscle groups. One other thing she has come up with is using her exercise ball as a chair while she is working at her desk. Since it requires her to keep her balance, she is working her core muscles as she does her various tasks.

I think it's important to point out that when Trisha uses weights for any type of exercise, she only uses small five-pound weights. She is not looking to be a body builder, but like most women as they age, keeping her arms firm presents a special challenge. Using these weights helps her achieve her goal and builds endurance. It's amazing and inspirational to watch Trisha enjoy doing exercises she could never have done just a few years ago. Most of us want a quick cure and are impatient to get results. She has done it the right way, which is to start slowly and increase repetitions over time.

There are a couple of other things I do which are easy and I find beneficial. Years ago we bought one of those little devices that allow you to do sit-ups without straining your neck. I hadn't used it in years, but recently I took it out of storage and find it works very well for me. I also keep a twenty-five-pound weight and a hand grip next to my chair. When I watch television, I often do sit-ups, a few sets of arm curls with each arm, and several sets with the hand grip. I'm very pleased with the added strength these simple exercises have given me.

I want to make sure to re-emphasize the most important principle in our approach to regular exercise. That principle is fun. Do something that is fun for you. If you like certain sports like golf or tennis, then you should play on a regular basis. Exercise by itself can be boring, and that is self-defeating. Just the other day, I found myself in a small town near our home. I had been there many times, but never really paid much attention. Since

I had some extra time, I parked my car and just walked around the town. I can't tell you how many little restaurants, shops, and interesting places I discovered. It was a really fun walk, and I didn't have to go to the health club that day.

Having fun while exercising reminds me of a recent trip to Hawaii in which our long-time friends invited us to their timeshare on the island of Kauai. We took full advantage of the beautiful scenery and went on long walks every morning. At our facility, there was an enormous circular pool that had a large island in the middle and was four feet deep all the way around. On the first day of our visit, I offered Trisha a head start and challenged her to a footrace around the inside of the pool. Being so much taller, I won easily. Well, of course she wanted more of a head start and a rematch. I agreed, and off we went again. This went on all afternoon. Each day after that, we could not wait for our water war. It was great fun and wonderful exercise. Be creative, keep your exercises fun, and you will stick with them. In a very short time you will feel better and look younger.

While we are talking about feeling and looking younger, did you know you can actually be younger than your age? "How many years younger?" you ask. Well, an eleven-year British study asked that very question. Researchers studied the behaviors of more than twenty thousand men and women. They came up with four categories considered to be the most important factors in determining a healthy lifestyle. They were:

- No smoking
- At least half an hour of daily physical activity
- Moderate drinking (between one and fourteen alcoholic drinks per week)
- Eating at least five daily servings of fruits and vegetables

And the answer to the question is. . . fourteen years! This long-term study found you can cut fourteen years off your age. Having all four of the habits "was equivalent to being 14 years younger," wrote Kay-Tee Khaw, Ph.D., and colleagues at Cambridge University. These researchers also concluded that having one, two, or three of these behaviors was better than none at all. Keep in mind, if you don't drink, most physicians would advise you not to start.

There you have it: four behaviors to shed fourteen years. Sounds like a pretty good deal to me. If you currently smoke, quit now. No arguments, no rationalizations, no procrastinating, just quit! Get help, do what you have to do, but quit. If you drink, drink in moderation. Be sure to eat plenty of veggies and fruits. Finally, make sure you are getting your daily exercise. I've already described our daily exercise routine, and we really enjoy the benefits.

## 4. Get enough sleep

There is an old Irish proverb that says, "A good laugh and a long sleep are the best cures in the doctor's book." The National Sleep Foundation, which conducts ongoing research on sleep habits and disorders, reports on their website, sleepfoundation.org, that seven out of ten Americans experience sleep problems. Over 40% of Americans report they sleep less than five hours per day. One of the most serious health consequences of lack of sleep has been determined by the University of Warwick Medical School in Great Britain. Their research, as reported in the journal *SLEEP,* concluded that people who do not get the proper sleep have a greater risk for stroke and heart attacks. The risk for heart failure was almost doubled.

The National Institute on Aging (NIA) has reported that 36% of women and 13% of men over sixty-five take thirty minutes or more to fall asleep. They also conclude that older persons require the same amount of sleep as young children, between seven and nine hours. One of their other findings, and this won't surprise many of you, is that older people sleep lighter and therefore awaken more easily. This is probably because as we age, we secrete less melatonin, which produces deeper sleep. This is why so many older people are more sensitive to environmental issues that disturb their sleep.

I think the following statements by the NIA, found on the website nihseniorhealth. gov, dramatically sum up the importance of sleep for older adults:

"Not sleeping well can lead to a number of problems. Older adults who have poor nighttime sleep are more likely to have a depressed mood, attention and memory problems, excessive daytime sleepiness, more nighttime falls, and use more over-the-counter or prescription sleep aids. Poor sleep is also associated with a poorer quality of life."

They go on to say:

"Many people believe that poor sleep is a normal part of aging, but it is not. In fact, many healthy older adults report few or no sleep problems. Sleep patterns change as we age, but disturbed sleep and waking up tired every day are not part of normal aging. If you are having trouble sleeping, see your doctor or a sleep specialist. There are treatments that can help."

As older adults, if we have a sleep disorder, it can be almost impossible to get a good night's sleep. Not only do these disorders make it difficult to sleep at night, they can cause us to be drowsy and irritable during the daytime. The most common sleep disorders for older adults are insomnia, sleep-disordered breathing, such as snoring and sleep apnea, and movement disorders such as restless leg syndrome. Here are descriptions of each sleep disorder and possible treatment suggestions:

## INSOMNIA

Older adults with insomnia have trouble falling asleep, have trouble getting back to sleep, and wake up too early. Occasional insomnia is normal, but chronic insomnia can be caused by stress, certain medications, and drinking alcohol or eating too close to bedtime. Although alcohol may make it easier to fall asleep, once the effects wear off, the person often wakes up. If your insomnia lasts most nights for a few weeks, see your doctor. Insomnia is most common in females, people with depression, and in adults over sixty. These treatment suggestions for insomnia come from the Mayo Clinic.

### Treatments for insomnia
- Go to bed and get up at about the same time every day
- Do not eat or drink large amounts before bedtime
- Avoid nicotine, caffeine, and alcohol in the evening

- Exercise regularly
- Sleep primarily at night
- Choose a comfortable mattress and pillow
- Develop a relaxing bedtime routine
- Go to bed when you're tired and turn out the lights
- Use sleeping pills only as a last resort

## SLEEP-DISORDERED BREATHING

## SNORING

Older adults with sleep-disordered breathing are those who snore or have sleep apnea. Snoring is noisy breathing during sleep that is caused by vibrations in the throat.

### Treatments for snoring
- Lose weight
- Cut down on smoking and alcohol
- Sleep on your side instead of your back

## SLEEP APNEA

There are two kinds of sleep apnea: obstructive sleep apnea and central sleep apnea. Obstructive sleep apnea occurs when the air enters the nose or mouth and is either partially or completely blocked because of obesity or extra tissue in the back of the throat or mouth. Central sleep apnea is less common and occurs when the brain doesn't send the right signals to start the breathing process. It is not uncommon for the same person to have both types of sleep apnea.

Obstructive sleep apnea is more common among older adults and people who are significantly overweight. It can greatly increase a person's risk for high blood pressure, strokes, heart disease, and cognitive problems.

### Treatments for sleep apnea
- Use an assisted breathing device called a CPAP
- Change your sleep position
- Avoid alcohol and sleeping pills
- Lose weight
- Have corrective surgery

## MOVEMENT DISORDERS

The most common of these disorders are PLMD (Periodic Limb Movement Disorder) and RLS (Restless Leg Syndrome). They both are characterized by frequent involuntary movement of limbs, typically the lower extremities. These disorders may also include feelings of itching, burning, tingling, and cramping in your limbs. Persons with these disorders should consult a physician.

**Treatments for movement disorders**
- Doctors may prescribe iron supplements
- Doctors may prescribe specific medications

In a review of the literature on aging and sleep, the most common advice seems to center around stress reduction, weight reduction, regular exercise, relaxation before bedtime, and developing a bedtime routine. We have already discussed several of these ideas. Remember my "no watching the news before bedtime" rule in Chapter 2? Developing a relaxing bedtime routine should go a long way in helping you get the proper sleep you require. Trisha and I follow one, and I can honestly tell you we sleep very soundly. Sweet dreams.

Let me conclude this section by once again cautioning you to check with your physician before making any nutritional changes or beginning any fitness program. Medical conditions, medications, and other individual needs may have to be addressed beyond the scope of the recommendations given here. With that said, these suggestions represent the current guidelines for persons over fifty years old from health, fitness, and nutritional experts.

## SENIOR SEX

Since it was our generation that opened the door to sexual liberation, it's not surprising that over the last three decades, sexual activity among seniors has seen a dramatic rise. One study, published in the *British Medical Journal*, investigated the sexual behavior of seventy-year-olds over a thirty year time span. The findings revealed that in the 1970s, 52% of married men in their seventies were engaging in sexual activity. Thirty years later, that number had jumped to 68%. For married women, the increase was even more dramatic. The percentage of married women in their seventies engaging in sexual activity rose from 38% to 56%. For unmarried men in the same age group, the increase was from 30% to 54%. For unmarried women, the figures increased from just below 1 percent to 12%. In addition, this study found that seniors' attitudes about their sex lives had also improved. The seniors describing their sex life as "very happy" improved from 40 percent to 57% for men, and 35% to 52% for women. Researcher and author of the study Nils Beckman is quoted as saying, "Our study shows that a large majority of elderly consider sexual activity and sexual feelings a natural part of late life."

More recently, a federally funded study published in the *New England Journal of Medicine* determined the following percentages of seniors that engage in sexual activity:

- 73% of seniors 57 to 64 years of age
- 53% of seniors 65 to 74 years of age
- 26% of seniors 75 to 85 years of age

"From a societal perspective, I would say that old people are young people later in life," said the lead researcher of the study, Dr. Stacy Tesler Lindau. In addition, this detailed study found that half of the sexually active subjects between the ages of fifty-seven and seventy-five reported engaging in oral sex. The study also discovered that half of all subjects, even those not sexually active, reported they had masturbated in the previous year. Coauthor and sociologist at the University of Chicago, Edward O. Laumann, reasoned that this information on masturbation "reflects a level of sexual need, even among men at very advanced ages, and speaks to the fact that sexuality is a lifelong proposition."

Let me summarize the findings of these and several other scientific studies on senior sex for you: *Most seniors are still interested in sex and are engaging in sexual activity.* Is anyone shocked by these findings? I didn't think so.

Regardless of the statistics, it's important we understand that aging does present certain obstacles and challenges to our sex lives. As a matter of fact, the same study also found that half of all seniors reported one or more problems hampering their sex lives. Half of all men and women in the study described low desire as a serious problem. Of the female respondents, 43% said that vaginal dryness posed a problem. Of the male respondents, 37% admitted having a problem gaining and maintaining an erection. Other reported problems included the effects of medications, diabetes, and other health issues.

Given all the different findings from my research on this topic, the next one is the most shocking and significant statistic for us all. Given the high percentages of seniors reporting sexual problems in this major study, only 38% of men and 22% of women had discussed their problems with a doctor. I am stunned and saddened by this statistic. As with any other aspects of our mental and physical health, problems with our sex lives are important and should be treated as such. I understand there are seniors out there who are embarrassed and uncomfortable discussing such a personal matter with anyone. Don't be. You deserve to live the life you want to live. If you currently have any mental or physical health problem hindering your sex life, seek medical attention. I remember the words of a radio psychologist who used to say, "This is your life, not the dress rehearsal." Take the appropriate action now.

I have found that most experts provide similar commonsense suggestions for seniors when it comes to sex. Hopefully, you will find these suggestions beneficial for improving and maintaining your sex life.

## Senior Sex Suggestions

- **Talk to your doctor**

Your doctor can advise you in managing your health issues and medications to help you achieve a healthy sex life. There are a number of new innovations in medicine aimed at improving sexual performance. Doctors, in most cases, will not ask you about your sex life, so it's your responsibility to initiate the discussion.

- **Stay positive**

During the aging process, some people become dissatisfied with their self-image, which results in a negative impact on their sex life. This is more prevalent with women, but men have similar image problems. The best advice is to be honest with your partner:

respect and encourage each other. If this becomes a serious problem, seek professional counseling.

- **Get healthy**

Proper nutrition and regular exercise are the keys to a healthy sex life. Avoiding alcohol and practicing safe sex are also important for seniors.

- **Talk to your partner**

Even though some people have been with the same partner for many years, they are still uncomfortable talking about sexual issues. You can begin by asking your partner about his or her sexual desires, concerns, and needs.

- **Try some variety**

If you usually have sex at night, try having it in the morning when you may have more energy. Spice things up by changing your routine and adding a little romance. Include a little more kissing and touching. Plan a date together and do something a bit wild. Some experts suggest dressing differently, changing your hairstyle, or role-playing. It's your sex life, so do what it takes to enjoy yourself.

I found this last suggestion quite interesting. Some time back, Trisha and I started to plan dates with each other. I don't mean expensive or elaborate dates, but romantic dates. We have planned such activities as walking on the beach, having a picnic lunch by ourselves in a remote setting, or simply watching a movie together. The key for us is not the activity itself, but the planning. The more we talk about our date, the more interesting and exciting it becomes. I should add that we also talk about how we want our date to evolve. You get the picture. Of course, until now, we have never told anyone about our dates. Not long ago, while driving and listening to a news program on the radio, we heard a psychologist describe a study which found that people who discuss and plan out their romantic activities report better sex lives. We looked at each other and smiled knowingly.

## ROUTINE CHECKUPS AND HEALTH SCREENINGS

While I hope you all follow a program of routine physical checkups and health screening tests, the fact is many people do not, even though the medical community tells us that following such a program is very important for prevention, early detection, and curing diseases or other possible health problems. Some people are still resistant due to ignorance, fear, or indifference.

As evidence of this resistant behavior, in a study conducted by the National Cancer Institute, researchers studied the records of 24,000 people who had undergone initial screening for colon cancer. Only 10% returned for follow-up testing, and only 34% of that group had both of the recommended follow-up procedures. This left only 774 patients who had both procedures; 241 of those were diagnosed with colon polyps and 32 had colon cancer. What is very scary in reporting these statistics to you is that there is no way to know what happened to the rest of the people involved in this study. They did not return for the recommended follow-up procedures, and we can make some very dire assumptions about the consequences of their behavior.

Please schedule routine physical checkups with your personal physician and follow his or her advice concerning health screening tests. While there is not always universal agreement about these tests, consult your physician and do what is best for you. Here are the most common recommendations:

**Women Over Age Fifty**
- Blood pressure at least every two years
- Cholesterol every five years (every three after age sixty-five)
- Skin exam every year
- Breast exam every year
- Mammogram every year
- Fecal occult blood test every year
- Pelvic exam every year
- Pap test every year or doctor's recommendation
- Bone mineral density test once as a baseline
- Fasting plasma glucose test for diabetes every three years
- Thyroid-stimulating hormone test every three to five years after age sixty-five
- Colorectal cancer test every five to ten years

**Men Over Age Fifty**
- Blood pressure at least every two years
- Cholesterol every five years (every three after age sixty-five)
- Skin exam every year
- Digital rectal exam every year
- Prostate specific antigen (PSA) test every year
- Fasting plasma glucose test for diabetes every three years
- Colorectal cancer test every five to ten years

Let me make a suggestion concerning regular checkups and screenings. I've found that not all physicians ask you about your family and work history during these procedures. My research and experience indicates these factors can be very important for a proper diagnosis. Be sure to consult your physician and provide him or her with any information you think beneficial. If you have not put yourself on a regular physical exam and screening test schedule, by all means do so right now.

Each year, the American Medical Association (AMA) provides recommendations for improving health. Here is a recent list:

Don't smoke
Eat fruits and vegetables
Cut back on salt
Limit fat in your diet
Check your cholesterol
Reduce amount of soda you drink

Check your blood pressure
Get a colonoscopy
Get a mammogram
Protect your skin

We've already touched on several of these issues, but a little more expert advice can't hurt. I've also included this list because it mentions protecting our skin. When retired, many of us spend much more time out in the sun. It is essential that you use sunscreen to protect yourself from skin cancer. At our age, you or one of your friends has probably already had to deal with skin cancer in some form. Be smart, protect yourself, and have your physician routinely check you for skin cancer. Every morning, as a matter of habit, Trisha applies a moisturizer that contains sunscreen. This way she knows she is getting a certain amount of protection should she go out into the sun, even for a short time.

Here are some other health and safety issues I consider to be important for those of us at retirement age:

## FLU AND PNEUMONIA VACCINATIONS

With your physician's approval, it's important to get a flu and pneumonia vaccination each year. The number of seniors who get seriously ill or die from flu each year is estimated to be near 200,000. Flu and pneumonia shots are usually covered by Medicare Part B and Medicaid, so be safe, check with your doctor, and make sure all your inoculations are current.

## DENTAL CARE

It's a fact of life that as we age, and with people now living much longer lives, many of us encounter serious problems with our teeth. Since most retired people don't have dental insurance, going to the dentist is an expense many try to avoid. The fact is, this strategy may be more costly in the long run. We have purchased an electric toothbrush, which does a good job of cleaning our teeth and massaging our gums. We've found this to be quite effective. Of course, regular cleanings and checkups with your dentist are essential. Seems like no one ever wants to go to the dentist, but we must be realistic and count it as one more regular checkup to add to our list.

## UNDERSTANDING STROKE

Another important health issue we seniors need to learn more about is stroke. Recently, I was present when my mother had what is called a transient ischemic attack (TIA), or ministroke. While at first I didn't realize what was happening, I did get her immediate medical attention. On reflection, I realized I lacked the proper understanding to more quickly recognize the symptoms of stroke. Stroke symptoms include:

- Numbness, weakness, or paralysis of the face, arm, or leg, especially on one side of the body

- Trouble seeing in one or both eyes
- Confusion or trouble understanding
- Slurred or garbled speech
- Trouble walking, dizziness, or clumsiness
- Severe headache

The most important advice concerning a stroke is to recognize it quickly and get immediate medical attention. Given my recent personal experience, I know this is extremely important information.

## HEARING

One of the most common age-related health problems is hearing loss. Recent research on this topic reveals that more than 30% of people over the age of sixty-five have significant hearing loss. At age seventy-five, this increases to almost 50%. Even more surprising is the fact that only one in five people who need hearing aids have them, and only one-third of those people actually use them.

We now know, based on recent research at Duke University (see Stewart in the References section), that hearing loss strains relationships, can lead to depression, and downgrades the quality of life. Having a father with severe hearing loss, I really didn't need the scientific evidence. Hearing loss is a severe health issue for seniors. Do everything you can to protect your hearing. Get tested, find the proper aids if needed, and use them.

## DEPRESSION

Unfortunately, depression in seniors is often very difficult to determine. Unlike a young person, in whom a serious mood change would arouse suspicion, with seniors, such behavior is often just assumed to be part of the aging process. Typical signs of depression in seniors are a lack of appetite, fatigue, and problems concentrating. Since these are also common aging factors, family and friends can't usually make the distinction. Experts advise us to look for changes in regular routine, such as not going to church or missing social gatherings. Depression is a health problem that can be medically treated. If you or someone you know suffers from depression, seek medical attention. Not treated, depression in seniors results in a severely degraded quality of life, and possible suicide.

## CPR

Every senior should know CPR (cardiopulmonary resuscitation), which is used to resuscitate persons when their hearts have stopped beating. This procedure can help save heart attack and drowning victims. You can sign up to learn CPR at local fire departments, the American Red Cross, and the American Heart Association (1-800-AHAUSA1).

## HEIMLICH MANEUVER

The Heimlich maneuver is a procedure that involves saving a person who is choking. This can be very serious, and unfortunately, I have firsthand experience. I actually had to perform the Heimlich maneuver on myself a few years ago. It was very scary and frustrating because I was not alone, but no one present knew how to perform this maneuver. I was so fortunate to know what to do. Your health care provider and the Red Cross can help you find the proper training. You could save a life, maybe your own.

Well, there you have it. Following the guidelines and suggestions presented in this chapter should start you on your way to good health and fitness. Remember, it's never too late to start leading a healthy lifestyle. One recent study found that the average person in the U.S. is now living to seventy-eight. In addition, there are numerous studies that contend people who lead healthy lifestyles in their seventies have a better than 50% chance to live into their nineties. As with any and all the information we present, evaluate it for yourself, check with your physician, find what works best for you, and come up with your own individual plan. As always, we wish you health, fitness, and happiness.

*Before you can really start setting financial goals, you need to
determine where you stand financially.*
—David Bach

CHAPTER 4

# MANAGING YOUR DAILY LIVING EXPENSES
*By Trisha*

At some point in your life you've most likely had the money woes, studied or read about the money whys, and wondered how you could become money wise. Given the unpredictable and volatile nature of our economy, managing our expenses and resources wisely has become essential for every retired person. Regardless of the amount of resources each individual has at his or her disposal, the principles of money management remain the same. We cannot control the economy, but we can make the best effort possible in protecting our personal resources. In preparing for and living *The Best of Our Lives*, it's important that we carefully manage our finances to ensure we have the funds available for daily living, enjoying life, and living out our dreams.

To become what I refer to as financially fit in retirement, we must clearly understand our personal financial situation, take responsibility for our financial future, and establish an effective financial plan. In this first chapter on financing our retirement, we will begin by learning how to manage daily living expenses. Simply stated, we are going to employ good financial common sense.

As we begin this series of chapters, I don't want anyone feeling lost or confused because of the terminology. While some of you may already have a working knowledge of finance, others may not. For that reason, I have provided definitions and explanations throughout each chapter, and provided a complete glossary of financial terms at the end of the book.

Before we go any further, let me assure you I'm well aware that every retired person has a unique amount of financial resources available for their retirement years. The advice and principles in each of these chapters is meant to be helpful for everyone, regardless of his or her financial situation.

Getting financially fit is not difficult, and once you have everything organized and in place, the rewards will be well worth your efforts. For John and me, the ideas presented in these financial chapters have made the dream of our early retirement come true. Now that we are retired, these financial practices have become even more important and allow us to enjoy life with peace of mind for ourselves and our family. Financial fitness truly allows us to live *The Best of Our Lives*.

I'm Trisha Parker and I'm happy to say I no longer work. In my previous career I had numerous corporate responsibilities, which included developing and implementing budgets, managing salary programs, and overseeing retirement benefits. Now that I'm retired, my job is managing our daily living expenses and making certain our money is working as hard for us as we worked for it. This is truly the most rewarding and fun job I've ever had. The benefit of my new job is having the time and resources to enjoy life more than ever before, and living out my dreams. As was mentioned previously, John and I live a comfortable life, but are not wealthy. We are constantly mindful of our spending and strive to be financially practical. I believe the following quote by financial planner and author Rajen Devadason sums up quite nicely what retirement planning is all about.

> Financial planning, I believe, is not exclusively about retirement planning or investing or even portfolio management. If distilled to its purest elements, this discipline is more accurately understood as one that involves applying guiding principles to deal with our past, present and future finances.
> Our past – because some of us may be carrying the baggage of yesterday's excesses that are costing us our future happiness and financial well-being;
> Our present – because now is the best time to act and change course toward a better destination; and
> Our future – because each of us is entitled to dream of a better tomorrow.

Do you really know where all your money is being spent? Even people who have budgets or spending plans don't always account for designer coffee, an afternoon at the driving range, a car wash, or a quick fix for a broken nail. It's time to get serious about taking control and managing your daily living expenses. While this may sound overwhelming, you can accomplish it by completing two important tasks: one, accurately record your spending; and two, create a budget.

## 1. Record Your Spending
In this first step, record the amount of money you are spending on each of the specific items listed on the Monthly Spending Worksheet (one of several worksheets and forms I have created to assist you in managing your finances). This should be done for at least three months so that you can properly analyze and track your spending patterns. Keep in mind that this is absolutely essential for developing an effective financial plan for your retirement. Without a detailed assessment of your current spending, developing an appropriate and specific financial plan will be virtually impossible. Make photocopies of this worksheet or go to our website, TheBestofOurLives.com, and download copies.

Before you begin recording your spending, you may want to take some time and familiarize yourself with the worksheet. You will notice I have also provided a sample Monthly Spending Worksheet. The figures used in the sample worksheet are arbitrary and have been used for demonstration purposes only. They are not meant to be anything more than samples.

## USING THE MONTHLY SPENDING WORKSHEET

- **Category item** – This first column lists an inventory of possible spending items. Go through this list and identify the items that do not pertain to your spending and simply cross them out. If you have spending items that are not listed, add them to your worksheet in the spaces provided.
- **Expected spending** – In this second column, record your spending on fixed items. Notice that Expected Spending is broken down into Monthly (rent, mortgage, car payment, etc.) and Periodic (property taxes, home warranty, car insurance, etc.) categories. Monthly refers to monthly spending that is unchanged each month. Periodic refers to nonmonthly spending (billed yearly, semiannually, or quarterly), which should be averaged and listed as a monthly expense. For example, a $600 annual car insurance bill should be recorded as $50 under Monthly Periodic Spending. You will need to have your periodic spending figures readily available for future tracking in your budget process, so I suggest you highlight them. I use the color green to highlight these items.
- **Estimated spending** – In this third column, record your estimated spending on nonfixed items (gasoline, food, entertainment, etc.). Don't get bogged down with your estimates; simply go through your checkbook or previous monthly statements and come up with an average.
- **Monthly spending totals** – In this last column, record your total monthly spending for each category item.

Once you have completed filling out your Monthly Spending Worksheet, go through each category item with a highlighter and identify the items you feel are controllable. Controllable Spending Items are those that you feel can be eliminated or that you can spend less on each month. I use the color yellow to highlight these items. Noncontrollable Items are those you consider necessary and spend a reasonable amount on each month. This process of sorting controllable and noncontrollable items establishes the baseline for creating your budget.

At this point, I would like to share some of my ideas on tracking your spending. These ideas concern special purchases, personal spending, and the use of credit cards.

## SPECIAL PURCHASES

You probably noticed a category item labeled Special Purchases. These are purchases that are not recurring, such as a television, an appliance, or a set of luggage. While they may not reoccur, it's necessary to track them on your Monthly Spending Worksheet—they will help you to budget and adjust spending on your controllable spending items—in order to pay for them.

## PERSONAL SPENDING

Because it's so easy to spend cash on smaller items without tracking your spending, I suggest you budget your spending cash, and each time you spend some, replace it with the receipt. Each day, deposit your change in a piggy bank. At the end of the week, record the spending from your receipts, and then deposit any leftover cash in your bank. Ours is a colorful Mexican piggy bank. We use the money as an "enjoy life fund." When we travel, we use it to buy a meal at a special restaurant, or on shorter trips, we usually have enough to pay for all our meals. If you don't have a piggy bank on hand, make one. Decorate an empty coffee container, use a vase, or wrap a shoe box. Remember the old days when we made our valentine mailboxes for school out of shoe boxes? (As I remember, some of them were very creative.)

As mentioned earlier, we are very frugal. When a rebate comes with a purchase, I immediately fill out the form and send it in. When the rebate check arrives, I cash it and deposit it directly into our piggy bank.

If you have never kept a bank like this, or perhaps think it's a bit trivial, it may help you to know that each time we "break the bank" we never cease to be amazed by how much money we have available to spend. If nothing else, it's lots of fun, and also helps get you in the habit of keeping your receipts for tracking purposes.

## TRACK SPENDING WITH CREDIT CARDS

Assign a specific credit card for the purchase or payment of items under the housing and utilities category, another for transportation and food, and another for entertainment and miscellaneous. This way, when the bill comes, it's very easy to track and see where the money was spent.

## CREDIT CARD REWARD PROGRAMS

We like to use credit cards that have reward programs, such as those that offer gift cards. The variety of gift cards available fits nicely into our spending item categories, such as home improvement, decorating, restaurants, and home entertainment.

If you haven't used these reward programs before, you may be surprised how quickly the rewards add up. At this point, we know which reward programs work best for us. Given that knowledge, we make it a practice of asking before each purchase if a specific card should be used. This is especially beneficial if you use your favorite card for large purchases. For example, did you know that most insurance companies will take a credit card for automobile and property insurance? Home warranties, utilities, cable TV, and communications services will also accept credit cards.

The key, of course, is to make certain you pay off the credit card each month. Let me be clear. **A credit card interest payment is a big no-no and is the root of financial destruction.** If you don't like credit cards, or don't trust yourself to control your charges and pay them off each month, find a bank with a debit card that has a reward program.

If you decide to use credit cards for tracking purposes and reward programs, here are a few example rewards and some important considerations:

- **If your credit card does not have a reward or cash rebate program, get a different card.** In one of our reward programs, if we accumulate an average of 1,250 reward points each month, after a year we will have 15,000 points. This reward program offers both $25 and $50 gift cards. We are able to redeem our 15,000 points for six $25 gift cards, giving us a total of $150. We like to put the gift cards in new wallets, making nice birthday or Christmas presents for our grandchildren. Some reward programs will let you apply the cash value to your account as a payment. You are spending your money, so you might as well get something for it.

- **Avoid credit cards that carry an annual fee.** While reward per-point value may be attractive, the cost of the annual fee eats away the value of the reward.
- **Avoid reward programs that have limits or cap the number of points you can earn annually.** If your credit card has these limitations, when you have reached your maximum point accumulation, you might want to consider switching to a different card.
- **Compare credit card programs to find the best value.** The point values to redeem a reward vary among programs. The fewer points needed to redeem a reward, the less money you spend to acquire the points, making it a better per-point value.
- **Donation rewards are not tax deductible.** Some reward programs allow you to make a donation to a nonprofit organization. These donations are not tax deductible. It is actually better to take the cash reward, if available, and write a donation check yourself.
- **Gift cards are the best rewards.** The key here is to pick the gift cards for restaurants and retailers you most often frequent and shop.
- **Cash gift certificates on a per-point value are not as good as gift cards.** Simply put, the cash value is typically not as good.
- **Airline tickets can be attractive on a per-point value but have restrictions.** For instance, if you are traveling a popular route or during a peak period, the availability of seats and other restrictions make the reality of travel next to impossible. Depending on your travel destinations, the time of the year, and the day of the week, you potentially will find purchasing cheap tickets a better deal than using airline points.
- **Redeeming points for merchandise is the worst deal.** The merchandise is often overpriced, so, if available, take the cash reward and purchase the item yourself.
- **Cash rewards are a better value when you save your points for the maximum benefit.** Typically, the more points you have, the bigger the cash reward on a per-point value.
- **Check your credit card statements each month for point promotions on gasoline, travel, or retail purchases.** This is an easy way to earn double or triple points. Be careful, however, and don't buy something you don't need just for the sake of points.

---

*A budget tells us what we can't afford,*
*but it doesn't keep us from buying it.*
—William Feather

---

## 2. Create a Budget

After recording your spending for three months, go through your Monthly Spending Worksheets and identify those items you can delete or cut back on. Having carefully tracked your spending, you will now be able to set appropriate spending limits and create your budget.

Use the Monthly Budget Tracking Form and fill in your monthly spending limits for each item in the column titled Monthly Budget. This is the form that will be used each month to track your spending. To demonstrate how the budget should be filled out, I have included a sample budget. Once again, these figures are arbitrary and are for demonstration purposes only. Make photocopies of this form or go to our website, TheBestofOurLives.com, and download necessary copies.

At this point, some of you may be asking yourselves why you are going through this process, especially if you have plenty of resources and can afford high levels of spending in any category you choose. Congratulations. Remember, however, we are going through this process to get a clear picture of your spending as part of developing an entire financial plan for your retirement. We will discuss your resources later, but for now, we are only concerned with spending. Here are some considerations to keep in mind while developing your budget:

- Focus on making changes in your controllable spending. It is possible to cut spending in other areas, but that requires major lifestyle changes, which will be discussed later.
- Prioritize spending items by what you consider to be most important.
- Understand which items are most important in maintaining your lifestyle.
- Try to be objective and realistic in setting your spending limits.
- Monitor and consider all items when cutting spending.
- Retired life should be enjoyable, so build as much flexibility into your budget as you deem necessary.

SAMPLE

# MONTHLY SPENDING WORKSHEET

**Controllable expenses are italic and bold.**

**Annual/semiannual expenses are uppercase and underlined.**

| Category<br>Item | Expected Spending Monthly | Periodic | Estimated Spending | Monthly Spending Totals |
|---|---|---|---|---|
| **Housing** | | | | |
| Mortgage/Rent | $ 1,000 | $ - | $ - | $ 1,000 |
| PROPERTY TAXES | $ - | $ 250 | $ - | $ 250 |
| INSURANCE | $ - | $ 25 | $ - | $ 25 |
| *Security System* | $ - | $ - | $ - | $ - |
| HOME WARRANTY | $ - | $ 25 | $ - | $ 25 |
| *Yard Maintenance* | $ - | $ - | $ - | $ - |
| *Pest Control* | $ - | $ - | $ - | $ - |
| *House Maintenance* | $ - | $ - | $ 50 | $ 50 |
| HOA | $ - | $ - | $ - | $ - |
| Other (be specific) | $ - | $ - | $ - | $ - |
| Other (be specific) | $ - | $ - | $ - | $ - |
| **Sub Total** | | | | **$ 1,350** |
| | | | | |
| **Utilities** | | | | |
| Gas/Electricity | $ - | $ - | $ 150 | $ 150 |
| Water | $ - | $ - | $ 30 | $ 30 |
| Waste Management | $ 8 | $ - | $ - | $ 8 |
| *Telephone* | $ - | $ - | $ 25 | $ 25 |
| *Cell Phone* | $ - | $ - | $ 30 | $ 30 |
| *Internet Service* | $ 30 | $ - | $ - | $ 30 |
| Other (be specific) | $ - | $ - | $ - | $ - |
| Other (be specific) | $ - | $ - | $ - | $ - |
| **Sub Total** | | | | **$ 273** |
| | | | | |
| **Medical Care** | | | | |
| Medical Insurance Premiums | $ 150 | $ - | $ - | $ 150 |
| Life Insurance Premiums | $ 200 | $ - | $ - | $ 200 |
| *Doctor* | $ - | $ - | $ 40 | $ 40 |
| *Dental* | $ - | $ - | $ 13 | $ 13 |
| *Vision* | $ - | $ - | $ 20 | $ 20 |
| *Prescriptions* | $ - | $ - | $ 40 | $ 40 |
| *Over the Counter Drugs* | $ - | $ - | $ 50 | $ 50 |
| LONG TERM CARE POLICIES | $ - | $ 250 | $ - | $ 250 |
| Other (be specific) | $ - | $ - | $ - | $ - |
| Other (be specific) | $ - | $ - | $ - | $ - |
| **Sub Total** | | | | **$ 763** |

**Transportation**

| | | | | | | | | |
|---|---|---|---|---|---|---|---|---|
| Car Payment | $ | - | $ | - | $ | - | $ | - |
| DMV | $ | - | $ | 13 | $ | - | $ | 13 |
| AUTO INSURANCE | $ | - | $ | 50 | $ | - | $ | 50 |
| *Gasoline* | $ | - | $ | - | $ | 125 | $ | 125 |
| *Auto Service* | $ | - | $ | - | $ | 13 | $ | 13 |
| *Car Wash* | $ | - | $ | - | $ | - | $ | - |
| *AAA* | $ | - | $ | - | $ | - | $ | - |
| Other (be specific) | $ | - | $ | - | $ | - | $ | - |
| Other (be specific) | $ | - | $ | - | $ | - | $ | - |
| **Sub Total** | | | | | | | **$** | **201** |

**Food/Beverage/Paper Products/etc**

| | | | | | | | | |
|---|---|---|---|---|---|---|---|---|
| *Grocery Store* | $ | - | $ | - | $ | 50 | $ | 50 |
| *Wholesale Club* | $ | - | $ | - | $ | 50 | $ | 50 |
| *Discount Store* | $ | - | $ | - | $ | 200 | $ | 200 |
| *Drug Store* | $ | - | $ | - | $ | - | $ | - |
| *Restaurants* | $ | - | $ | - | $ | 75 | $ | 75 |
| *Fast Food* | $ | - | $ | - | $ | 25 | $ | 25 |
| Other (be specific) | $ | - | $ | - | $ | - | $ | - |
| Other (be specific) | $ | - | $ | - | $ | - | $ | - |
| **Sub Total** | | | | | | | **$** | **400** |

**Entertainment**

| | | | | | | | | |
|---|---|---|---|---|---|---|---|---|
| *Cable TV* | $ | 80 | $ | - | $ | - | $ | 80 |
| *Club Dues* | $ | - | $ | - | $ | - | $ | - |
| *Movies* | $ | - | $ | - | $ | - | $ | - |
| *Concerts/Sporting Events* | $ | - | $ | - | $ | - | $ | - |
| *Vacations* | $ | - | $ | - | $ | 250 | $ | 250 |
| *Computer Service* | $ | - | $ | - | $ | - | $ | - |
| *Newspaper* | $ | - | $ | - | $ | - | $ | - |
| Other (be specific) | $ | - | $ | - | $ | - | $ | - |
| Other (be specific) | $ | - | $ | - | $ | - | $ | - |
| **Sub Total** | | | | | | | **$** | **330** |

**Miscellaneous**

| | | | | | | | | |
|---|---|---|---|---|---|---|---|---|
| *Charity* | $ | - | $ | - | $ | 100 | $ | 100 |
| *Gifts* | $ | - | $ | - | $ | 100 | $ | 100 |
| *Holiday Purchases* | $ | - | $ | - | $ | 150 | $ | 150 |
| *Household Purchases* | $ | - | $ | - | $ | 50 | $ | 50 |
| *Clothing* | $ | - | $ | - | $ | 75 | $ | 75 |
| *Athletic Club* | $ | - | $ | - | $ | - | $ | - |
| Other (be specific) | $ | - | $ | - | $ | - | $ | - |
| Other (be specific) | $ | - | $ | - | $ | - | $ | - |
| **Sub Total** | | | | | | | **$** | **475** |

| | | |
|---|---|---|
| **MONTHLY EXPENSES** | **$** | **3,792** |

| | | | |
|---|---|---|---|
| Special Purchases | TIVO / DVR Replacement | $ | 65 |
| Special Purchases | | $ | - |
| Special Purchases | | $ | - |
| **Sub Total** | | **$** | **65** |

| | | |
|---|---|---|
| **TOTAL MONTHLY EXPENSES** | **$** | **3,857** |

# MONTHLY SPENDING WORKSHEET

**Highlight controllable expenses.**

**Highlight annual/semiannual expenses.**

| Category<br>Item | Expected Spending<br>Monthly | Expected Spending<br>Periodic | Estimated<br>Spending | Monthly<br>Spending<br>Totals |
|---|---|---|---|---|
| **Housing** | | | | |
| Mortgage/Rent | $ - | $ - | $ - | $ - |
| Property Taxes | $ - | $ - | $ - | $ - |
| Insurance | $ - | $ - | $ - | $ - |
| Security System | $ - | $ - | $ - | $ - |
| Home Warranty | $ - | $ - | $ - | $ - |
| Yard Maintenance | $ - | $ - | $ - | $ - |
| Pest Control | $ - | $ - | $ - | $ - |
| House Maintenance | $ - | $ - | $ - | $ - |
| HOA | $ - | $ - | $ - | $ - |
| Other (be specific) | $ - | $ - | $ - | $ - |
| Other (be specific) | $ - | $ - | $ - | $ - |
| **Sub Total** | | | | $ - |
| | | | | |
| **Utilities** | | | | |
| Gas/Electricity | $ - | $ - | $ - | $ - |
| Water | $ - | $ - | $ - | $ - |
| Waste Management | $ - | $ - | $ - | $ - |
| Telephone | $ - | $ - | $ - | $ - |
| Cell Phone | $ - | $ - | $ - | $ - |
| Internet Service | $ - | $ - | $ - | $ - |
| Other (be specific) | $ - | $ - | $ - | $ - |
| Other (be specific) | $ - | $ - | $ - | $ - |
| **Sub Total** | | | | $ - |
| | | | | |
| **Medical Care** | | | | |
| Medical Insurance Premiums | $ - | $ - | $ - | $ - |
| Life Insurance Premiums | $ - | $ - | $ - | $ - |
| Doctor | $ - | $ - | $ - | $ - |
| Dental | $ - | $ - | $ - | $ - |
| Vision | $ - | $ - | $ - | $ - |
| Prescriptions | $ - | $ - | $ - | $ - |
| Over the Counter Drugs | $ - | $ - | $ - | $ - |
| Long Term Care Policies | $ - | $ - | $ - | $ - |
| Other (be specific) | $ - | $ - | $ - | $ - |
| Other (be specific) | $ - | $ - | $ - | $ - |
| **Sub Total** | | | | $ - |

**Transportation**

| | | | | | | | | |
|---|---|---|---|---|---|---|---|---|
| Car Payment | $ | - | $ | - | $ | - | $ | - |
| DMV | $ | - | $ | - | $ | - | $ | - |
| Auto Insurance | $ | - | $ | - | $ | - | $ | - |
| Gasoline | $ | - | $ | - | $ | - | $ | - |
| Auto Service | $ | - | $ | - | $ | - | $ | - |
| Car Wash | $ | - | $ | - | $ | - | $ | - |
| AAA | $ | - | $ | - | $ | - | $ | - |
| Other (be specific) | $ | - | $ | - | $ | - | $ | - |
| Other (be specific) | $ | - | $ | - | $ | - | $ | - |
| **Sub Total** | | | | | | | $ | - |

**Food/Beverage/Paper Products/etc**

| | | | | | | | | |
|---|---|---|---|---|---|---|---|---|
| Grocery Store | $ | - | $ | - | $ | - | $ | - |
| Wholesale Club | $ | - | $ | - | $ | - | $ | - |
| Discount Store | $ | - | $ | - | $ | - | $ | - |
| Drug Store | $ | - | $ | - | $ | - | $ | - |
| Restaurants | $ | - | $ | - | $ | - | $ | - |
| Fast Food | $ | - | $ | - | $ | - | $ | - |
| Other (be specific) | $ | - | $ | - | $ | - | $ | - |
| Other (be specific) | $ | - | $ | - | $ | - | $ | - |
| **Sub Total** | | | | | | | $ | - |

**Entertainment**

| | | | | | | | | |
|---|---|---|---|---|---|---|---|---|
| Cable TV | $ | - | $ | - | $ | - | $ | - |
| Club Dues | $ | - | $ | - | $ | - | $ | - |
| Movies | $ | - | $ | - | $ | - | $ | - |
| Concerts/Sporting Events | $ | - | $ | - | $ | - | $ | - |
| Vacations | $ | - | $ | - | $ | - | $ | - |
| Computer Service | $ | - | $ | - | $ | - | $ | - |
| Newspaper | $ | - | $ | - | $ | - | $ | - |
| Other (be specific) | $ | - | $ | - | $ | - | $ | - |
| Other (be specific) | $ | - | $ | - | $ | - | $ | - |
| **Sub Total** | | | | | | | $ | - |

**Miscellaneous**

| | | | | | | | | |
|---|---|---|---|---|---|---|---|---|
| Charity | $ | - | $ | - | $ | - | $ | - |
| Gifts | $ | - | $ | - | $ | - | $ | - |
| Holiday Purchases | $ | - | $ | - | $ | - | $ | - |
| Household Purchases | $ | - | $ | - | $ | - | $ | - |
| Clothing | $ | - | $ | - | $ | - | $ | - |
| Athletic Club | $ | - | $ | - | $ | - | $ | - |
| Other (be specific) | $ | - | $ | - | $ | - | $ | - |
| Other (be specific) | $ | - | $ | - | $ | - | $ | - |
| **Sub Total** | | | | | | | $ | - |

**MONTHLY EXPENSES**                                         $        -

| | | |
|---|---|---|
| Special Purchases | $ | - |
| Special Purchases | $ | - |
| Special Purchases | $ | - |
| **Sub Total** | $ | - |

**TOTAL MONTHLY EXPENSES**                          $        -

# SAMPLE
# MONTHLY BUDGET TRACKING FORM

**Highlight controllable expenses.**

| Category / Item | Monthly Budget | 1st Month | 2nd Month | → | 12th Month | Annual Totals |
|---|---|---|---|---|---|---|
| **Housing** | | | | | | |
| Mortgage/Rent | $1,000.00 | $1,000.00 | $1,000.00 | | $    - | $2,000.00 |
| Security System - quarterly | $    - | $    - | $    - | | $    - | $    - |
| Yard Maintenance | $    - | $    - | $    - | | $    - | $    - |
| Pest Control | $    - | $    - | $    - | | $    - | $    - |
| House Maintenance | $  50.00 | $    - | $  50.00 | | $    - | $  50.00 |
| HOA | $    - | $    - | $    - | | $    - | $    - |
| Other (be specific) | $    - | $    - | $    - | | $    - | $    - |
| Other (be specific) | $    - | $    - | $    - | | $    - | $    - |
| **Sub Total** | **$1,050.00** | **$1,000.00** | **$1,050.00** | → | **$    -** | **$  2,050** |
| Variance = /- | | $  (50) | $    - | | $ (1,050) | |
| **Utilities** | | | | | | |
| Gas/Electricity | $ 150.00 | $ 160.00 | $ 135.00 | | $    - | $ 295.00 |
| Water | $  30.00 | $  20.00 | $  20.00 | | $    - | $  40.00 |
| Waste Management - quarterly | $   8.00 | $   8.00 | $   8.00 | | $    - | $  16.00 |
| Telephone | $  25.00 | $  20.00 | $  30.00 | | $    - | $  50.00 |
| Cell Phone | $  30.00 | $  30.00 | $  30.00 | | $    - | $  60.00 |
| Internet Service | $  30.00 | $  30.00 | $  30.00 | | $    - | $  60.00 |
| Other (be specific) | $    - | $    - | $    - | | $    - | $    - |
| Other (be specific) | $    - | $    - | $    - | | $    - | $    - |
| **Sub Total** | **$ 273.00** | **$ 268.00** | **$ 253.00** | → | **$    -** | **$   521** |
| Variance = /- | | $   (5) | $  (20) | | $  (273) | |
| **Medical Care** | | | | | | |
| Medical Insurance Premiums | $ 150.00 | $ 150.00 | $ 150.00 | | $    - | $ 300.00 |
| Life Insurance Premiums | $ 200.00 | $ 200.00 | $ 200.00 | | $    - | $ 400.00 |
| Doctor | $  40.00 | $  10.00 | $  30.00 | | $    - | $  40.00 |
| Dental | $  13.00 | $    - | $    - | | $    - | $    - |
| Vision | $  20.00 | $    - | $    - | | $    - | $    - |
| Prescriptions | $  40.00 | $  10.00 | $  30.00 | | $    - | $  40.00 |
| Over the Counter Drugs | $  50.00 | $  30.00 | $  25.00 | | $    - | $  55.00 |
| Other (be specific) | $    - | $    - | $    - | | $    - | $    - |
| Other (be specific) | $    - | $    - | $    - | | $    - | $    - |
| **Sub Total** | **$ 513.00** | **$ 400.00** | **$ 435.00** | → | **$    -** | **$   835** |
| Variance = /- | | $ (113) | $  (78) | | $  (513) | |
| **Transportation** | | | | | | |
| Car Payment | $    - | $    - | $    - | | $    - | $    - |
| Gasoline | $ 150.00 | $ 100.00 | $  75.00 | | $    - | $ 175.00 |
| Auto Service | $  13.00 | $    - | $    - | | $    - | $    - |
| Car Wash | $    - | $    - | $    - | | $    - | $    - |
| AAA | $    - | $    - | $    - | | $    - | $    - |
| Other (be specific) | $    - | $    - | $    - | | $    - | $    - |
| Other (be specific) | $    - | $    - | $    - | | $    - | $    - |
| **Sub Total** | **$ 163.00** | **$ 100.00** | **$  75.00** | → | **$    -** | **$   175** |
| Variance = /- | | $  (63) | $  (88) | | $  (163) | |

**Highlight controllable expenses.**

| Category / Item | Monthly Budget | 1st Month | 2nd Month | ⇒ | 12th Month | Annual Totals |
|---|---|---|---|---|---|---|
| **Food/Beverage/Paper Products/etc.** | | | | | | |
| Grocery Stores | $ 50.00 | $ 25.00 | $ 50.00 | | $ - | $ 75.00 |
| Wholesale Club | $ 50.00 | $ - | $ - | | $ - | $ - |
| Discount Store | $ 200.00 | $ 175.00 | $ 200.00 | | $ - | $ 375.00 |
| Drug Store | $ - | $ - | $ - | | $ - | $ - |
| Restaurants | $ 75.00 | $ - | $ 50.00 | | $ - | $ 50.00 |
| Fast Food | $ 25.00 | $ - | $ - | | $ - | $ - |
| Other (be specific) | $ - | $ - | $ - | | $ - | $ - |
| Other (be specific) | $ - | $ - | $ - | | $ - | $ - |
| | | | | | | |
| **Sub Total** | **$ 400.00** | **$ 200.00** | **$ 300.00** | ⇒ | **$ -** | **$ 500** |
| Variance = /- | | $ (200) | $ (100) | | $ (400) | |
| **Entertainment** | | | | | | |
| Cable TV | $ 80.00 | $ 80.00 | $ 80.00 | | $ - | $ 160.00 |
| Club Dues | $ - | $ - | $ - | | $ - | $ - |
| Movies | $ - | $ - | $ - | | $ - | $ - |
| Concerts/Sporting Events | $ - | $ - | $ - | | $ - | $ - |
| Vacations | $ 250.00 | $ - | $ - | | $ - | $ - |
| Computer Service | $ - | $ - | $ - | | $ - | $ - |
| Newspaper | $ - | $ - | $ - | | $ - | $ - |
| Other (be specific) | $ - | $ - | $ - | | $ - | $ - |
| Other (be specific) | $ - | $ - | $ - | | $ - | $ - |
| | | | | | | |
| **Sub Total** | **$ 330.00** | **$ 80.00** | **$ 80.00** | ⇒ | **$ -** | **$ 160** |
| Variance = /- | | $ (250) | $ (250) | | $ (330) | |
| **Miscellaneous** | | | | | | |
| Charity | $ 100.00 | $ 100.00 | $ 100.00 | | $ - | $ 200.00 |
| Gifts | $ 100.00 | $ - | $ 25.00 | | $ - | $ 25.00 |
| Holiday Purchases | $ 150.00 | $ - | $ - | | $ - | $ - |
| Household Purchases | $ 50.00 | $ - | $ 50.00 | | $ - | $ 50.00 |
| Clothing | $ 75.00 | $ - | $ - | | $ - | $ - |
| Athletic Club | $ - | $ - | $ - | | $ - | $ - |
| Other (be specific) | $ - | $ - | $ - | | $ - | $ - |
| Other (be specific) | $ - | $ - | $ - | | $ - | $ - |
| | | | | | | |
| **Sub Total** | **$ 475.00** | **$ 100.00** | **$ 175.00** | ⇒ | **$ -** | **$ 275** |
| Variance = /- | | $ (375) | $ (300) | | $ (475) | |
| | | | | | | |
| **ROUTINE MONTHLY EXPENSES** | $3,204.00 | $2,148.00 | $2,368.00 | ⇒ | $ - | $ 4,516 |
| Variance = /- | | $ 1,056) | $ (836) | | $ (3,204) | |
| **ROUTINE ANNUAL EXPENSES** | $ 38,448 | | | | | |
| | | | | | | |
| **Non Routine - Special Purchases** | | | | | | |
| Be Specific | $ - | $ - | $ - | | $ - | $ - |
| Be Specific | $ - | $ - | $ - | | $ - | $ - |
| Be Specific | $ - | $ - | $ - | | $ - | $ - |
| Be Specific | $ - | $ - | $ - | | $ - | $ - |
| | | | | | | |
| **Sub Total** | **$ -** | **$ -** | **$ -** | | **$ -** | **$ -** |
| | | | | | | |
| **TOTAL MONTHLY EXPENSES** | | **$2,148.00** | **$2,368.00** | ⇒ | **$ -** | **$ 4,516** |

**Highlight controllable expenses.**

| Periodic Expenses | Standard | 1st Month | 2nd Month | | 12th Month | Annual Totals |
|---|---|---|---|---|---|---|
| Property Taxes | $ 250.00 | $ - | $ - | | $ - | $ - |
| House Insurance | $ 25.00 | $ - | $ - | | $ - | $ - |
| Home Warranty | $ 25.00 | $ - | $ - | | $ - | $ - |
| Long Term Care Policies | $ 250.00 | $ - | $3,000.00 | | $ - | $3,000.00 |
| DMV - Car # 1 | $ 13.00 | $ - | $ - | | $ - | $ - |
| Car #1 - Insurance | $ 25.00 | $ - | $ - | | $ - | $ - |
| DMV - Car # 2 | $ - | $ - | $ - | | $ - | $ - |
| Car #2 - Insurance | $ - | $ - | $ - | | $ - | $ - |
| | | | | | | |
| **PERIODIC EXPENSES** | **$ 588.00** | **$ -** | **$3,000.00** | | **$ -** | **$ 3,000** |
| **Running Total** | | | **$3,000.00** | | **$ -** | |
| | | | | | | |
| **PERIODIC ANNUAL EXPENSES** | **$ 7,056** | | | | | |
| | | | | | | |
| **MONTHLY BUDGET** | **$ 3,792** | | | | | |
| | | | | | | |
| **ANNUAL BUDGET** | **$ 45,504** | | | | | **$ 7,516** |

# MONTHLY BUDGET TRACKING FORM

**Highlight controllable expenses.**

| Category / Item | Monthly Budget | 1st Month | 2nd Month | 3rd Month | 4th Month | 5th Month |
|---|---|---|---|---|---|---|
| **Housing** | | | | | | |
| Mortgage/Rent | $ - | $ - | $ - | $ - | $ - | $ - |
| Security System - quarterly | $ - | $ - | $ - | $ - | $ - | $ - |
| Yard Maintenance | $ - | $ - | $ - | $ - | $ - | $ - |
| Pest Control | $ - | $ - | $ - | $ - | $ - | $ - |
| House Maintenance | $ - | $ - | $ - | $ - | $ - | $ - |
| HOA | $ - | $ - | $ - | $ - | $ - | $ - |
| Other (be specific) | $ - | $ - | $ - | $ - | $ - | $ - |
| Other (be specific) | $ - | $ - | $ - | $ - | $ - | $ - |
| **Sub Total** | $ - | $ - | $ - | $ - | $ - | $ - |
| Variance = /- | | $ - | $ - | $ - | $ - | $ - |
| **Utilities** | | | | | | |
| Gas/Electricity | $ - | $ - | $ - | $ - | $ - | $ - |
| Water | $ - | $ - | $ - | $ - | $ - | $ - |
| Waste Management - quarterly | $ - | $ - | $ - | $ - | $ - | $ - |
| Telephone | $ - | $ - | $ - | $ - | $ - | $ - |
| Cell Phone | $ - | $ - | $ - | $ - | $ - | $ - |
| Internet Service | $ - | $ - | $ - | $ - | $ - | $ - |
| Other (be specific) | $ - | $ - | $ - | $ - | $ - | $ - |
| Other (be specific) | $ - | $ - | $ - | $ - | $ - | $ - |
| **Sub Total** | $ - | $ - | $ - | $ - | $ - | $ - |
| Variance = /- | | $ - | $ - | $ - | $ - | $ - |
| **Medical Care** | | | | | | |
| Medical Insurance Premiums | $ - | $ - | $ - | $ - | $ - | $ - |
| Life Insurance Premiums | $ - | $ - | $ - | $ - | $ - | $ - |
| Doctor | $ - | $ - | $ - | $ - | $ - | $ - |
| Dental | $ - | $ - | $ - | $ - | $ - | $ - |
| Vision | $ - | $ - | $ - | $ - | $ - | $ - |
| Prescriptions | $ - | $ - | $ - | $ - | $ - | $ - |
| Over the Counter Drugs | $ - | $ - | $ - | $ - | $ - | $ - |
| Other (be specific) | $ - | $ - | $ - | $ - | $ - | $ - |
| Other (be specific) | $ - | $ - | $ - | $ - | $ - | $ - |
| **Sub Total** | $ - | $ - | $ - | $ - | $ - | $ - |
| Variance = /- | | $ - | $ - | $ - | $ - | $ - |
| **Transportation** | | | | | | |
| Car Payment | $ - | $ - | $ - | $ - | $ - | $ - |
| Gasoline | $ - | $ - | $ - | $ - | $ - | $ - |
| Auto Service | $ - | $ - | $ - | $ - | $ - | $ - |
| Car Wash | $ - | $ - | $ - | $ - | $ - | $ - |
| AAA | $ - | $ - | $ - | $ - | $ - | $ - |
| Other (be specific) | $ - | $ - | $ - | $ - | $ - | $ - |
| Other (be specific) | $ - | $ - | $ - | $ - | $ - | $ - |
| **Sub Total** | $ | $ | $ | $ | $ | $ |
| Variance = /- | | $ - | $ - | $ - | $ - | $ - |

**Highlight controllable expenses.**

| Category<br>Item | Monthly<br>Budget | 1st<br>Month | 2nd<br>Month | 3rd<br>Month | 4th<br>Month | 5th<br>Month |
|---|---|---|---|---|---|---|
| **Food/Beverage/Paper Products/etc.** | | | | | | |
| Grocery Stores | $ - | $ - | $ - | $ - | $ - | $ - |
| Wholesale Club | $ - | $ - | $ - | $ - | $ - | $ - |
| Discount Store | $ - | $ - | $ - | $ - | $ - | $ - |
| Drug Store | $ - | $ - | $ - | $ - | $ - | $ - |
| Restaurants | $ - | $ - | $ - | $ - | $ - | $ - |
| Fast Food | $ - | $ - | $ - | $ - | $ - | $ - |
| Other (be specific) | $ - | $ - | $ - | $ - | $ - | $ - |
| Other (be specific) | $ - | $ - | $ - | $ - | $ - | $ - |
| **Sub Total** | $ - | $ - | $ - | $ - | $ - | $ - |
| Variance = /- | | $ - | $ - | $ - | $ - | $ - |
| **Entertainment** | | | | | | |
| Cable TV | $ - | $ - | $ - | $ - | $ - | $ - |
| Club Dues | $ - | $ - | $ - | $ - | $ - | $ - |
| Movies | $ - | $ - | $ - | $ - | $ - | $ - |
| Concerts/Sporting Events | $ - | $ - | $ - | $ - | $ - | $ - |
| Vacations | $ - | $ - | $ - | $ - | $ - | $ - |
| Computer Service | $ - | $ - | $ - | $ - | $ - | $ - |
| Newspaper | $ - | $ - | $ - | $ - | $ - | $ - |
| Other (be specific) | $ - | $ - | $ - | $ - | $ - | $ - |
| Other (be specific) | $ - | $ - | $ - | $ - | $ - | $ - |
| **Sub Total** | $ - | $ - | $ - | $ - | $ - | $ - |
| Variance = /- | | $ - | $ - | $ - | $ - | $ - |
| **Miscellaneous** | | | | | | |
| Charity | $ - | $ - | $ - | $ - | $ - | $ - |
| Gifts | $ - | $ - | $ - | $ - | $ - | $ - |
| Holiday Purchases | $ - | $ - | $ - | $ - | $ - | $ - |
| Household Purchases | $ - | $ - | $ - | $ - | $ - | $ - |
| Clothing | $ - | $ - | $ - | $ - | $ - | $ - |
| Athletic Club | $ - | $ - | $ - | $ - | $ - | $ - |
| Other (be specific) | $ - | $ - | $ - | $ - | $ - | $ - |
| Other (be specific) | $ - | $ - | $ - | $ - | $ - | $ - |
| **Sub Total** | $ - | $ - | $ - | $ - | $ - | $ - |
| Variance = /- | | $ - | $ - | $ - | $ - | $ - |
| **ROUTINE MONTHLY EXPENSES** | $ - | $ - | $ - | $ - | $ - | $ - |
| Variance = /- | | $ - | $ - | $ - | $ - | $ - |
| **ROUTINE ANNUAL EXPENSES** | $ - | | | | | |
| **Non Routine - Special Purchases** | | | | | | |
| Be Specific | $ - | $ - | $ - | $ - | $ - | $ - |
| Be Specific | $ - | $ - | $ - | $ - | $ - | $ - |
| Be Specific | $ - | $ - | $ - | $ - | $ - | $ - |
| Be Specific | $ - | $ - | $ - | $ - | $ - | $ - |
| **Sub Total** | $ - | $ - | $ - | $ - | $ - | $ - |
| **TOTAL MONTHLY EXPENSES** | | $ - | $ - | $ - | $ - | $ - |

**Highlight controllable expenses.**

| Periodic Expenses | Standard | | 1st Month | | 2nd Month | | 3rd Month | | 4th Month | | 5th Month | |
|---|---|---|---|---|---|---|---|---|---|---|---|---|
| Property Taxes | $ | - | $ | - | $ | - | $ | - | $ | - | $ | - |
| House Insurance | $ | - | $ | - | $ | - | $ | - | $ | - | $ | - |
| Home Warranty | $ | - | $ | - | $ | - | $ | - | $ | - | $ | - |
| Long Term Care Policies | $ | - | $ | - | $ | - | $ | - | $ | - | $ | - |
| DMV - Car # 1 | $ | - | $ | - | $ | - | $ | - | $ | - | $ | - |
| Car #1 - Insurance | $ | - | $ | - | $ | - | $ | - | $ | - | $ | - |
| DMV - Car # 2 | $ | - | $ | - | $ | - | $ | - | $ | - | $ | - |
| Car #2 - Insurance | $ | - | $ | - | $ | - | $ | - | $ | - | $ | - |
| | | | | | | | | | | | | |
| **PERIODIC  EXPENSES** | $ | - | $ | - | $ | - | $ | - | $ | - | $ | - |
| **Running Total** | | | | | $ | - | $ | - | $ | - | $ | - |

**PERIODIC ANNUAL EXPENSES**     $   -

**MONTHLY BUDGET**     $   -

**ANNUAL BUDGET**     $   -

# MONTHLY BUDGET TRACKING FORM

**Yellow Highlight controllable expenses.**

| Category Item | Monthly Budget | | 6th Month | | 7th Month | | 8th Month | | 9th Month | |
|---|---|---|---|---|---|---|---|---|---|---|
| **Housing** | | | | | | | | | | |
| Mortgage/Rent | $ | - | $ | - | $ | - | $ | - | $ | - |
| Security System - quarterly | $ | - | $ | - | $ | - | $ | - | $ | - |
| Yard Maintenance | $ | - | $ | - | $ | - | $ | - | $ | - |
| Pest Control | $ | - | $ | - | $ | - | $ | - | | |
| House Maintenance | $ | - | $ | - | $ | - | $ | - | $ | - |
| HOA | $ | - | $ | - | $ | - | $ | - | $ | - |
| Other (be specific) | $ | - | $ | - | $ | - | $ | - | $ | - |
| Other (be specific) | $ | - | $ | - | $ | - | $ | - | $ | - |
| **Sub Total** | **$** | **-** | **$** | **-** | **$** | **-** | **$** | **-** | **$** | **-** |
| Variance = /- | | | $ | - | $ | - | $ | - | $ | - |
| **Utilities** | | | | | | | | | | |
| Gas/Electricity | $ | - | $ | - | $ | - | $ | - | $ | - |
| Water | $ | - | $ | - | $ | - | $ | - | $ | - |
| Waste Management - quarterly | $ | - | $ | - | $ | - | $ | - | $ | - |
| Telephone | $ | - | $ | - | $ | - | $ | - | $ | - |
| Cell Phone | $ | - | $ | - | $ | - | $ | - | $ | - |
| Internet Service | $ | - | $ | - | $ | - | $ | - | $ | - |
| Other (be specific) | $ | - | $ | - | $ | - | $ | - | $ | - |
| Other (be specific) | $ | - | $ | - | $ | - | $ | - | $ | - |
| **Sub Total** | **$** | **-** | **$** | **-** | **$** | **-** | **$** | **-** | **$** | **-** |
| Variance = /- | | | $ | - | $ | - | $ | - | $ | - |
| **Medical Care** | | | | | | | | | | |
| Medical Insurance Premiums | $ | - | $ | - | $ | - | $ | - | $ | - |
| Life Insurance Premiums | $ | - | $ | - | $ | - | $ | - | $ | - |
| Doctor | $ | - | $ | - | $ | - | $ | - | $ | - |
| Dental | $ | - | $ | - | $ | - | $ | - | $ | - |
| Vision | $ | - | $ | - | $ | - | $ | - | $ | - |
| Prescriptions | $ | - | $ | - | $ | - | $ | - | $ | - |
| Over the Counter Drugs | $ | - | $ | - | $ | - | $ | - | $ | - |
| Other (be specific) | $ | - | $ | - | $ | - | $ | - | $ | - |
| Other (be specific) | $ | - | $ | - | $ | - | $ | - | $ | - |
| **Sub Total** | **$** | **-** | **$** | **-** | **$** | **-** | **$** | **-** | **$** | **-** |
| Variance = /- | | | $ | - | $ | - | $ | - | $ | - |
| **Transportation** | | | | | | | | | | |
| Car Payment | $ | - | $ | - | $ | - | $ | - | $ | - |
| Gasoline | $ | - | $ | - | $ | - | $ | - | $ | - |
| Auto Service | $ | - | $ | - | $ | - | $ | - | $ | - |
| Car Wash | $ | - | $ | - | $ | - | $ | - | $ | - |
| AAA | $ | - | $ | - | $ | - | $ | - | $ | - |
| Other (be specific) | $ | - | $ | - | $ | - | $ | - | $ | - |
| Other (be specific) | $ | - | $ | - | $ | - | $ | - | $ | - |
| **Sub Total** | **$** | **-** | **$** | **-** | **$** | **-** | **$** | **-** | **$** | **-** |
| Variance = /- | | | $ | - | $ | - | $ | - | $ | - |

**Yellow Highlight controllable expenses.**

| Category Item | Monthly Budget | | 6th Month | | 7th Month | | 8th Month | | 9th Month | |
|---|---|---|---|---|---|---|---|---|---|---|
| **Food/Beverage/Paper Products/etc.** | | | | | | | | | | |
| Grocery Stores | $ | - | $ | - | $ | - | $ | - | $ | - |
| Wholesale Club | $ | - | $ | - | $ | - | $ | - | $ | - |
| Discount Store | $ | - | $ | - | $ | - | $ | - | $ | - |
| Drug Store | $ | - | $ | - | $ | - | $ | - | $ | - |
| Restaurants | $ | - | $ | - | $ | - | $ | - | $ | - |
| Fast Food | $ | - | $ | - | $ | - | $ | - | $ | - |
| Other (be specific) | $ | - | $ | - | $ | - | $ | - | $ | - |
| Other (be specific) | $ | - | $ | - | $ | - | $ | - | $ | - |
| **Sub Total** | $ | - | $ | - | $ | - | $ | - | $ | - |
| Variance = /- | | | $ | - | $ | - | $ | - | $ | - |
| **Entertainment** | | | | | | | | | | |
| Cable TV | $ | - | $ | - | $ | - | $ | - | $ | - |
| Club Dues | $ | - | $ | - | $ | - | $ | - | $ | - |
| Movies | $ | - | $ | - | $ | - | $ | - | $ | - |
| Concerts/Sporting Events | $ | - | $ | - | $ | - | $ | - | $ | - |
| Vacations | $ | - | $ | - | $ | - | $ | - | $ | - |
| Computer Service | $ | - | $ | - | $ | - | $ | - | $ | - |
| Newspaper | $ | - | $ | - | $ | - | $ | - | $ | - |
| Other (be specific) | $ | - | $ | - | $ | - | $ | - | $ | - |
| Other (be specific) | $ | - | $ | - | $ | - | $ | - | $ | - |
| **Sub Total** | $ | - | $ | - | $ | - | $ | - | $ | - |
| Variance = /- | | | $ | - | $ | - | $ | - | $ | - |
| **Miscellaneous** | | | | | | | | | | |
| Charity | $ | - | $ | - | $ | - | $ | - | $ | - |
| Gifts | $ | - | $ | - | $ | - | $ | - | $ | - |
| Holiday Purchases | $ | - | $ | - | $ | - | $ | - | $ | - |
| Household Purchases | $ | - | $ | - | $ | - | $ | - | $ | - |
| Clothing | $ | - | $ | - | $ | - | $ | - | $ | - |
| Athletic Club | $ | - | $ | - | $ | - | $ | - | $ | - |
| Other (be specific) | $ | - | $ | - | $ | - | $ | - | $ | - |
| Other (be specific) | $ | - | $ | - | $ | - | $ | - | $ | - |
| **Sub Total** | $ | - | $ | - | $ | - | $ | - | $ | - |
| Variance = /- | | | $ | - | $ | - | $ | - | $ | - |
| **ROUTINE MONTHLY EXPENSES** | $ | - | $ | - | $ | - | $ | - | $ | - |
| Variance = /- | | | $ | - | $ | - | $ | - | $ | - |
| **ROUTINE ANNUAL EXPENSES** | $ | - | | | | | | | | |
| **Non Routine - Special Purchases** | | | | | | | | | | |
| Be Specific | $ | - | $ | - | $ | - | $ | - | $ | - |
| Be Specific | $ | - | $ | - | $ | - | $ | - | $ | - |
| Be Specific | $ | - | $ | - | $ | - | $ | - | $ | - |
| Be Specific | $ | - | $ | - | $ | - | $ | - | $ | - |
| **Sub Total** | $ | - | $ | - | $ | - | $ | - | $ | - |
| **TOTAL MONTHLY EXPENSES** | | | $ | - | $ | - | $ | - | $ | - |

**Yellow Highlight controllable expenses.**

| Periodic Expenses | Standard | | 6th Month | | 7th Month | | 8th Month | | 9th Month | |
|---|---|---|---|---|---|---|---|---|---|---|
| Property Taxes | $ | - | $ | - | $ | - | $ | - | $ | - |
| House Insurance | $ | - | $ | - | $ | - | $ | - | $ | - |
| Home Warranty | $ | - | $ | - | $ | - | $ | - | $ | - |
| Long Term Care Policies | $ | - | $ | - | $ | - | $ | - | $ | - |
| DMV - Car # 1 | $ | - | $ | - | $ | - | $ | - | $ | - |
| Car #1 - Insurance | $ | - | $ | - | $ | - | $ | - | $ | - |
| DMV - Car # 2 | $ | - | $ | - | $ | - | $ | - | $ | - |
| Car #2 - Insurance | $ | - | $ | - | $ | - | $ | - | $ | - |
| **PERIODIC EXPENSES** | $ | - | $ | - | $ | - | $ | - | $ | - |
| **Running Total** | | | $ | - | $ | - | $ | - | $ | - |

**PERIODIC ANNUAL EXPENSES**    $   -

**MONTHLY BUDGET**    $   -

**ANNUAL BUDGET**    $   -

# MONTHLY BUDGET TRACKING FORM

**Yellow Highlight controllable expenses.**

| Category<br>Item | Monthly<br>Budget | 10th<br>Month | 11th<br>Month | 12th<br>Month | Annual<br>Totals |
|---|---|---|---|---|---|
| **Housing** | | | | | |
| Mortgage/Rent | $ - | $ - | $ - | $ - | $ - |
| Security System - quarterly | $ - | $ - | $ - | $ - | $ - |
| Yard Maintenance | $ - | $ - | $ - | $ - | $ - |
| Pest Control | $ - | $ - | $ - | $ - | $ - |
| House Maintenance | $ - | $ - | $ - | $ - | $ - |
| HOA | $ - | $ - | $ - | $ - | $ - |
| Other (be specific) | $ - | $ - | $ - | $ - | $ - |
| Other (be specific) | $ - | $ - | $ - | $ - | $ - |
| **Sub Total** | $ - | $ - | $ - | $ - | $ - |
| Variance = /- | | $ - | $ - | $ - | |
| **Utilities** | | | | | |
| Gas/Electricity | $ - | $ - | $ - | $ - | $ - |
| Water | $ - | $ - | $ - | $ - | $ - |
| Waste Management - quarterly | $ - | $ - | $ - | $ - | $ - |
| Telephone | $ - | $ - | $ - | $ - | $ - |
| Cell Phone | $ - | $ - | $ - | $ - | $ - |
| Internet Service | $ - | $ - | $ - | $ - | $ - |
| Other (be specific) | $ - | $ - | $ - | $ - | $ - |
| Other (be specific) | $ - | $ - | $ - | $ - | $ - |
| **Sub Total** | $ - | $ - | $ - | $ - | $ - |
| Variance = /- | | $ - | $ - | $ - | |
| **Medical Care** | | | | | |
| Medical Insurance Premiums | $ - | $ - | $ - | $ - | $ - |
| Life Insurance Premiums | $ - | $ - | $ - | $ - | $ - |
| Doctor | $ - | $ - | $ - | $ - | $ - |
| Dental | $ - | $ - | $ - | $ - | $ - |
| Vision | $ - | $ - | $ - | $ - | $ - |
| Prescriptions | $ - | $ - | $ - | $ - | $ - |
| Over the Counter Drugs | $ - | $ - | $ - | $ - | $ - |
| Other (be specific) | $ - | $ - | $ - | $ - | $ - |
| Other (be specific) | $ - | $ - | $ - | $ - | $ - |
| **Sub Total** | $ - | $ - | $ - | $ - | $ - |
| Variance = /- | | $ - | $ - | $ - | |
| **Transportation** | | | | | |
| Car Payment | $ - | $ - | $ - | $ - | $ - |
| Gasoline | $ - | $ - | $ - | $ - | $ - |
| Auto Service | $ - | $ - | $ - | $ - | $ - |
| Car Wash | $ - | $ - | $ - | $ - | $ - |
| AAA | $ - | $ - | $ - | $ - | $ - |
| Other (be specific) | $ - | $ - | $ - | $ - | $ - |
| Other (be specific) | $ - | $ - | $ - | $ - | $ - |
| **Sub Total** | $ - | $ - | $ - | $ - | $ - |
| Variance = /- | | $ - | $ - | $ - | |

**Yellow Highlight controllable expenses.**

| Category<br>Item | Monthly<br>Budget | | 10th<br>Month | | 11th<br>Month | | 12th<br>Month | | Annual<br>Totals | |
|---|---|---|---|---|---|---|---|---|---|---|
| **Food/Beverage/Paper Products/etc.** | | | | | | | | | | |
| Grocery Stores | $ | - | $ | - | $ | - | $ | - | $ | - |
| Wholesale Club | $ | - | $ | - | $ | - | $ | - | $ | - |
| Discount Store | $ | - | $ | - | $ | - | $ | - | $ | - |
| Drug Store | $ | - | $ | - | $ | - | $ | - | $ | - |
| Restaurants | $ | - | $ | - | $ | - | $ | - | $ | - |
| Fast Food | $ | - | $ | - | $ | - | $ | - | $ | - |
| Other (be specific) | $ | - | $ | - | $ | - | $ | - | $ | - |
| Other (be specific) | $ | - | $ | - | $ | - | $ | - | $ | - |
| **Sub Total** | $ | - | $ | - | $ | - | $ | - | $ | - |
| Variance = /- | | | $ | - | $ | - | $ | - | | |
| **Entertainment** | | | | | | | | | | |
| Cable TV | $ | - | $ | - | $ | - | $ | - | $ | - |
| Club Dues | $ | - | $ | - | $ | - | $ | - | $ | - |
| Movies | $ | - | $ | - | $ | - | $ | - | $ | - |
| Concerts/Sporting Events | $ | - | $ | - | $ | - | $ | - | $ | - |
| Vacations | $ | - | $ | - | $ | - | $ | - | $ | - |
| Computer Service | $ | - | $ | - | $ | - | $ | - | $ | - |
| Newspaper | $ | - | $ | - | $ | - | $ | - | $ | - |
| Other (be specific) | $ | - | $ | - | $ | - | $ | - | $ | - |
| Other (be specific) | $ | - | $ | - | $ | - | $ | - | $ | - |
| **Sub Total** | $ | - | $ | - | $ | - | $ | - | $ | - |
| Variance = /- | | | $ | - | $ | - | $ | - | | |
| **Miscellaneous** | | | | | | | | | | |
| Charity | $ | - | $ | - | $ | - | $ | - | $ | - |
| Gifts | $ | - | $ | - | $ | - | $ | - | $ | - |
| Holiday Purchases | $ | - | $ | - | $ | - | $ | - | $ | - |
| Household Purchases | $ | - | $ | - | $ | - | $ | - | $ | - |
| Clothing | $ | - | $ | - | $ | - | $ | - | $ | - |
| Athletic Club | $ | - | $ | - | $ | - | $ | - | $ | - |
| Other (be specific) | $ | - | $ | - | $ | - | $ | - | $ | - |
| Other (be specific) | $ | - | $ | - | $ | - | $ | - | $ | - |
| **Sub Total** | $ | - | $ | - | $ | - | $ | - | $ | - |
| Variance = /- | | | $ | - | $ | - | $ | - | | |
| **ROUTINE MONTHLY EXPENSES** | $ | - | $ | - | $ | - | $ | - | $ | - |
| Variance = /- | | | $ | - | $ | - | $ | - | | |
| **ROUTINE ANNUAL EXPENSES** | $ | - | | | | | | | | |
| **Non Routine - Special Purchases** | | | | | | | | | | |
| Be Specific | $ | - | $ | - | $ | - | $ | - | $ | - |
| Be Specific | $ | - | $ | - | $ | - | $ | - | $ | - |
| Be Specific | $ | - | $ | - | $ | - | $ | - | $ | - |
| Be Specific | $ | - | $ | - | $ | - | $ | - | $ | - |
| **Sub Total** | $ | - | $ | - | $ | - | $ | - | $ | - |
| **TOTAL MONTHLY EXPENSES** | | | $ | - | $ | - | $ | - | $ | - |

**Yellow Highlight controllable expenses.**

| Periodic Expenses | Standard | 10th Month | 11th Month | 12th Month | Annual Totals |
|---|---|---|---|---|---|
| Property Taxes | $ - | $ - | $ - | $ - | $ - |
| House Insurance | $ - | $ - | $ - | $ - | $ - |
| Home Warranty | $ - | $ - | $ - | $ - | $ - |
| Long Term Care Policies | $ - | $ - | $ - | $ - | $ - |
| DMV - Car # 1 | $ - | $ - | $ - | $ - | $ - |
| Car #1 - Insurance | $ - | $ - | $ - | $ - | $ - |
| DMV - Car # 2 | $ - | $ - | $ - | $ - | $ - |
| Car #2 - Insurance | $ - | $ - | $ - | $ - | $ - |
| | | | | | |
| **PERIODIC EXPENSES** | $ - | $ - | $ - | $ - | $ - |
| **Running Total** | | $ - | $ - | $ - | |
| | | | | | |
| **PERIODIC ANNUAL EXPENSES** | $ - | | | | |
| | | | | | |
| **MONTHLY BUDGET** | $ - | | | | |
| | | | | | |
| **ANNUAL BUDGET** | $ - | | | $ - | |

After retiring, you should be able to cut your expenses by 20% without experiencing any major changes in your lifestyle. Small savings can add up. Casual clothes cost less than work clothes and are less expensive to maintain. If you are a couple, you may be able to get by with just one automobile. That's a lot of savings on gas, maintenance, and insurance. There are other things you can do, such as prepare coffee at home, have less-expensive lunches, do less commuting, etc. If you have not yet retired and are planning your budget for the future, simply multiply your monthly budget total by 80%. This is the figure you should use as you work through the exercises in the next chapter, "Funding Your Retirement."

In recording your spending and developing your budget, you may be alarmed at some of what you discover. Don't despair. It can be worked out and is all part of a necessary process. In working through our budget each month, I try to follow certain cost-cutting principles. I've listed them here and included some actual examples:

## Cost-Cutting Principles

- **Always look for a better deal.** We recently needed to have two windows replaced in our house. Since we like to do business with local people, we called a company near our home. The estimate they gave us seemed high, so we began to look for another company. The next company came out, did a great job, and, better yet, charged us $180 less than the first company.
- **Let competition work for you.** The competition among retailers is such that many will now meet or beat a price if given the opportunity. Keep in mind, it's up to you to give them that opportunity.
- **Shop online.** Each year we make more and more of our purchases online. Typically the items are less expensive, shipping is often free, there is often no tax, and we save money on gas by staying at home. We bought a new big screen television recently and saved nearly $800 on the purchase price alone.
- **Don't buy it if you don't need it.** Beware of coupons and sales. It's easy to talk yourself into buying things that you don't need just because it's a good deal. I save only the coupons for products we use, restaurants we frequent, and stores we regularly shop in. I keep them in an expanding file folder, categorized into grocery, paper products, restaurants, and store sale promotions. I keep this folder in our car in case we find ourselves out and spontaneously decide to pick up an item or have lunch or dinner at a restaurant. I always have my coupons ready, and it saves us a lot of money. Be sure to always tip your server based upon the original bill when using coupons.
- **Do it yourself.** If you need to have something done, and you have the physical or mental capability, do it yourself. It feels good. It's important that we stay active and use our god-given capabilities as long as we can. We enjoy working around the house and in the yard. People that don't know us would probably be surprised that we don't have a gardener. John has always done our gardening and landscaping. He takes pride in keeping everything planted, watered, trimmed, cut, and fed. He even figured out how to keep our potted plants watered while

we are away from home. You would be impressed with some of his inventions. Our house is always presentable because of some simple practices we follow. The basic idea is to keep things clutter-free, and don't let things get out of control. If you see a dirty dish or glass, wash it. The house is always in order before we go to bed each night. My mom always said, "You never know who will ring the doorbell in the morning; don't embarrass yourself." In terms of deep cleaning, I thoroughly clean one room a day. This way it doesn't become overwhelming. My mom would not have approved of this approach, complaining that some rooms would always be in need of attention. Fortunately for us, our family and friends typically don't show up wearing white gloves.

- **Use what you have.** Have you ever purchased any everyday dishes? I hope it wasn't recently. A few years back, I began to wonder why I was saving dishes (indoor and outdoor), china from our wedding, serving dishes, table linens, and treasures handed down from parents. Was I saving them for my children to store? Or, heaven forbid, give away or sell to someone who doesn't know their history? That would be a shame. So instead of buying any more dishes and other such items, I simply use the ones I have, all of them. A nicely set table turns an average meal into a lovely dining experience. When I come across a family treasure, as an ongoing project, I write notes detailing its history, such as original ownership, occasion received or purchased, etc. I feel these items should be used and enjoyed, and future generations might enjoy knowing their history.

- **Eat most meals at home.** Most economists will tell you one of the biggest expenses in our society today is eating meals outside the home. Please understand, we have our favorite places to go out for lunch or dinner, but we really do eat the majority of meals at home. I was very flattered not long ago when a friend asked John why we didn't go out to eat more often. His response was, "With Trisha cooking my meals, why would I want to go out?" Of course this made me feel wonderful, but the fact is I try very hard to cook good meals and try new recipes on a regular basis. I enjoy cooking and entertaining, so I've pulled out old recipes and dusted off all my cookbooks. For a recent family gathering, I fixed many of our old family favorites. Some guests had not enjoyed them for years and others, such as new family members, had only heard about them. It was fun for me and tasty for everyone.

- **Bundle your communications.** Check out communication companies that bundle services. If you travel for extended periods of time, ask about seasonal service or the flexibility to suspend and activate the service based on travel periods. Make certain that you are familiar with all the services your current provider offers within your existing contract. As an example, if your internet provider offers an e-mail account, don't buy another one. Recently we had a need to purchase an emergency response system for John's parents. We had heard about several different systems from friends and in commercials. While the cost varied, they averaged about $175 per quarter after purchasing the equipment. Our first call was to our home security service. Guess what? They offered an emergency response system that could be connected to our existing system. While we did have to purchase the wireless equipment, the cost increase to our monthly security bill was only $4. Always check out solutions that might work with existing services before you purchase another service.

- **Find savings in a home warranty.** First of all, if you don't have a home warranty, consider buying one, especially if your home is older. For a yearly fee, you will be covered for most major home repair expenses. In our last home, the central heating and air conditioning system went out twice in the short while we lived there. We saved thousands of dollars by having a home warranty. In addition, you can work within your policy in terms of the items covered to save money. As an example, when it was time to renew our last home warranty policy, since we had replaced the old refrigerator with a new one which came with a manufacturer's warranty, we were able to remove the cost of the refrigerator coverage from our home warranty. At the same time, our dealer warranty for our washer and dryer was going to expire, so it was time to add them to the policy.

- **Share your home with family and friends.** John once had an idea that after retirement, family and friends should each buy a home or condo in a nice location. Then, he reasoned, we could swap and share these places with one another. Guess what? That didn't happen, but it almost did. We share our home and love to entertain as often as possible. Our family and friends also invite us to their homes, and some even invite us to their vacation homes or time-shares. Since retiring, we have been to visit family and friends in such places as Arizona, Hawaii, Palm Desert, Lake Tahoe, and even South America. While it was never our intention to get anything in return for our invitations, we certainly enjoy the kindness and hospitality of others.

A friend of ours recently described this time in her life as the time for needs and wants to come together. This is the time in our lives when we don't want to be wasteful, but we do want to enjoy ourselves. We always strive to find a balance and be financially practical. This doesn't mean we do without something we really need or want. We track our spending, maintain a budget, and make the financial decisions we need to make.

---

*The only way regular people can stay ahead of inflation's voracious appetite is to curb their own.*
—Rajen Devadason

---

While everyone says the costs of living and inflation really take their toll on those living on fixed incomes, unnecessary spending is a bigger threat. We simply prioritize our purchases and try to stay in budget. We often will put a purchase on hold if there have been unexpected expenses in a given month or if we have been invited to join friends on an unplanned trip. It's all about choices in an attempt to stay within budget and remain financially fit while living *The Best of Our Lives*.

*Money is like a sixth sense, and you can't*
*make use of the other five without it.*
—William Somerset Maugham

CHAPTER 5

# FUNDING YOUR RETIREMENT
*By Trisha*

Everything worth having requires a certain amount of effort. Think of all the time and work you have put into school, career, family, hobbies, and everything else you value. In order to live *The Best of Our Lives*, we need to put that same kind of effort into funding our retirement. Now that you have completed your budget and tracked your spending patterns, you must determine if the funds you have are sufficient to support your lifestyle, and for how long. Let's first look at your spendable income.

## SPENDABLE INCOME

Spendable income is the amount of money you have or will have at your disposal to fund your daily living expenses, now and in the future. A pension, rental property income, or social security benefits are examples of spendable income. As a side note, I suggest you contact your bank about their direct deposit program. Direct deposit of a pension check, social security check, or even a tax refund will give you immediate access to your spendable income and put your money to work for you faster in an interest-bearing account.

To determine your spendable income, simply list the income you receive each month and when you receive it. Keep your list handy because we will be using it later.

Here is a sample list (remember, all dollar amounts in samples are arbitrary):

**SPENDABLE INCOME**

| DATE | SOURCE | AMOUNT |
|------|--------|--------|
| 1st | Annuity | $750 |
| 15th | Pension | $1,200 |
| 15th | Pension | $700 |
| 23rd | Rental Income | $1,100 |
| | | |
| **TOTAL MONTHLY SPENDABLE INCOME** | | **$3,750** |

Many will tell you the cost of your retirement and living The Best of Our Lives will be the greatest expense of your lifetime. If you choose to think of it that way, that's fine. We prefer to think of it as the price of an adventure we have worked and saved for our entire lives. That's why we consider our financial assets as savings. Whether you are still working or already retired, you need to make sure you understand savings and how they work toward funding your retirement.

## SAVINGS

Any and all assets you have access to now, or will have in the future, can to be put into one of three savings categories.

1. *Spendable Savings:* This is money that is easily accessible for monthly draws to supplement your spendable income and fund your monthly budget or special events, such as a travel adventure.
2. *Invested Savings:* These are financial products you have purchased with earnings that have already been taxed or were not subject to being taxed, for example, last year's bonus that you used to purchase some stock or a CD, or the nontaxable realized capital gain from the sale of a primary residence you put into an investment fund. Make certain you understand the tax liability before you sell or liquidate investments.
3. *Deferred Savings:* These are earnings that have been deposited into a deferred account 401(k), IRA, or annuity. These earnings and the realized gain from these investments are not subject to taxes until the money is withdrawn. Usually these funds will be available to you without penalty when you reach the age of 59 1/2.

At this point, list your spendable savings, your invested savings, and deferred savings. Keep this list available.

Here is a sample list:

**SAVINGS**

| | |
|---|---|
| Spendable Savings | $30,000 |
| Invested Savings | $150,000 |
| Deferred Savings | $290,000 |

Now, as part of this process, let's see if we can answer those two questions every retired person must ask. "Do I have enough money to retire, and how long will my money last?" Of course, I can't answer for you, but I can share the four-step process we went through to get our answers. The four steps are:

1. Balance your income and budget
2. Phase your savings
3. Calculate your funding

4. Track your spending and savings

## 1. Balance Your Income and Budget

In this first step, you want to find out if you are spending more or less than your income can cover. You do this by comparing the figures from your monthly spendable income list and your total monthly budget figure. Given this comparison, calculate the variance, which is simply the difference between the two figures.

In the sample comparison below, the calculation indicates a negative variance of $42. This means that the individual or couple in our example is spending $42 more than their monthly spendable income can cover.

### INCOME TO BUDGET COMPARISON

|  | Monthly |
|---|---|
| Monthly Spendable Income | $3,750 |
| Total Monthly Budget | $3,792 |
| Variance | $-42 |

In your calculation, if you come up with a positive variance, then, as the Australians say, "No worries." If, as in the sample comparison, you come up with a negative variance, you have two choices. Make the necessary spending cutbacks and adjust your total monthly budget, or take a monthly draw from spendable savings to cover the shortfall.

## 2. Phase Your Savings

In this step, you are going to record your spendable savings and short, intermediate, and long-term invested and deferred savings (financial assets) using the age-related financial timetable found on the Phase Your Savings Worksheet. Make photocopies of this worksheet or go to our website, TheBestofOurLives.com, and download copies.

Before you begin recording your savings, you may want to take some time and familiarize yourself with the worksheet and the following age-related financial triggers. I have provided you with a sample Phase Your Savings Worksheet in which I have recorded the figures from the spendable income and savings lists. These are only sample figures for demonstration purposes.

Please note that in this example we assumed phasing savings began at age fifty-five. Begin your phasing based on your age or the age you plan to retire. Start by recording one-fourth of the current value of your invested and deferred savings under age groups 59 1/2 and 62; the remaining one-half should be recorded under age group 70 1/2.

### Age-Related Financial Triggers

- **Age 55** is typically the qualifying age requirement in most retirement programs.
- **Age 59 1/2** is the typical age milestone for deferred investment withdrawals without penalty.
- **Age 62** is the first opportunity for a Social Security benefit. The percentage that your benefit will be reduced depends on your age at the time you start to receive

the benefit and your full retirement age. Your full retirement age is based on your year of birth.

The following table, based upon information provided by the Social Security Administration, will allow you to determine your full retirement age.

**FULL RETIREMENT AGE**

| Year of Birth | Full Retirement Age |
| --- | --- |
| 1943–1954 | 66 |
| 1955 | 66 and 2 months |
| 1956 | 66 and 4 months |
| 1957 | 66 and 6 months |
| 1958 | 66 and 8 months |
| 1959 | 66 and 10 months |
| 1960 | 67 |

**Retiring Early** – If your full retirement age is sixty-six and you elect to start receiving benefits prior to your full retirement age, your benefits will be reduced as follows:

| | |
| --- | --- |
| 25% | at age 62 |
| 20% | at age 63 |
| 13.33% | at age 64 |
| 6.66% | at age 65 |

Please consider this next statement very carefully:

**The cash value of taking your Social Security benefit at age sixty-two, with the 25% reduction, as opposed to waiting until age sixty-six, equals out at age seventy-seven.**

Do you have a good reason not to take the benefit at age sixty-two and keep your savings working for you? If you factor in your untouched principal at age seventy-seven, funding your four years at the back end, you would receive the full retirement value until age eighty-nine. The real benefit of taking your Social Security benefit early comes with the compounding interest you will earn.

**If you invest the value of the benefit you receive at ages sixty-two, sixty-three, sixty-four, and sixty-five in a fund that earns 5% per year, at the age of seventy-seven your money would have doubled.**

Applying what some refer to as **The Rule of 72** will determine the term of growth necessary for your investment to double given the rate of return on your investment product.

## THE RULE OF 72

| RULE OF | / | %<br>RATE OF<br>RETURN | = | YEARS<br>TERM OF<br>GROWTH | -OR- | RULE OF | / | YEARS<br>TERM OF<br>GROWTH | = | %<br>RATE OF<br>RETURN |
|---|---|---|---|---|---|---|---|---|---|---|
| 72 | / | 5% | = | 14.4 | | 72 | / | 10 | = | 7.2 |

If you are aiming for a specific investment time frame, apply the Rule of 72 with the term of growth to determine your required rate of return.

- **Age 65:** If you purchased a deferred invested annuity with a lump sum pension distribution, record the value under this age group.
- **Age 70 1/2:** The age at which minimum distributions are required for tax-deferred assets. It is important to note that The Worker, Retiree, and Employer Recovery Act of 2008 suspended the minimum required distribution rules for qualified retirement plans and traditional IRAs for the tax year 2009. Since these rules can change from year to year, make sure you stay abreast of the current distribution rules.

While most or all of your savings will be available to you at age 59 1/2, it's important to plan the phasing of your savings. This will ensure the balance of taxable (deferred savings) and nontaxable (invested savings) distributions, as well as funding your retirement throughout each age-related budgeting period.

## 3. Calculate Your Funding

A simple calculation will tell you how many years your current financial assets will last based on your current budget with no fluctuation in your total principal. In the following example, I have used figures from the previous sample tables and worksheets to demonstrate the calculation. They are not meant to be considered anything more than samples.

| | Monthly | Annual |
|---|---|---|
| **Funded budget** | $ 4,050 | **$48,600** |
| *Total cash principal* | | *$470,000* |
| **Principal divided by budget = Years of simple funding** | | **10** |

Another calculation will determine the percent of gain you would need from your investments to cover your annual budget.

|  | Monthly | Annual |
|---|---|---|
| **Funded budget** | | $48,600 |
| *Total cash principal* | | $470,000 |
| **Principal divided by budget = Years of simple funding** | | 10 |
| **Budget divided by principal = Annual rate of return** | | 10.3% |
| **needed to cover annual expenses** | | |

The ten years of simple funding, and the 10.3% necessary annual rate of return to cover your annually funded budget, does not include your current level of spendable income or social security benefits. It's very important to be realistic in planning the funding for your retirement. This approach provides you with both a mental and actual financial buffer zone. This financial buffer zone will help to cushion the impact of inflation on your cash flow, it will soften the emotional blow if in a given year your annual rate of return does not cover your annual expenses, and it will fund events and adventures as you live out your dreams.

Keep in mind that each year you are able to cover the cost of your budget with your investment earnings, you have added an additional year to your funding. Your goal is to make your principal work for you and cover most or all of your expenses.

Let's look at the impact that real estate, as an investment strategy, can have on your funding years and rate of return needs.

| | |
|---|---|
| *Total cash principal* | $470,000 |
| **Principal divided by budget = Years of simple funding** | 10 |
| **Budget divided by principal = Annual rate of return** | 10.3% |
| **needed to cover annual expenses** | |

**INVESTMENT PROPERTY: Current Value – Mortgage = Asset**

| | |
|---|---|
| *Second home* | $250,000 |
| *Rental property* | $200,000 |
| *Real estate adjusted principal* | $920,000 |
| **Adjusted principal divided by budget = Years of simple funding** | 19 |
| **Budget divided by principal = Annual rate of return** | 5.3% |
| **needed to cover annual expenses** | |

As with all other financial assets, as the value increases, your years of funding increase and your needed rate of return decreases. Depending on where you live and where you want to invest, this may or may not be a good option for you. Real estate investments take time to manage, require a certain amount of luck and a lot of patience, and are not for everyone. As we have all seen, real estate markets can sometimes go down more quickly than they go up. Always be cautious and do your homework. Never find yourself investing more than you can afford, because then you are gambling. This is not the time of life to gamble.

If you are still working and trying to figure out how much you need to retire, a different calculation using rate of return assumptions and your current budget will give you a total principal target range to shoot for. While we all want to earn as much as we can, it's important that we be realistic as we plan for how much money we will need. Don't overstate or understate your potential for gain; be realistic.

Here are three sample rate of return calculations:

### CONSERVATIVE: 3% RATE OF RETURN = BUDGET FACTOR OF 33

| ANNUAL BUDGET | | *BUDGET FACTOR* | | TOTAL PRINCIPAL |
|---|---|---|---|---|
| $45,504 | X | *33* | = | $1,501,632 |

### MODERATE: 5% RATE OF RETURN = BUDGET FACTOR OF 20

| ANNUAL BUDGET | | *BUDGET FACTOR* | | TOTAL PRINCIPAL |
|---|---|---|---|---|
| $45,504 | X | *20* | = | $910,080 |

### AGGRESSIVE: 7% RATE OF RETURN = BUDGET FACTOR OF 14.3

| ANNUAL BUDGET | | *BUDGET FACTOR* | | TOTAL PRINCIPAL |
|---|---|---|---|---|
| $45,504 | X | *14.3* | = | $650,707 |

Here is additional information I consider important for funding your retirement. I've also included suggestions that have been beneficial for funding our retirement by increasing our savings and improving our earnings.

## SAVINGS ACCUMULATION CONSIDERATIONS

- **Check your contributions.** If you are not retired, I encourage you to look at your retirement plan contribution level. Currently, the maximum annual tax-deferred contribution to a 401(k) or 403(b)(7) retirement plan is $16,500, and those individuals who are at least fifty by year end can contribute an additional $5,500.
- **Check your spendable savings amount.** The sample Phase Your Savings Worksheet reported $30,000 under spendable savings. While the income-to-budget variance in this sample is $42 a month, I suggest you factor in some budget flexibility. In the example, I have allowed for a $300 spendable savings monthly draw. Based on a draw of $300 a month, or $3,600 annually, this amount should be reduced to $20,000. In most instances, it probably will not be necessary to cover your budget

funding for more than five years ($3,600 X 5 = $18,000). The other $10,000 could be used to purchase a short-term or intermediate-term savings product with earnings greater than those realized from your spendable savings account.

- **Analyze your investment terms.** Review the current term and level of earnings for each of your invested products. If you own stocks that produce poor earnings or dividends, consider selling and purchasing different stocks or another product. You should make your decision on each investment separately. Before you take any action, make certain you know when the investment can be sold and/or when the funds will become available for withdrawal without penalty. Again I remind you, make sure you understand the issues of tax liability for every financial transaction you make.

## 4. Track Your Spending and Saving

Now that you have created your monthly budget and recapped your savings, it's time to record your spending and track your savings progress each and every month.

Record your spending on the Monthly Budget Tracking Form, which was introduced in Chapter 4, or download the form from our website, TheBestofOurLives.com. Before you begin, review the following sample Monthly Budget Tracking Form. This form is designed to track month-to-month spending against your monthly budget, cumulative spending by item throughout the year, and annual spending.

### SAMPLE
### MONTHLY BUDGET TRACKING FORM

**Highlight controllable expenses.**

| Category Item | Monthly Budget | 1st Month | 2nd Month | 12th Month | Annual Totals |
|---|---|---|---|---|---|
| ROUTINE MONTHLY EXPENSES | $3,204.00 | $2,148.00 | $2,368.00 | $ - | $ 4,516 |
| Variance = /- | | $ (1,056) | $ (836) | $ (3,204) | |
| ROUTINE ANNUAL EXPENSES | $ 38,448 | | | | |
| ANNUAL BUDGET | $ 45,504 | | | | $ 7,516 |

If you are consistently over your budget, you need to figure out why. Was your planning faulty or did you overspend? Did you have some unusual expenses that might have been recorded in the special purchases category? I don't want you to massage the numbers to simply make them look good. I do want you to reasonably categorize your expenses so that your routine and nonroutine monthly expenses are accurately reported.

Record your savings on the Savings Tracking Form. Make photocopies of this form or go to our website, TheBestofOurLives.com, and download necessary copies.

Before you actually begin recording your savings, you may want to take some time and familiarize yourself with the form. You will notice I have also provided you with a sample Savings Tracking Form. I have used the sample figures from previous tables and worksheets. They are not meant to be considered anything more than samples. This form is designed to track month-to-month savings and to calculate your years of simple funding and rate of return needed to cover annual expenses, as well as the savings performance for the year.

A month-to-month review is simply the first step in managing your plan and getting yourself organized. There is no right or wrong number. At this stage of your planning, it is what it is. Remember, when it comes to tracking your savings results, you need to take the long view.

---

*Financial planning is the process of meeting your life goals through the proper management of your finances.*
—Certified Financial Planner Board of Standards

---

SAMPLE
# PHASE YOUR SAVINGS WORKSHEET

| TERM | SHORT | INTERMEDIATE | LONG |
|---|---|---|---|
| **AGE 55** | | | |
| Spendable Savings Account | $  30,000 | | |
| | | | |
| **AGE 59 1/2** | | | |
| Invested Savings | $  25,000 | $  25,000 | |
| Managed Account, CD's, Stock | | | |
| Deferred Savings | $  25,000 | $  25,000 | |
| 401K / IRA / Annuity | | | |
| | | | |
| **AGE 62** | | | |
| Social Security Income | | $  20,000 | |
| Invested Savings | | $  25,000 | $  25,000 |
| Managed Account, CD's, Stock | | | |
| Deferred Savings | | $  25,000 | $  25,000 |
| 401K / IRA / Annuity | | | |
| | | | |
| **AGE 65** | | | |
| Deferred Savings | | $  90,000 | |
| Annuity | | | |
| | | | |
| **AGE 70 1/2** | | | |
| Invested Savings | | | $  50,000 |
| Managed Account, CD's, Stock | | | |
| Deferred Savings | | | $ 100,000 |
| 401K / IRA / Annuity | | | |
| | | | |
| **Cash by Term** | $  80,000 | $ 190,000 | $ 200,000 |
| **Cumulative Cash Principal** | | $ 270,000 | $ 470,000 |

Record but do not include the amount of your social security benefit in the totals for either cash by term or cumulative cash principal.

# PHASE YOUR SAVINGS WORKSHEET

| TERM | SHORT | INTERMEDIATE | LONG |
|---|---|---|---|
| **AGE 55** | | | |
| Spendable Savings Account | | | |
| | | | |
| **AGE 59 1/2** | | | |
| Invested Savings | | | |
|   Managed Account, CD's, Stock | | | |
| Deferred Savings | | | |
|   401K / IRA / Annuity | | | |
| | | | |
| **AGE 62** | | | |
| Social Security Income | | | |
| Invested Savings | | | |
|   Managed Account, CD's, Stock | | | |
| Deferred Savings | | | |
|   401K / IRA / Annuity | | | |
| | | | |
| **AGE 65** | | | |
| Deferred Savings | | | |
|   Annuity | | | |
| | | | |
| **AGE 70 1/2** | | | |
| Invested Savings | | | |
|   Managed Account, CD's, Stock | | | |
| Deferred Savings | | | |
|   401K / IRA / Annuity | | | |
| | | | |
| **Cash by Term** | $ - | $ - | $ - |
| **Cumulative Cash Principal** | | $ - | $ - |

Record but do not include the amount of your social security benefit in the totals for either cash by term or cumulative cash principal.

SAMPLE
# SAVINGS TRACKING FORM

Annual Funded Budget      $    48,600

| | Current Month | 1st Month | 2nd Month | | 12th Month |
|---|---|---|---|---|---|
| Spendable Savings Account | $ 30,000 | $ 20,000 | $ - | ⟹ | $ - |
| **Age 59 1/2** | | | | | |
| Invested Savings | $ 50,000 | $ 60,000 | $ - | ⟹ | $ - |
| Managed Account, CDs, Stock | | | | | |
| Deferred Savings | $ 50,000 | $ 50,125 | $ - | | $ - |
| 401(k) / IRA / Annuity | | | | | |
| **Age 62** | | | | | |
| Invested Savings | $ 50,000 | $ 50,125 | $ - | ⟹ | $ - |
| Managed Account, CDs, Stock | | | | | |
| Deferred Savings | $ 50,000 | $ 50,125 | $ - | | $ - |
| 401(k) / IRA / Annuity | | | | | |
| **Age 65** | | | | | |
| Deferred Savings | $ 90,000 | $ 90,225 | $ - | ⟹ | $ - |
| Annuity | | | | | |
| **Age 70 1/2** | | | | | |
| Invested Savings | $ 50,000 | $ 50,125 | $ - | ⟹ | $ - |
| Managed Account, CDs, Stock | | | | | |
| Deferred Savings | $ 100,000 | $ 100,250 | $ - | | $ - |
| 401(k) / IRA / Annuity | | | | | |
| **Total Cash Principal** | $ 470,000 | $ 470,975 | $ - | ⟹ | $ - |
| **$ Variance in Cash Principal** | | $ 975 | $ (470,975) | | $ - |
| **% Variance in Cash Principal** | | 0.2% | -100.0% | ⟹ | #DIV/0! |
| **Years of simple funding*** | 10 | 10 | 0 | | 0 |
| **Needed Annual Rate of Return** | 10.3% | 10.3% | #DIV/0! | | #DIV/0! |
| **Annual Rate of Inflation** | 4% | 4% | 4% | | 4% |
| **Year End % of Variance** | | | | | 1.0021 |
| **Actual Rate of Return** | | | | | 0.21% |

# SAVINGS TRACKING FORM

Annual Funded Budget

|  | Current Month | 1st Month | 2nd Month | 3rd Month | 4th Month |
|---|---|---|---|---|---|
| Spendable Savings Account | $ - | $ - | $ - | $ - | $ - |
| **Age 59 1/2** | | | | | |
| Invested Savings | $ - | $ - | $ - | $ - | $ - |
| Managed Account, CDs, Stock | | | | | |
| Deferred Savings | $ - | $ - | $ - | $ - | $ - |
| 401(k) / IRA / Annuity | | | | | |
| **Age 62** | | | | | |
| Invested Savings | $ - | $ - | $ - | $ - | $ - |
| Managed Account, CDs, Stock | | | | | |
| Deferred Savings | $ - | $ - | $ - | $ - | $ - |
| 401(k) / IRA / Annuity | | | | | |
| **Age 65** | | | | | |
| Deferred Savings | $ - | $ - | $ - | $ - | $ - |
| Annuity | | | | | |
| **Age 70 1/2** | | | | | |
| Invested Savings | $ - | $ - | $ - | $ - | $ - |
| Managed Account, CDs, Stock | | | | | |
| Deferred Savings | $ - | $ - | $ - | $ - | $ - |
| 401(k) / IRA / Annuity | | | | | |
| **Total Cash Principal** | $ - | $ - | $ - | $ - | $ - |
| **$ Variance in Cash Principal** | | $ - | $ - | $ - | $ - |
| **% Variance in Cash Principal** | | #DIV/0! | #DIV/0! | #DIV/0! | #DIV/0! |
| **Years of simple funding\*\*\*** | #DIV/0! | #DIV/0! | #DIV/0! | #DIV/0! | #DIV/0! |
| **Needed Annual Rate of Return** | #DIV/0! | #DIV/0! | #DIV/0! | #DIV/0! | #DIV/0! |
| **Annual Rate of Inflation** | 4% | 4% | 4% | 4% | 4% |
| **Year End % Variance Actual Rate of Return** | | | | | |

# SAVINGS TRACKING FORM

Annual Funded Budget

| | Current Month | 5th Month | 6th Month | 7th Month | 8th Month |
|---|---|---|---|---|---|
| Spendable Savings Account | $        - | $        - | $        - | $        - | $        - |
| **Age 59 1/2** | | | | | |
| Invested Savings | $        - | $        - | $        - | $        - | $        - |
| Managed Account, CDs, Stock | | | | | |
| Deferred Savings | $        - | $        - | $        - | $        - | $        - |
| 401(k) / IRA / Annuity | | | | | |
| **Age 62** | | | | | |
| Invested Savings | $        - | $        - | $        - | $        - | $        - |
| Managed Account, CDs, Stock | | | | | |
| Deferred Savings | $        - | $        - | $        - | $        - | $        - |
| 401(k) / IRA / Annuity | | | | | |
| **Age 65** | | | | | |
| Deferred Savings | $        - | $        - | $        - | $        - | $        - |
| Annuity | | | | | |
| **Age 70 1/2** | | | | | |
| Invested Savings | $        - | $        - | $        - | $        - | $        - |
| Managed Account, CDs, Stock | | | | | |
| Deferred Savings | $        - | $        - | $        - | $        - | $        - |
| 401(k) / IRA / Annuity | | | | | |
| **Total Cash Principal** | $        - | $        - | $        - | $        - | $        - |
| **$ Variance in Cash Principal** | | $        - | $        - | $        - | $        - |
| **% Variance in Cash Principal** | | #DIV/0! | #DIV/0! | #DIV/0! | #DIV/0! |
| **Years of simple funding***** | #DIV/0! | #DIV/0! | #DIV/0! | #DIV/0! | #DIV/0! |
| **Needed Annual Rate of Return** | #DIV/0! | #DIV/0! | #DIV/0! | #DIV/0! | #DIV/0! |
| **Annual Rate of Inflation** | 4% | 4% | 4% | 4% | 4% |
| **Year End % Variance Actual Rate of Return** | | | | | |

# SAVINGS TRACKING FORM

Annual Funded Budget

| | Current Month | 9th Month | 10th Month | 11th Month | 12th Month |
|---|---|---|---|---|---|
| Spendable Savings Account | $ - | $ - | $ - | $ - | $ - |
| **Age 59 1/2** | | | | | |
| Invested Savings | $ - | $ - | $ - | $ - | $ - |
| Managed Account, CDs, Stock | | | | | |
| Deferred Savings | $ - | $ - | $ - | $ - | $ - |
| 401(k) / IRA / Annuity | | | | | |
| **Age 62** | | | | | |
| Invested Savings | $ - | $ - | $ - | $ - | $ - |
| Managed Account, CDs, Stock | | | | | |
| Deferred Savings | $ - | $ - | $ - | $ - | $ - |
| 401(k) / IRA / Annuity | | | | | |
| **Age 65** | | | | | |
| Deferred Savings | $ - | $ - | $ - | $ - | $ - |
| Annuity | | | | | |
| **Age 70 1/2** | | | | | |
| Invested Savings | $ - | $ - | $ - | $ - | $ - |
| Managed Account, CDs, Stock | | | | | |
| Deferred Savings | $ - | $ - | $ - | $ - | $ - |
| 401(k) / IRA / Annuity | | | | | |
| | | | | | |
| **Total Cash Principal** | $ - | $ - | $ - | $ - | $ - |
| | | | | | |
| **$ Variance in Cash Principal** | | $ - | $ - | $ - | $ - |
| | | | | | |
| **% Variance in Cash Principal** | | #DIV/0! | #DIV/0! | #DIV/0! | #DIV/0! |
| | | | | | |
| **Years of simple funding\*\*\*** | #DIV/0! | #DIV/0! | #DIV/0! | #DIV/0! | #DIV/0! |
| | | | | | |
| **Needed Annual Rate of Return** | #DIV/0! | #DIV/0! | #DIV/0! | #DIV/0! | #DIV/0! |
| | | | | | |
| **Annual Rate of Inflation** | 4% | 4% | 4% | 4% | 4% |

**Year End**
   **% Variance**                                                      #DIV/0!
   **Actual Rate of Return**                                           #DIV/0!

*Retirement is like a long vacation in Las Vegas. The goal is to enjoy*
*it to the fullest, but not so fully as you run out of money.*
—Jonathan Clements

CHAPTER 6

# MANAGING YOUR FINANCIAL RETIREMENT PLAN
## *By Trisha*

In living *The Best of Our Lives,* we like to describe our retirement as spontaneous and adventurous. Financially, we would probably use the terms cautious and responsible. Everything we do in our retirement must be supported by our financial position. In this chapter, I share my ideas on managing a financial retirement plan to assist you in keeping your financial position secure. As stated previously, while we all have different levels of resources, the information presented here is intended to be beneficial for all retirees.

While getting an early start on your financial planning for retirement is certainly preferable, a late start is still better than the alternative. After all, plans start with dreams, and dreams can become reality. As with all plans, there is a certain amount of preparation that is required. It should be noted, as we are all painfully aware, there are always unknown factors that can play a role in your financial management and security. A downturn in financial markets can have a devastating effect, especially on retired persons. For that reason, having a financial plan for retirement and actively managing that plan through good times and bad is essential. The world of finance comes with few guarantees, but those wise persons who take the time to understand their financial situation, and take control of it, have a better chance of surviving financial downturns. Here are the five steps that we follow to manage our retirement finances:

## STEPS OF FINANCIAL MANAGEMENT

1. Create a financial decision-making model
2. Establish a financial advisory team
3. Do your retirement homework
4. Develop a personal financial plan
5. Manage your personal financial plan

### 1. Create a Financial Decision-Making Model
Create a financial decision-making model and then apply the model each time you make a financial decision. We actually use one of two models. Every significant financial

action we take, or decision we make, is guided by one of our models and one of two desired and required outcomes. These outcomes are either savings accumulation or savings preservation. We are only going to make significant financial moves to accumulate more money, property, etc., or we are going to make moves that help us preserve what we have. In either case, we are going to first research and gather enough information to make an informed decision.

**OUR FINANCIAL DECISION-MAKING MODELS**

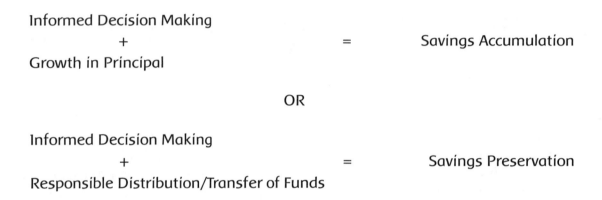

Informed Decision Making
  +                                               =          Savings Accumulation
Growth in Principal

OR

Informed Decision Making
  +                                               =          Savings Preservation
Responsible Distribution/Transfer of Funds

For example, if we were to consider making an investment in a stock or piece of property, we would get all the information we could find, educate ourselves adequately, and convince ourselves the decision would create a growth in our principal, resulting in savings accumulation. All investments are gambles to an extent, but we are not gamblers. When we follow our model properly, we are more cautious and careful in how we invest our money. Isn't everyone cautious and careful? No, many people invest on tips, rumors, hearsay, emotions, etc. You might as well go to Las Vegas.

In another example, we might consider making a financial move that would involve the transfer of certain funds. With our other model as a guide, we would be sure to factor in the tax liability before we made the final decision. You would probably be surprised how little we typically pay in taxes each year. Following this model helps us to preserve our savings.

Once again, the point is to create a model that works for you. Some financial opportunities might sound very tempting, but aren't right for you. Your model will keep you consistent. How much risk can you take? Do you always consider the tax liability? To establish your criteria, evaluate your past investments, get a clear picture of your available resources, and incorporate this information into your decision-making model.

## 2. Establish a Financial Advisory Team
Regardless of your financial resources, you should have professionals looking out for your financial interests. There are always going to be changes in the real estate market, economic conditions, tax laws, and investment opportunities. By putting together a financial advisory team, you can better enjoy your life while they handle the daily financial responsibilities.

In uncertain financial times, it is even more important you put together a financial advisory team you can trust. Of course, given the nature of financial markets, there are never any 100% guarantees. The best you can do is get as much information as possible, get recommendations from those you already trust, and remember, **if it sounds too good to be true, it probably is.**

If you are still employed, consider the firms that administer your financial benefit programs. If you are fully retired and don't have a financial advisor, ask your accountant or insurance agent for the name of their advisor or firm. Contact these firms and obtain brochures of their services. It is my firm opinion that once retired, you need to establish a financial advisory team that includes a financial firm and advisor, an accountant, a trust attorney, and an insurance agent or broker. While you will always have the final responsibility for your financial dealings, having a professional team in place will make your job much easier. Here are some key suggestions for selecting the members of your team:

## SUGGESTIONS FOR SELECTING YOUR FINANCIAL FIRM AND ADVISOR

**Select a financial firm that provides a variety of services.** What you really want is one-stop shopping for the majority of your financial service needs. Look for these services:

- Banking
- Bill pay and electronic funds transfer
- Credit card with reward program
- Stock purchase and sale
- Investment products—IRAs, annuities
- Flexible distribution options
- Managed accounts
- Mortgage services
- Consolidated record keeping
- Excellent tax reporting
- Online services—24 hours a day, 7 days a week

**Rank the firms.** Rank the firms being considered based on the following criteria listed in order of importance:

- Meets your financial service needs
- Recommended by your accountant
- Recommended by your insurance agent
- Currently administers your financial benefit programs
- Currently manages your investments

**Personally evaluate each financial advisor.** Contact each advisor and evaluate him or her on these criteria:

- **Experience** – Look for an advisor who has been in the business for at least ten years and has managed a team for at least five years.
- **Expertise** – You will need to know the level of expertise that each advisor has within the broad range of services you require.
- **Credentials** – You may want to know if the advisor is a Certified Financial Planner (CFP), Certified Public Accountant (CPA), Personal Financial Specialist (PFS), or Chartered Financial Consultant (ChFC). Keep in mind, these credentials are not mandatory, but may play a role in your decision.
- **Type of fee structure** – Typical fee structures are fee only, fee and commission, fee-based, or commission only. Make sure you understand the fee structure before you do business.
- **Your gut reaction** – Did they answer your questions? Do you feel like you could work with them? Would you feel comfortable providing them with your personal information? Do your financial goals and their ideas sound compatible? Do you feel they will be committed to developing and implementing your financial plans? These are important questions, and your reactions and answers to them are an important part of your decision-making.

The point of having a financial team is to free you up from the day-to-day task of monitoring your money and investments. While you can do your own monitoring, in order to live *The Best of Our Lives* it would be a very difficult and time-consuming task. When we retired, we went through the evaluation process I just shared and selected a financial team that worked for us. Since that time, we have kept that same team in place and continue to trust them. We have developed both personal and professional relationships with the members of our team. When we need money (our money), it's amusing that we have to call and request it, but it's so beneficial to have the counsel of our advisors. Our team actively manages our relatively limited funds quite professionally.

## OTHER MEMBERS OF YOUR FINANCIAL ADVISORY TEAM

### Your accountant

In addition to handling your financial accounts accurately, I feel the most important function an accountant provides is to make sure you don't pay one cent more in taxes than necessary. Please don't get the wrong idea. I'm as patriotic as the next person, but at this point in our lives, any financial worth we have has already been taxed repeatedly. I'm a big believer in the philosophy of "It's our money," and the government has certainly gotten their fair share. In retirement, it's a matter of economic survival. Make sure you have an accountant with a sharp pencil and a complete understanding of tax liability.

### Your insurance agent/broker

In retirement, we have found our insurance professional to be invaluable. This person keeps us advised of services that protect our health, welfare, possessions, and liability, and also supports our estate planning strategies. Some time back, we sat down with our insurance professional and decided to purchase a long-term-care policy. It was expensive and a major decision, but it gives us tremendous peace of mind. This is the kind of decision we may not have made on our own.

### Your trust attorney

This is the professional who will help you protect your assets during your lifetime. The trust attorney will also help you plan for the distribution of your assets upon your death (sorry, but we all have to go sometime). Obviously, it's important to have a good working relationship with your trust attorney, because through the rest of your lifetime laws and regulations will change, and you will be making changes to your trust.

## GOAL OF YOUR FINANCIAL ADVISORY TEAM

Regardless of the team you select, their goal should be to help you financially support your lifestyle for the rest of your life. Along the way, they should help you to live within your budget and prioritize spending. They should make every effort to protect your assets and grow your invested and deferred savings. Select the best team, and together you can put into action a financial plan that will allow you to live *The Best of Our Lives.*

### 3. Do Your Retirement Homework

Retirement is a time when financial mistakes can be disastrous. Before or shortly after retiring, you need to do your homework on all matters financial. Your objective is to limit financial surprises, to the best of your ability, during your retirement.

If you are considering retirement within the next five years and you work for an employer, I encourage you to meet with your benefits representative prior to making any retirement decision. Fully research, understand, and get the following in writing:

- All benefits to which you are entitled
- All benefits for which you are eligible
- All benefits that will continue after you retire
- All benefits that will end when you retire
- Specific plan or summary plan documents for each program you have participated in, such as savings, 401(k), pension, medical, dental, life insurance, etc.
- Vesting and eligibility requirements. These can differ, and you don't want to stop working if a benefit is just around the corner.
- Information on options for deferral, rollovers, distributions, and methods of payment.
- Information concerning in-service distributions. An in-service distribution allows you to transfer 401(k) assets into an Individual Retirement Account (IRA) while you are still employed. If available, this is a good option if you plan to work after you retire from your current employer.
- Information about distributions as a retiree under your company plan. Retiree distributions under the plan can be taken without penalty beginning at age 55. This means that if you retire from your employer and leave your money in their

plan, you should be able to take distributions without penalty once you reach age 55. If you were to transfer the funds out of your employer plan into an IRA, distributions prior to age 59 1/2 would be subject to a 10 percent federal tax penalty.

## RETIREMENT VS. TERMINATION

Discussing the difference between retirement and termination with a friend of mine a few years back made me realize how uninformed some employees are about their benefits. My friend was planning to leave her organization and go to work for another company. While she knew she was eligible for retirement with her current company, her comment to me was she didn't need her money yet. My immediate question to her was, "Why not?" Clearly her decision was based on what she did not know.

I quickly got her on the right track. She was going to defer her pension to a later date, which meant that it would be frozen, and not realize any gain for several years. I suggested she roll her benefit into a deferred invested annuity. In addition, with her new employer, she was going to have to pay toward her health care premiums, with a large deductible and substantial copay for each doctor visit. I advised her she was already eligible for employer-paid health care at the point she activated her retirement from her current employer. She was surprised, and she immediately contacted human resources and changed her reason for termination to retirement. She now owns an annuity that is working hard for her while she continues to work elsewhere, and is receiving health care benefits with very small copayments for doctor visits and prescriptions from her previous employer.

## DEFERRALS, ROLLOVERS, AND PLAN PAYMENTS

Don't wait until you have made the decision to retire to understand the differences between deferrals, rollovers, and plan payments. If you have already retired, it's time to understand these concepts.

**Deferrals** – While many plans will allow you to defer receipt of your benefit, you need to be aware of what happens with the funds during the deferral period. Many plans simply freeze the value of the benefit. With an assumption of 4% inflation, this means that you are losing purchasing power each and every year and that your money is no longer working for you.

**Rollovers** – Most plans meet the criteria for rollover into an individual retirement account or an annuity, which provides for postponed taxation. Not all plans meet the criteria for rollover into another employer plan. Make certain that your rollover will be accepted prior to requesting a distribution. Check to see if you can rollover part of your account balance in one product and the rest in another. This is a great approach if you want to stage your investments for disbursement to coordinate with age-related events, earmark them for a special activity, or put them aside as part of your family savings transfer plan (discussed in the next chapter).

**Plan payments** – Make certain that you fully understand tax consequences, benefits, and penalties. For example, if you meet the requirements for retirement eligibility under the plan, you may be able to take a distribution without penalty beginning at age 55. In many cases a payment prior to age 59 1/2 results in a 10% federal tax penalty. If you meet the eligibility for retirement there are usually several different methods of payment available to you. Consider the pros and cons of each relative to your personal and financial situation. These forms of payment are:

- **Annuities** – Once an annuity is annuitized, you receive regular payments over your life expectancy. You can choose a life annuity in which the benefit stops upon your death and there are no beneficiaries. You can also choose a joint and survivor annuity in which the benefit is reduced upon death of either recipient, or stops upon the death of both. (Don't get confused—rolling over your benefit to purchase an invested annuity is different from taking a life or joint and survivor annuity distribution.)
- **Installments** – Your account balance can be taken in periodic installments over a period of years. You choose the frequency and the number of years.
- **Lump sum payment** – You receive your account balance in a single payment.

The moment that you take physical receipt of the benefit/savings from your plan, your money stops working for you. It's no longer invested and it's taxable. This applies to lump sum payments, periodic installments, life annuities, and joint and survivor annuities. You should separately examine each of the benefits for which you are eligible. Consider when the funds will become available with and without penalty, and know the penalty for withdrawal, any transfer fees, and the current rate of earnings.

Be aware: **a guaranteed pension from an employer may not be guaranteed.** Pension plans, also known as defined benefit plans, are becoming a benefit of the past. Many organizations are limiting eligibility for participation in the plan, phasing out participation to employee groups, modifying the defined benefit for new and active participants, or, in some cases, modifying (reducing or eliminating) the benefit for retirees. The best way to protect your pension value is to roll over a lump sum payment into a product offered outside of your employer plan. Your financial advisors can help you select the product that is best for you.

## 4. Develop a Personal Financial Plan

With your financial advisory team in place, and after doing your financial homework, it's now time to develop a personal financial plan to protect your savings and grow your assets. Work with your team and create a personal plan that you can live with comfortably. Here are some of my considerations for developing your personal financial plan:

- *Diversification*

Most financial experts will tell you that diversification is the key to planning and safeguarding your money. While this is important, perhaps even critical, it's not your job. Diversification is the responsibility of your financial advisor. Your responsibility, once you have selected your financial advisory team, is to oversee their actions and monitor their performance in growing your savings. How much or how little you want to be involved with buying, selling, holding, disbursing, and diversification on a day-to-day basis is up to you. Consider your time, interest, and skill level when making this decision.

- *If you are still working*

For those of you who are still working, the current maximum annual contribution to an IRA is $5000. If you are over fifty you can contribute up to $6000 to an IRA. If you purchase and IRA before the end of the year, you will lower your taxable income and lower your tax liability. The added benefit is that the money you have invested will produce a yield free from taxes and will compound each year. Talk to your financial advisor about adding this product to your portfolio.

- *Fold your benefits into your financial plan*

Determine which will best support your financial plan and investment strategy: one of your employer's plan distribution options or consolidation and reallocation of assets. Create a checks and balances process for review and peace of mind.

Many of us have had more than one employer during our career. Chances are you left assets in your employer's plan when you terminated. Historically, not all company plans have allowed for in-service distributions or rollovers into another employer plan at termination. Plan rules have most likely changed since your termination. Your financial adviser will provide you with insight and recommendations for consolidating your assets, taking into consideration current rates of return, penalties for withdrawal or rollover, accessibility of funds, and ease of distribution or withdrawal.

Additionally, if your employer plan accepts rollover contributions, this is one option to consider. If you plan on retiring over the next couple of years, an IRA may be a better choice. Your financial advisor will be able to guide you in the right direction based on your specific situation. If you are married, your spouse should go through a similar exercise. While you may choose to have different investment profiles, having all of your investments within a common account will provide a tremendous advantage when it comes to record keeping and quick reviews of your assets relative to your plan, and it will ultimately be a critical tool to keep your plan on track.

- *Bundle investments*

Over the years, we had purchased IRAs to supplement our retirement contribution levels, benefiting both from tax liability and retirement savings. At one point, I realized that the perceived small fee attached to each IRA was a not such a small percentage of the principal. Given my realization, we promptly rolled them all into one IRA with one fee, simple and effective.

• **Make your money work for you**

While your spendable, taxable income may be fixed, you want to make certain that your savings (spendable, invested, and deferred) are working hard for you. Keep your focus on your objective and manage your savings to ensure availability of funds for your lifetime. Your financial adviser may recommend reallocating or rebalancing your savings to realize greater gain or improved flexibility.

Keep in mind, if you are not in a position to add to your savings, it is never too late to take advantage of the time you have to improve your earnings and enjoy the yearly compounding. Each year your investments yield a return. Those earnings are reinvested or rolled back into investments so that you are making money not only on your investment but on the earnings from your investment as well. The tax liability of your earnings depends on the investment category (invested or deferred savings).

• **Inflation**

When making investment decisions, it is important that you consider the impact of inflation. As a result of the cost-of-living rise each year, a dollar today will be worth less in the future. If the annual rate of inflation is running 4%, then you need to invest in financial products that earn at least 4%. In an ideal world, your asset growth will outpace inflation and your principal will be fully protected.

• **Be realistic**

While we all want to create as much wealth and make our savings last for as long as possible, it's important that we be realistic as we develop our plans. In retirement, we shouldn't expect our money to last forever. That's OK, because we won't, either. Try not to overstate or understate your potential for gain.

• **Keep your emotions in check**

Be responsible when it comes to your investments, follow your gut and the advice of your financial advisors, and do not let your emotions trip you up. Avoid the temptation to move funds around too often in times of volatile markets. If you have a sound plan, don't be too quick to change your investment strategy. Keep in mind there is a big difference between being informed about market trends and being overwhelmed with information. If something is relevant, a responsible financial advisor will keep you informed. While there are never any guarantees, making your decisions based on current information and sound advice is the best anyone can do.

• *Track your plan's performance*

A month-to-month review is an easy way to check your plan's performance against your goals. There is no right answer or wrong answer. It is what it is. If you see significant swings, contact your advisor for an explanation. Be sure to ask your financial advisor when the management fees will be drawn from your accounts. I've made a call more than once to find out that a reduction in principal was due to our fee payment.

As John noted in Chapter 2, we need to take the long view. When it comes to the market, you can either be grateful and patient, or greedy and panic. For your sake, and for those around you, take the long view and be grateful and patient.

## 5. Manage Your Personal Financial Plan

Managing your plan is all about being financially practical. Remember, a plan is just a plan. You should check it out at least twice a year to make sure that it's working for you and still in line with your goals. Take a close look at your current, short, intermediate, and long-term funding by age-related events. If you identify deficiencies or gaps in your funding strategy, consider all available alternatives, such as changing your distribution schedule, consolidating or reallocating your assets, purchasing new investment products, etc. Here are some considerations for managing your plan:

• **Selecting the best time to review your plan**

We like to review our financial plan in both March and October. Tax time enables us to look at how well we did on balancing the invested savings and deferred savings. We can tweak our plan to increase or decrease tax deductions, reaping a nine-month benefit. October enables us enough time to make some corrections, if necessary, to minimize the impact of taxes. For these reasons, I am not a fan of year-end planning.

• **Managing your cash flow and the impact of taxes**

The key to making your invested savings and your deferred savings work for you is in the balance. The balance comes from managing your cash flow and the impact of taxes.

Taxable income is reduced by tax-deductible expenses, such as property taxes, mortgage interest, and charitable donations. Know the impact of your deductions on your taxable income. If you have the opportunity, make certain that you draw just enough taxable deferred income to cover your deductions. We try to never take more than we really need. The more you can reduce your taxable income, the smaller your tax liability. What would you rather do, go on a travel adventure or pay state and federal taxes? We go on travel adventures.

If you find yourself needing a few more deductions to offset your taxable income, consider accelerating your property tax payment. If you typically have to pay state income tax, consider a prepayment. As you know, state income taxes are a federal tax deduction.

Remember, reducing your taxable income could save you 10 to 15% on each dollar. If you don't think it's that big a deal, consider this: A property tax payment of $7000 prepaid could save you $700 to $1050 in taxes. If you are close to meeting the required 7.5% in health care expenses to qualify for a deduction, consider prepaying toward next year's cost. Work with your accountant to find ways to balance your income with deductions for a positive tax impact.

If managed properly, your deferred savings will last longer and continue to work for you. Ask your financial advisor about investing in products that pay interest that is exempt from some or all taxes.

- **Financing a purchase**

When making major purchases, consider the available finance interest rates. If the interest rate is less than the percent you're currently earning, finance the purchase. This will keep your savings working for you.

Several years ago, we decided to purchase a new car. We didn't want to, but our other car caught fire due to a leaky gas line. There was a promotional 1.99% interest rate being offered. Since we were making more than that on our investments, we took the loan and continued to let our money work for us.

In contrast, when we decided to purchase our latest vehicle, it was at a time when interest rates for car loans were 9% plus. Nine percent, plus the rate of inflation, was more than we were earning on our investments. Rather than pay the high rate of interest, we liquidated some funds and paid cash for the car.

- **Planning for the short-term**

While cash reserves pay relatively low returns, they can be effective over the short-term. We all need access to spendable savings for such things as monthly draws, vacations, family events, and special purchases. Instead of letting your spendable savings rest in a savings account earning pennies, consider investing in CDs.

As an example, if you are planning a budget for your big anniversary trip two years out, purchase a CD with moderate-term maturity. If you're considering a new car to fit your lifestyle in the next year, purchase a short-term CD. Mentally, you have reserved the funds for a specific need but you are not tied to it. This approach puts your cash reserves to work and provides you with purchasing flexibility, and your only risk is the impact of inflation.

- **Longevity and annuities**

We've touched on the financial risk of a volatile market, the financial impact of investments not yielding a return equal to the rate of inflation, and the impact of taxes on accumulated savings. There is yet another risk to consider: the risk of longevity.

The rumor is that we are all going to live longer than expected. The question is, "What's expected?" You should consider incorporating one or more annuities into your asset portfolio. Annuities can be purchased through your financial advisor or your insurance agent. There are different types of annuities that can be structured to support your financial plan. They also provide you with income protection by transferring the risk of outliving your assets to an insurance company.

*Fixed annuities* are structured with a guaranteed rate of return and the option to elect a guaranteed income (over a number of years, your lifetime, or lifetime of longest living spouse) at some point in the future. You can assign a beneficiary to be eligible for a death benefit of the initial investment and earnings during the investment period. When you elect to receive a guaranteed income, you are transferring your risk of longevity to the insurance company.

Be sure you are clear on the term of the benefit. Is the payment period based on your life expectancy or your lifetime? Are you agreeing to a life annuity or a joint and survivor annuity? This type of annuity does not allow for contingent beneficiaries. If you are concerned that a death benefit is not provided with this product, take out a term life insurance policy equal to 50 percent of the annuitized value. Keep in mind, life insurance benefits are not taxable. It's important you understand that with a fixed annuity, the insurance company assumes the risk of your longevity, and you are assured guarantees on your principal, a rate of return, and payments when annuitized.

*Variable annuities* contain a variety of investment funds that you have selected. Money can be moved between funds and earnings are tax-deferred during the investment period. This type of annuity provides you with benefits during your lifetime, along with a death benefit protecting your investment for your beneficiaries. Generally, you can choose from a variety of payment options. Variable annuities are long-term investments structured to meet your long-range goals. As a result, taxes, fees, and penalties may apply if funds are withdrawn early.

The bottom line is you assume the risk with a variable annuity. You choose the investments; your value will fluctuate and could be worth more or less than the invested principal, as you have no guaranteed rate of return. When annuitized, payments will fluctuate based on investment performance.

*A variable annuity with a guaranteed annual minimum rate of return* provides the best of both fixed and variable annuities. Your principal is protected, your rate of return is fixed with an upside potential each year, and payments will be guaranteed when annuitized.

You should discuss the advantages (guaranteed income, etc.) and disadvantages (subject to inflation risk, etc.) of annuities with your financial advisor or your insurance agent.

- **Keep your eye on the prize**

Remember, your goal is to grow your savings to cover your spending. Teaming up with your financial advisory team to develop and manage a return strategy that will financially support your living *The Best of Our Lives* will be well worth your time and effort.

Once you have mastered sticking to your budget, realized earnings to cover your spending, and learned to manage the impact of taxes, you have become financially practical. Now it's time to put your plan into action and reap the benefits from your hard work.

---

*My retirement money is sort of like my vegetable garden. I can't always predict how much it will grow, but I try to do everything I can to help it along.*
—Trisha Parker

---

*You cannot escape the responsibility*
*of tomorrow by evading it today.*
—Abraham Lincoln

CHAPTER 7

# THE RESPONSIBLE RETIREE
*By Trisha*

For John and me, *Living the Best of Our Lives* has meant enjoying everyday life to-gether, traveling, spending time with family and friends, and working on projects like this book. It's been great fun for us, very rewarding and mentally stimulating. After we retired, because we consider ourselves to be responsible people, we made sure one of the first projects we completed was the establishment of our financial retirement plan. To do this, we followed the financial recommendations detailed in the previous three chapters. Retirement brings with it certain responsibilities that, once completed, will provide a sense of accomplishment and peace of mind.

I believe there are three areas in which we seniors need to assume responsibility. I have identified these areas as Taking Care of Me, Taking Care of Loved Ones, and Gifting. Accepting and following through on these responsibilities will require a certain amount of effort and informed decision-making. In this chapter, I provide you with information and considerations to help you make the best decisions possible. Meeting these responsibilities will not only benefit you in your retirement, it will benefit your loved ones when you are no longer around.

## 1. Taking Care of Me
Once you are on track with your spending and confident in funding your retirement, it's time to realistically examine your lifestyle and make the necessary changes. I suggest you examine the following areas:

## WHERE WILL YOU LIVE?

Where you decide to live will most likely be your biggest expense during the course of your retirement. While most people stay in their same home, in retirement you have lots of options. Before you make the decision of where you will live, ask yourself the following questions and answer them very honestly. Let your answers guide you in your decision-making process.

- What are my special needs in choosing a home?

- If I could live anywhere, where would it be?
- Why do I want to live there?
- Can I afford it?
- Should I buy or rent?
- What other expenses will I incur?
- Should I downsize?
- How will I pay for it?
- How long will I be able to pay for it?
- Will this change have an impact on my medical coverage?
- What effect will my decision have on my family relationships?
- What will be the effect, positive or negative, on my social life?
- Will making a change have any consequences for my health?
- Will this decision make me happy?

I'm sure you can think of more questions, but these will give you a good start. As mentioned, we have known several retired people who stayed in their homes with what appeared to be very little consideration for how it might impact their retirement years. Hopefully, if you decide to stay in the same house, it's because you have very good reasons. While it's understandable that some people have an aversion to change, there are so many possible and exciting things that can be gained from a change in living arrangements. Perhaps path-of-least-resistance thinking and having that settled feeling keep so many in one place. I'm not a crystal ball reader and claim no special ability to predict anyone's future. What I do know, and have experienced, is that change can sometimes be wonderful. If there is a better option, why not take it? Laziness and indifference are not acceptable answers. While we can't all live on Malibu Beach or along the French Riviera, there may be some place in this wonderful world that would fulfill your dreams and make you extremely happy. Isn't that the ultimate goal?

## DOWNSIZING

While I'm not advocating every retired person downsize, there are a number of attractive reasons to do so. For your consideration, here are some of the reasons retired people have downsized.

- Ownership is less expensive in most cases
- Utility costs are less
- Takes less time, effort, and expense to maintain
- Allows more time for family, friends, hobbies, and travel
- Forces you to go through your belongings and make decisions
- Reduces stress because you have less to worry about

## SELLING YOUR HOUSE

If you currently own a house and are considering selling, you may potentially free up a lot of equity to provide for your retirement lifestyle. Perhaps the most important financial consideration is: Capital gain on real estate equity up to $250,000 per person on a primary residence is not taxable. For this reason, some of the realized equity can be used for purchasing another house or condo, a vacation home, or investment products to enhance your future income. Of course, market trends will play an important role in your decision to sell, so obtain the best real estate advice available. When John and I retired, we decided to sell our home and brought in the top real estate professional in our area. It was a very good decision and we were well represented in every aspect of the process.

## REVERSE MORTGAGES

I'm not a big fan of the reverse mortgage, but I do realize it may be an appropriate option for some. Before making a decision, do your homework, get expert advice, and consult your family members.

I can better rationalize this option if an individual is seventy-five or older and needs money for living expenses or medical bills. The amount of money you receive is almost always related to your age. The older you are, the larger amount of money you will receive each month. Personally, given the ability to do so, I would rather chart my own destiny, sell my home, take the equity, and manage the funding of my life.

## MORTGAGES

Paying on a mortgage is not necessarily a bad thing, especially if the percent of interest you are paying is less than the percent of interest you are earning on your investments. Paying on a mortgage allows your savings to continue working for you and provide you with income.

Many people have asked me about my thoughts on mortgages, and I believe there are two approaches. The first approach, and I mean no disrespect, is guided by what I refer to as old-style thinking. This is when a person decides to pay off a mortgage as quickly as possible. The reasoning is, "I won't have to worry about a place to live when I'm retired." Some even double up on their mortgage payments. That's one approach.

The other approach, continuing to pay regular mortgage payments, is one I prefer. The interest payment on a mortgage is a tax-deductible event and will count toward reducing your taxable income. As I stated before, if the interest rate you are paying is less than the interest rate you are receiving from savings or investments, why change anything? If you are worried about your home being paid off in the event of your death, take out a term life insurance policy equal to the loan amount. Life insurance benefits are not taxable and are available immediately to your beneficiary. Both approaches are certainly acceptable and each retiree should select the one best for him or her.

## HEALTH CARE

Medical costs for consumers are currently increasing faster than the rate of inflation. The responsibility for medical care costs for retirees continues to shift toward us as consumers. As a percent of our spending, these costs will increase as we age. For this reason, as retirees, we should look for supplemental health care alternatives that offer wellness and healthy living programs. Unfortunately, these types of programs and therapies are not typically covered by many health care providers.

In making your health care decisions, make sure that in your budget you reasonably project the cost for medical care. While your health care cost will be reduced when you qualify for Medicare coverage, you will need to maintain a supplemental insurance plan to cover your additional out-of-pocket costs. Medical costs can make or break your budget. This is such an important issue that I encourage every retiree to review their current plan and compare it to other available plan options. Of course, these options will differ based upon your health history, age, and place of residence. During your retirement, it would be unfortunate if you had to make a medical decision based upon the cost of your treatment. We belong to an HMO that places emphasis on preventative care. For us, prepaid health insurance with predetermined minimal point of service copays makes medical decisions easier. If we need to see a doctor, we go. If we need a prescription, we are able to obtain it.

## LONG-TERM CARE

Long-term care insurance is something every retired person should at least consider. Get together with your insurance agent and family members and determine if such a plan is right for you. For more information on these plans, there are a number of long-term care insurance websites to answer your specific questions.

Typically, this kind of coverage goes into effect when you are over sixty-five or experience a disabling or chronic medical condition that requires professional health care supervision. Services can be provided in-home, at a nursing home, or at an assisted living facility. Generally, rates are less expensive if you sign up at an earlier age. As with all types of insurance, an unexpected illness could result in a condition that might disqualify you from obtaining long-term care coverage or impact the cost, making it too expensive. For the men reading this, it appears you cannot arrange for members of the Swedish Bikini Team to be your long-term health care attendants. We know this because John actually asked. Very embarrassing.

Keep in mind there are several design features to a long-term care policy that will impact the premium cost. Here are a few:

- **Waiting period** – If you have funds set aside for assisted care, it may be advisable to select a longer waiting period, thereby lowering your premiums.
- **Benefit period** – Be cautious in selecting the benefit period. While selecting a shorter benefit period means lower premiums, we can't predict the future. Remember, the purpose of a long-term care policy is to ensure that care will be

provided when needed, and to financially protect your family assets. Don't be penny-wise and select too short a benefit period and suffer a financially devastating extended hospital or nursing home stay.

- **Benefit level** – Talk to your agent about your desired level of care. Most policies offer a per-day benefit range. If you have funds set aside for assisted care, selecting a lower daily benefit level will lower your premiums.
- **Cost of medical care protection** – Make sure that your premiums are fixed and that the daily benefit is adjusted annually for inflation so it doesn't erode your purchasing power.

By purchasing a long-term care policy, you are offsetting the risk of uncertain costs for future medical-related care expenses with a known premium cost. Once again, do your homework, and discuss these and other features with your family and insurance agent.

For us, long-term care made sense and met our financial criteria of savings preservation. We wanted to protect our assets from the cost of assisted or long-term care due to some future illness or disability. We also wanted to protect our family from the emotional and potential financial responsibility of providing our health care. To the extent possible, we wanted to control when needed care would be provided, who would provide the care, and where the care would be delivered.

As you research long-term care programs, pay close attention to how different types and levels of care coordinate or overlap. While you do not want any gaps in coverage, you certainly don't want to pay for duplicate coverage.

## MAKING YOUR HOME SAFE AND SECURE

Whether you decide to stay in your current home, remodel, or downsize, it's imperative you make your home safe and secure for your retirement years. Since we are all predicted to live longer lives than people of previous generations, it's responsible for us to think about our comfort, convenience, and safety.

I recently came across some shocking statistics concerning seniors and falling. Of all age groups, senior citizens have the highest mortality rate due to injury. Among these deaths, 50% are due to falling. One-third of women sixty-five and older and half of women eighty-five and older will be injured in a fall. For men, the statistics are slightly less, but the fact is, the National Institute on Aging reports that more than 1.6 million seniors are treated at hospitals each year due to falls. Half of those falls occur at home.

Because we believe it is a responsible thing to do, we recently prepared our home for retirement. To be completely honest, we don't yet need all the changes we've made, but we have been pleasantly surprised at how much these changes have already made life easier and more convenient. I suggest you assess your safety and security needs and create a list of changes you think will be suitable for you. Here is our list for your consideration:

- Arrange your furniture with wide walking paths
- Make your home as clutter-free as possible
- Reconsider low tables, plants, and other possible hazards
- Widen doorways and gates where possible
- Secure and recheck area rugs with slip-resistant backing
- Safely reposition electrical and telephone cords
- Check your flooring for cracks, slippery tiles, etc.
- If you have steps, place nonslip strips on each one
- Replace soft furniture with solid, supportive pieces
- Replace low chairs and sofas with higher ones
- Replace low toilets with higher ones
- Eliminate any sharp edges on furnishings and decorations
- Replace outdoor steps with gentle inclines where possible
- Install walk-in tubs, or replace tubs with walk-in showers
- Install grab bars in toilet areas, tubs, and showers
- Make sure your tubs and showers have nonskid strips
- Make sure all stairways have handrails on both sides
- Place light switches at the tops and bottoms of stairs
- Consider motion detector lights where necessary
- Store everyday items such as dishes at levels easy to reach
- Have appropriate step stools handy for objects placed up high
- Keep flashlights and battery-operated lanterns for emergencies
- Strategically place nightlights around your home
- Strategically place your telephones throughout your home (always have one next to your bed)
- Install and maintain smoke alarms
- Install or update a security system
- Consider adding a panic button to your security system
- Replace old cooking utensils with the easy-grip types
- Purchase easy-grip or one-touch bottle and can openers
- Frequently replace the air filters on your heating and air conditioning systems
- Consider purchasing an efficient air filtration system if you live in an area with poor air quality

You will probably come up with more changes to benefit your lifestyle. Of course, these don't have to be completed tomorrow, but looking at those scary statistics makes preparing our homes for retirement a very responsible task to accomplish. Our family physician recently sent a person to help John's parents prepare their living area. Check with your health care provider and see if they provide such a service to assist you.

## 2. Taking Care of Loved Ones
After you make the responsible decisions that will take care of yourself, I suggest you next make the decisions that will take care of loved ones. Let me be clear, by taking care

of loved ones I mean creating for them a financial protection and transfer plan. If you are like us, you probably don't have the kind of estate that will make your heirs wealthy. Like most folks, however, you probably do have assets you want to pass on to your family and not the government.

While I believe sharing the information we have gained from our experiences will benefit you in taking care of your loved ones, I strongly advise every retiree seeks out and develops a relationship with a trust attorney. As I mentioned in the last chapter, a trust attorney will provide the legal expertise you need in planning the distribution and protection of your assets during your lifetime and beyond. As I've stated previously, your financial team should include a trust attorney, a financial advisor, a tax accountant, and an insurance agent. Here are the most important considerations for taking care of loved ones.

## TRANSFERRING YOUR PERSONAL AND FINANCIAL POSSESSIONS

As the saying goes, you can't take it with you. You can, however, create a plan to transfer your assets to the loved ones you leave behind. Your goal should be to protect them from taxes, fees, probate, and family feuds. I never imagined we would be in a position to need a financial transfer plan. I always thought they were just for rich people. The fact is, if your assets, including your home, total $100,000 or more, you need a plan.

If you have gone through the experience of being a trustee or beneficiary as I have, I'm sure you understand the importance of this process. Having a plan in place is both financially responsible and emotionally comforting for those left to handle your finances and possessions.

When discussing this topic, one of the first questions everyone asks is, "Do I need a will or a trust?" The answer is, you need both. Here are brief descriptions of wills and trusts, along with some advantages and limitations. Remember, this is just an overview, and a trust attorney can provide you with much more detailed legal information.

## WILLS

A will is a statement of your intent and provides directions for the distribution of your life insurance and financial and personal possessions to named beneficiaries upon your death.

- **A will** is a public document and assets are subject to probate. Probate can be long, and if assets are in multiple states, the will is subject to probate in each state. Fees are expensive.
- **A will** does not provide for or protect the transfer of your financial and personal possessions to your heirs.
- **A will** is a very flexible document and it is typically less expensive than establishing a trust.
- **A will** works best when it is supplemented with a trust.

It's important to review your will periodically. Life-changing events, geographic re-locations, and frequent changes in tax laws might necessitate changes in your will. You may also want to revisit your choice of whomever you've chosen to manage your estate and serve as guardian for children or parents if needed.

## TRUSTS

A trust is a legal document in which you designate an individual or individuals to man-age your assets should you become incapacitated, or to supervise the distribution of your assets when you pass on. Typically, you are the designated trustee while you are living. A trust is designed to benefit you and your family in the event of illness, disability, or incapacity, and distribute your assets according to your wishes upon your death. A trust is personal and will only achieve the desired results if it is created to meet your specific needs. Once again, I suggest you find a trust attorney to assist you in this task.

- **A trust** will avoid probate.
- **A trust** will keep your beneficiaries out of the courts.
- **A trust** will ensure privacy.
- **A trust** will provide protection from disputes and reduce unnecessary stress on your beneficiaries.
- **A trust** will simplify the distribution of your assets to your beneficiaries.
- **A trust** will reduce the impact of taxes on your estate.
- **A trust** can be amended or revoked by you at anytime.

As described, a trust is personal. Here are the most common types of trusts:

*Revocable living trust* – A revocable living trust provides for a smooth delivery of your assets to your beneficiaries. During your lifetime you are responsible for manag-ing the assets in the trust. This is a key role for you and your financial advisor. If you consolidated your financial assets as previously discussed, you will have a tremendous advantage when it comes to record keeping, quick reviews of your assets in trust, and maintaining a current trust document. A relative is usually named to supervise the dis-tribution of your finances and personal possessions upon your passing. Choose wisely; this is a very important responsibility that not everyone can or should handle. While you may be asked to do so, I suggest you do not designate a lawyer or a bank as your successor trustee. They are usually very expensive, and to be quite frank, may not always have your or your heirs' best interests in mind.

*Bypass trust* – A bypass trust is a legal document that protects the assets of a couple for the surviving member. It is actually an extension of a revocable living trust: it goes into effect when one member of a couple dies. If you are married and a homeowner, you probably should consider a bypass trust, sometimes referred to as a unified credit shelter. The way this type of trust works is when one member of a couple passes on, the assets are divided. One portion of the assets remains with the surviving member and the rest goes into the trust. Here are a couple of the advantages of this type of trust:

- Currently minimizes federal estate taxes up to $7 million
- Ensures your heirs receive the full benefit of their inheritance upon the death of the surviving member

## WHAT WE HAVE DONE

After reviewing our personal situation and getting advice from a trust attorney, we decided on a revocable living trust that includes a bypass trust. Here is a diagram and explanation of how our trust will work when one, or both, of us passes on.

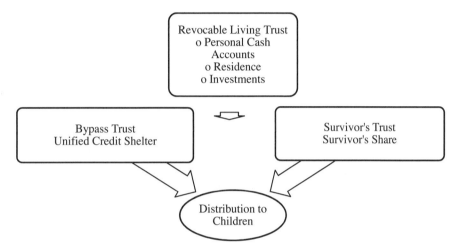

> Assets are recorded in the name of the trust.

> After the first death the joint trust is divided into two trusts.

    ✓ One portion passes directly to the survivor's trust and is not subject to taxation because of the unlimited marital deduction.

    ✓ The second portion passes to the bypass trust or credit shelter. The unified credit exclusion, currently $1 million, will be credited. If assets in this trust are less than or equal to the exclusion amount, no estate tax will be assessed.

        ■ The assets placed in the bypass trust are available to the survivor. A disbursement schedule for lifetime income payments can be created. You can restrict withdrawal of assets for general purposes such as health, insurance and other quality of life concerns.

        ■ By limiting the amount placed in the bypass trust to the amount of the unified credit exclusion no tax will be assessed upon distribution.

> After the second death the assets in the:

    ✓ bypass trust are distributed to the named beneficiaries and are not taxed;

    ✓ survivor's trust is included in the survivor's estate. The unified credit exclusion will be applied. If the estate is less than or equal to the exclusion amount, no estate tax will be assessed.

If you have special needs that you would like to have met for your grandchildren, friends, or a charity, consider a life insurance trust.

**Irrevocable Life Insurance Trust** – An irrevocable life insurance trust is created during a person's, or grantor's, lifetime. Once created, this type of trust cannot be modified or terminated by the grantor. The trust actually becomes the owner and beneficiary of the life insurance on the grantor, spouse, or other member(s) of the grantor's family. Some of the advantages of this type of trust are:

- Policy proceeds are tax-free and estate tax-free
- Cash is instantly available for any estate settlement costs
- Avoids probate administration
- Protects proceeds and assets from creditors
- Maintains confidentiality
- Provides income for family members

As you have probably concluded, our family is very important to us. Our children are supportive of our travel adventures. They encourage us to experience life, visit family and friends, and pursue anything that makes us happy. They admire our ability to be spontaneous, are proud to be our children, and never question the wisdom of our spending. They know that by creating a financial protection and transfer plan we have made certain that whatever is left in the piggy bank will go directly to them, not to the government or attorneys.

The choice is yours: either you plan for the direction and distribution of your family assets or the government does it for you. By investing time and thought in planning, you will spare those you love from the added emotional stress of fighting for what you intended them to have.

Over the last several years the federal estate tax exemption amount has increased and will continue to do so until 2010. What happens in 2010 is anyone's guess. Regardless of the new law that will be put into place, you need to create your plan and take whatever actions you can to minimize the tax liability and maximize the amount you leave to your beneficiaries. While there is no way around the income tax liability on tax-deferred retirement accounts, there are multiple ways to minimize the liability. Leave specific directions for your beneficiaries to seek tax advice prior to taking receipt of their inheritance.

Knowing what assets to place in joint tenancy, to distribute via a will, and to transfer via a trust are critical in the development and funding of your family savings transfer plan. Your trust attorney will advise you on this process.

Once your family savings transfer plan has been created, it will need to be maintained. All information, names, addresses, beneficiaries, properties, financial institutions, etc. need to be kept current. Several personal information worksheets will be shared with you in the next chapter. They are for you to use or modify as you see fit. They can also be found on our website, TheBestofOurLives.com. Your primary objective is to record the information and keep it current and accessible to your executor(s). You also need to be diligent on applying your financial decision-making model, discussed in Chapter 6, keeping an eye on savings accumulation and savings preservation.

It is important that you have a durable power of attorney for both personal property and medical care. A legally executed durable power of attorney enables the person(s) you have authorized to act on your behalf.

- Durable powers of attorney for personal property ensure that your financial affairs and assets can be attended to if your capability is limited.
- Durable powers of attorney for medical care ensure that decisions related to life-sustaining treatment can be made on your behalf, based on your stated directions, in the event you become incapacitated.

Your trust attorney will work with you to execute powers of attorney and seek clarification on your health care directives.

In addition to these responsibilities, I believe creating a family savings transfer plan and personal information file are essential in giving you and your loved ones peace of mind. Both of these important procedures will be discussed in detail in the next chapter.

---

*We make a living by what we get,*
*we make a life by what we give.*
—Sir Winston Churchill

---

## 3. Gifting

Most of us have lived the majority of our lives figuring out how to make ends meet. John often recalls an event that occurred shortly after we were married. He was serving in the United States Air Force and we were living in San Antonio, Texas. It was a Sunday and he got a craving for some potato chips. He decided to go down to the corner store and buy a small ten-cent bag. There was only one problem. We didn't have the ten cents. Payday wasn't until the next week, and we were completely out of money. Our kids have never really identified with that story, and let's face it; most people wouldn't even bend over to pick up a dime these days.

Fortunately for us, every once in a while someone came along and gave us a helping hand. It wasn't usually money, but an invite to dinner or hand-me-down clothes for the kids. We had family and friends that helped us, and I don't know where we would have been without them. Throughout our lives, when able, we've tried to help others as we were helped. Now that we've retired, we have begun to look at gifting as something we want to do for our loved ones. Let's look at some options for those of you who want to consider this practice.

## LIFE INSURANCE

As discussed previously, life insurance can play an important role in protecting your assets. Life insurance proceeds are not considered part of your estate. You should review your level of coverage annually. Have there been changes in your life, new family members, new mortgages, or a desire to leave charitable donations? Your insurance agent can work with you to set up a policy or policies that will provide the protection and financial support to benefit your family and heirs upon your passing. Life insurance proceeds can provide the liquid dollars to cover many expenses at death and financially protect the lives of those you leave behind.

If you gift in the form of an insurance policy, you can prioritize the use of the tax-free benefit in your will. For example, this is how I would prioritize the use of this benefit:

- Pay for the expenses related to your funeral and burial
- Pay outstanding bills
- Pay for probate and other related legal costs
- Pay estate taxes prior to disposition of assets

Note: An insurance policy that will pay the estate taxes prior to disposition of assets will ensure that your heirs are not forced to sell property or possessions that have sentimental value to simply cover the cost of the estate taxes. Spare them the need to make immediate emotional decisions on the family estate.

- If you have educational funds established for children or grandchildren that are not fully funded, life insurance can provide additional funding to these accounts.

As I'm sure you all know, there are two different types of life insurance: term and permanent. I suggest you work with your insurance agent and select the program that financially fits your current situation and supports your family savings transfer plan objectives.

**Term life insurance** – This is a policy that covers a specified period of time. At this time of our lives it is probably the best insurance buy you will find. The benefit provided is that of a death benefit. There is no money accumulation with this type of policy. While the policy can be renewed at the conclusion of the contract period, the new premiums will most likely increase with each renewal period. Strongly consider the longest time period offered to you.

**Permanent life insurance** – This is a policy that covers your lifetime. This type of policy can accumulate a cash value that can be withdrawn, borrowed against, or added to your death benefit. You perhaps have one or more permanent life insurance policies. Many young people feel that they are immortal and have not taken out permanent life insurance policies. There are several permanent life insurance products available. Consult your insurance agent for the product that fits your financial and personal situation.

## WHAT WE HAVE DONE

We have decided to purchase a universal life insurance policy for each of our children. In discussions with our insurance agent, it became clear this was a responsible form of gifting for children regardless of their age. This type of policy does not expire and does not have to be renewed as long as the insurance premiums are paid. Premiums are fixed and typically due annually. The policy will accumulate a cash value and will often pay dividends. An annual premium payment makes a great birthday gift and provides peace of mind that your child's family has a level of financial protection.

## TAX-FREE GIFTS

It is often said, "It's better to give than receive." This is especially true if your cash gifts are tax-free and/or deductible. Let me suggest three possible gifting strategies for your consideration.

The first gifting strategy involves each year granting to as many recipients as you like a tax-free gift up to that year's tax exclusion amount. Currently, the amount is $13,000 for a single filer and $26,000 for married couples. All gift transactions must be completed by December 31.

Should you find yourself flush with cash or need to liquidate funds to balance your taxable deductions, consider taking advantage of the gift-tax exclusion. To make sure you are never faced with missing the year-end deadline, set up investment funds for each of your children, their spouses, and your grandchildren, with you as the beneficiary. Your financial advisor can help you with this. This is a great way to move money tax-free to your heirs from your estate. The contributions are not taxable and the earnings are tax-deferred.

Another approach, if you want to determine the investment period, is to purchase CDs. Interest-bearing certificates of deposit are purchased at a bank. A short-term certificate of deposit matures in twelve months or less. A long-term certificate of deposit matures in twelve months or more.

The second gifting strategy involves passing tax-deferred IRA assets that have required minimum distributions at age 70 1/2 onto and through two or three generations. If this is something that suits your situation, you can contribute tax-deferred assets to an IRA, roll an amount of tax deferred assets from a 401(k) into a separate account, or purchase an annuity. Document a distribution schedule for you and your heirs to follow. Here is a sample distribution schedule:

- At age 70 1/2 you begin taking the RMD (required minimum distribution); your spouse is your primary beneficiary
- Upon your death, your spouse receives ownership of the IRA and begins taking the RMD at 70 1/2; your children become the primary beneficiaries
- Upon the death of your spouse, your living children receive ownership of the IRA that is to be equally allocated and distributed based on their individual life expectancy; their children (your grandchildren) become the primary beneficiaries

- Upon the death of your children, their living children receive ownership of the IRA, which is to be equally allocated; the distribution continues based on their parent's (or parents') remaining life expectancy

The principal and the earnings are not subject to taxes until the money is withdrawn. Required minimum distributions must be taken by December 31 of each year. This approach will make a wonderful Christmas gift each year of distribution and a lasting memory of you.

As part of a third gifting strategy, if you want to support your children's or grandchildren's education, there are several education savings products available, some for elementary or secondary schools and others for college or trade schools. These can be purchased through your financial advisor or your insurance agent. As an example, 529 plans allow you to withdraw earnings tax-free. Therefore, all the money you deposit into the plan and all the earnings from the plan go directly to the student for their educational expenses. Given the variety of programs, you should be able to find one that meets your goals.

This third strategy of gifting to our grandchildren's education is one both John and I favor. When blessed with an addition to our family, we open a savings plan. All you need is a social security number and a minimal initial deposit. You can make deposit slips available to other family members. You can also make up gift certificates to enclose in birthday and other special occasion cards, noting that a deposit has been made to their account. Trust me, they will appreciate it and so will their parents. To make it easy for us to remember when and how much to deposit, we crafted a plan. We agreed that a set amount of money times the child's age would be deposited each year on their birthday. A set amount of money would also be deposited each Christmas. This approach has freed us of worry. It's easy and fair, and you will have the peace of mind knowing that everyone is being treated equally.

Whether the situation is about Taking Care of Me, Taking Care of Loved Ones, or Gifting, your financial team of advisors (financial advisor, accountant, insurance agent, and trust attorney), can be a valuable resource to you as you continue your retirement journey. They can help you consider all programs and products available to you as you create your family savings transfer plan. Remember, your plan should always be a work in progress. It is important to keep your financial team informed and up-to-date on life-changing events and geographic relocations. They will keep you informed and up-to-date on new programs and products, as well as changes in the tax laws. Together you can maintain a fluid plan that addresses your desires and makes your dreams become reality for you and your loved ones. By addressing your retiree responsibilities, you will be ready to embrace your future and enjoy *The Best of Our Lives* with peace of mind.

*The greatest gift you can possibly give your family is the gift of love.*
*The most thoughtful gift you can provide them is a well-organized*
*personal information file.*
—Trisha Parker

CHAPTER **8**

# PERSONAL INFORMATION FILE
*By Trisha*

By now you know John and I strongly advocate that everyone should enjoy their retirement years to the fullest. We also believe retired people have certain important responsibilities. Regardless of age, there is always the possibility of illness, disability, incapacity, or death. Now retired, we have all accumulated various amounts of money, property, possessions, etc. If something happened to you, do your loved ones know what you have, who to contact, or where to go to find out? I've gone through this experience, as probably many of you have, with loved ones in my family. In this chapter, I demonstrate how to develop a personal information file. Developing this file will give you great peace of mind and be of tremendous assistance to your loved ones.

A personal information file is a resource file intended to provide your loved ones with the important information they will need should you become incapacitated or die. It is designed to provide answers to questions and locations of legal documents for you, your spouse, and your trustee(s) or executor(s). This file is a summary of your financial and personal possessions. In a stressful time for your loved ones, it will be an invaluable resource. Once completed, I suggest you share a copy with your financial team (financial advisor, accountant, insurance agent, and trust attorney), as they may have ideas that would enhance the value of the file for your estate and your family.

Be advised, in addition to your personal information file, you will also need to maintain separate files for:

- Your legally executed documents (will, trust, powers of attorney)
- Health care policies
- Financial contracts
- Real estate documents
- Life insurance policies

To assist you in preparing a complete personal information file, I have developed several forms to simplify the process. To give you an overview, here is the table of contents for the forms that will comprise your file. I suggest you look them over, determine which information pertains to you, and fill out the forms as completely as possible. If you are married, both you and your spouse should fill out forms that pertain to you as individuals. As always, you can photocopy these forms or download them at TheBestofOurLives. com.

## TABLE OF CONTENTS

Personal Information
Health Insurance Information
    Medical
    Supplemental
    Dental
    Long-Term Care
Account Information
    Financial Institutions
    Mortgages
    Utilities
    Credit Cards
Loans to Others Information
Advisor Contact Information
    Spiritual
    Medical
    Financial Team
    Others
Life Insurance Information
    Individually Owned
    Group
    Annuities
Final Wishes and Arrangements

    If your family finds this subject difficult to discuss, be patient and understanding, but persistent. Start with the basic information and discuss only one topic at a time. Perhaps your spiritual advisor can be of assistance. While planning your arrangements, remember that the service is primarily for those you leave behind. Be sensitive and respectful of their wishes.

    When a loved one dies, several death certificates will be required. I suggest you initially request a minimum of twelve.

Final Wishes Participation Directory
Beneficiary Information
    Primary
    Contingent
    Grandchildren
    Friends/Organizations
Financial Assets

Life Insurance

Bank Accounts – Spendable Savings

This is money that is easily accessible for daily living or monthly draws to supplement your spendable income. In addition to cash on hand and funds in your checking and savings accounts, it's a good idea for both you and your spouse to have a credit card in your own name with a substantial line of credit. Should there be delays in receiving life insurance proceeds or the distribution of liquid assets, you could find yourself financially stretched.

Securities – Deferred Savings

These are earnings that have been deposited into a deferred account 401(k), IRA, or annuity. These earnings and the realized gain from these investments are not subject to taxes until the money is withdrawn.

Securities – Invested Savings

These are financial products you have purchased with earnings that have already been taxed or were not subject to being taxed. The gain from these investments is taxable and is recorded in the form of periodic interest or dividend payments, and realized as capital gain at the point of sale or surrender.

Real Estate

    Primary Residence

    Vacation Home

    Rental Property

Motor Vehicles Information

    Automobile

    Recreational Vehicle

    Boat

    Trailer

Valuables Inventory

# PERSONAL INFORMATION FORM

In the event of your illness, disability, incapacity or death, this form will provide vital information for your family, trustee(s) or executor(s).

| | |
|---|---|
| Full Name | |
| Social Security Number<br>•    Location of Social Security Card | |
| Date and place of birth<br>•    Location of Certified Copy of Birth<br>     Certificate | |
| | |
| Driver's license number<br>•    Location of copy of driver's license | |
| | |
| Your Will<br>•    Date of execution<br>•    Date of last review<br>•    Location of document<br>•    Executor(s)<br>   -   Phone Number<br>•    Alternate Executor(s)<br>   -   Phone Number<br>•    Lawyer who drew up will<br>   -   Phone Number | |
| Your Trust<br>•    Name of Trust<br>•    Type of Trust<br>•    Date of execution<br>•    Date of last review<br>•    Location of document<br>•    Trustee(s)<br>   -   Phone Number<br>•    Successor Trustee(s)<br>   -   Phone Number<br>•    Lawyer who drew up trust<br>   -   Phone Number<br>•    Tax ID number, if one exists | |
| | |
| Durable Power of Attorney<br>•    Date of execution<br>•    Location of document | |
| Medical Power of Attorney<br>•    Date of execution<br>•    Location of document | |
| | |
| Marriage information<br>•    Date of marriage<br>•    Place of marriage<br>•    Location of Marriage Certificate | |
| | |
| Veteran information<br>•    Branch of service<br>•    Date of discharge<br>•    Service ID Number<br>•    Location of discharge papers | |

## HEALTH INSURANCE FORM – Medical, Supplemental, Dental and Long-term Care

It is important to pay close attention to how different types and levels of care coordinate or overlap. While you do not want any gaps in coverage you certainly do not want to pay for duplicate coverage.

## MEDICAL INSURANCE

| | |
|---|---|
| Insured Name | |
| Insurance Company | |
| | |
| Type of policy<br>• Group [ ], Individual [ ]<br>• Group or policy number | |
| Billing<br>• Address<br>• Phone Number | |
| Premium due date and amount | |
| | |
| Location of policy and benefit plan booklet | |
| Briefly describe the type and level of coverage provided | |
| Claims<br>• Address<br>• Phone Number | |
| | |
| Nearest<br>• Medical Office<br>  - Address<br>  - Phone Number<br>• Hospital<br>  - Address<br>  - Phone Number | |
| | |
| Additional Information<br>• Blood type<br>• Allergic to medication(s)?<br>• Chronic illness(es) | |
| Medical history problems or abnormalities of your immediate family<br>• Name<br>• Relationship<br>• Medical condition or issue | |

## SUPPLEMENTAL INSURANCE

| | |
|---|---|
| Insured Name | |
| Insurance Company | |
| | |
| Type of policy<br>• Group [ ], Individual [ ]<br>• Group or policy number | |
| Billing<br>• Address<br>• Phone Number | |
| Premium due date and amount | |
| | |
| Location of policy and benefit plan booklet | |
| Briefly describe the type and level of coverage provided | |
| Claims<br>• Address<br>• Phone Number | |

## DENTAL INSURANCE

| | |
|---|---|
| Insured Name | |
| Insurance Company | |
| | |
| Type of policy<br>• Group [ ], Individual [ ]<br>• Group or policy number | |
| Billing<br>• Address<br>• Phone Number | |
| Premium due date and amount | |
| | |
| Location of policy and benefit plan booklet | |
| Briefly describe the type and level of coverage provided | |
| Claims<br>• Address<br>• Phone Number | |

## LONG-TERM CARE

| | |
|---|---|
| Insured Name | |
| Location of policy and benefit plan booklet | |
| Policy date and number | |
| | |
| Insurance Company | |
| Insurance Agent<br>• Phone Number | |
| | |
| Billing<br>• Address<br>• Phone Number | |
| Premium due date and amount | |
| | |
| Briefly describe<br>• Waiting period<br>• Benefit period<br>• Benefit level<br>• Cost protection provisions | |
| Additional provisions | |
| Claims<br>• Address<br>• Phone Number | |
| | |
| Additional Information<br>• Blood type<br>• Allergic to medication(s)?<br>• Chronic illness(es) | |
| Medical history problems or abnormalities of your immediate family<br>• Name<br>• Relationship<br>• Medical condition or issue | |

## ACCOUNT INFORMATION FORM

It is important to record and keep current information on all accounts for which you have a financial relationship or obligation. Recording the following information will serve multiple purposes.

I carry this worksheet on my person when we travel. If I need to do online bill pay, or in the event of a misplaced, lost or stolen credit card, the information is at my fingertips.

In the event of your illness, disability, incapacity or death, this form will be useful for your trustee(s) or executor(s) in paying your bills, managing your accounts and other financial obligations.

## FINANCIAL INSTITUTIONS

| Firm | Bank of XXX | On Line ID | what ever |
|---|---|---|---|
| Account # | XXXXXXXX | Password | something cute |
| Website | www.xxxxxxxx.com | Security ?'s | home town, best friend |
| Phone # | (800) xxx-xxxx | Pin | XXXX |

| Firm | | On Line ID | |
|---|---|---|---|
| Account # | | Password | |
| Website | | Security ?'s | |
| Phone # | | Pin | |

| Firm | | On Line ID | |
|---|---|---|---|
| Account # | | Password | |
| Website | | Security ?'s | |
| Phone # | | Pin | |

## MORTGAGES

| Firm | Bank of XXX | On Line ID | what ever |
|---|---|---|---|
| Loan # | XXXXXXXX | Password | something cute |
| Website | www.xxxxxxxx.com | Security ?'s | home town, best friend |
| Phone # | (800) xxx-xxxx | Due Date | 1st |

| Firm | | On Line ID | |
|---|---|---|---|
| Loan # | | Password | |
| Website | | Security ?'s | |
| Phone # | | Due Date | |

# UTILITIES

| Company | Gas / Electric | On Line ID | what ever |
|---|---|---|---|
| Account # | XXXXXXXX | Password | something cute |
| Website | www.xxxxxxxx.com | Security ?'s | home town, best friend |
| Phone # | (800) xxx-xxxx | Due Date | 12th |

| Company | | On Line ID | |
|---|---|---|---|
| Account # | | Password | |
| Website | | Security ?'s | |
| Phone # | | Due Date | |

| Company | | On Line ID | |
|---|---|---|---|
| Account # | | Password | |
| Website | | Security ?'s | |
| Phone # | | Due Date | |

# CREDIT CARDS

| Credit Card | XXX Mastercard | On Line ID | what ever |
|---|---|---|---|
| Card Number | xxxx xxxx xxxx xxxx | Password | something cute |
| Website | www.xxxxxxxx.com | Security ?'s | home town, best friend |
| Phone # | (800) xxx-xxxx | Due Date | 20th |

| Credit Card | | On Line ID | |
|---|---|---|---|
| Card Number | | Password | |
| Website | | Security ?'s | |
| Phone # | | Due Date | |

| Credit Card | | On Line ID | |
|---|---|---|---|
| Card Number | | Password | |
| Website | | Security ?'s | |
| Phone # | | Due Date | |

| Credit Card | | On Line ID | |
|---|---|---|---|
| Card Number | | Password | |
| Website | | Security ?'s | |
| Phone # | | Due Date | |

# LOANS TO OTHERS FORM

List both secured and unsecured loans so that your trustee(s) or executor(s) can continue collection of your loan payments on your behalf.

| | |
|---|---|
| Borrower's Name<br>• Address<br>• Phone Number | |
| | |
| Loan Information<br>• Date of loan<br>• Amount of loan<br>• Interest rate | |
| Is the loan secured:  yes [ ], no [ ]<br>• If yes, description of collateral | |
| Location of note | |
| | |
| Repayment agreement | |
| Payment Information<br>• Due date<br>• Amount<br>• Final payment due | |

| | |
|---|---|
| Borrower's Name<br>• Address<br>• Phone Number | |
| | |
| Loan Information<br>• Date of loan<br>• Amount of loan<br>• Interest rate | |
| Is the loan secured:  yes [ ], no [ ]<br>• If yes, description of collateral | |
| Location of note | |
| | |
| Repayment agreement | |
| Payment Information<br>• Due date<br>• Amount<br>• Final payment due | |

# ADVISOR CONTACT INFORMATION FORM

It is important to record and keep your advisor contact information current. These are the individuals with whom you have a trusted personal relationship and can count on to provide you or your survivor(s) with advice and counsel.

## SPIRITUAL ADVISOR

| Advisor | | Address | |
|---|---|---|---|
| Name | | City, State | |
| Place of Worship | | 2nd Contact | |
| Phone # | | Fax # | |

| Advisor | | Address | |
|---|---|---|---|
| Name | | City, State | |
| Place of Worship | | 2nd Contact | |
| Phone # | | Fax # | |

| Advisor | | Address | |
|---|---|---|---|
| Name | | City, State | |
| Place of Worship | | 2nd Contact | |
| Phone # | | Fax # | |

## MEDICAL ADVISOR – List by specialty

| Advisor | | Address | |
|---|---|---|---|
| Name | | City, State | |
| Specialty | | 2nd Contact | |
| Phone # | | Fax # | |

| Advisor | | Address | |
|---|---|---|---|
| Name | | City, State | |
| Specialty | | 2nd Contact | |
| Phone # | | Fax # | |

| Advisor | | Address | |
|---|---|---|---|
| Name | | City, State | |
| Specialty | | 2nd Contact | |
| Phone # | | Fax # | |

## FINANCIAL TEAM

| Advisor | Financial | Address | |
|---|---|---|---|
| Name | | City, State | |
| Firm | | 2nd Contact | |
| Phone # | | Fax # | |

| Advisor | Accountant | Address | |
|---|---|---|---|
| Name | | City, State | |
| Firm | | 2nd Contact | |
| Phone # | | Fax # | |

| Advisor | Insurance Agent | Address | |
|---|---|---|---|
| Name | | City, State | |
| Firm | | 2nd Contact | |
| Phone # | | Fax # | |

| Advisor | Trust Attorney | Address | |
|---|---|---|---|
| Name | | City, State | |
| Firm | | 2nd Contact | |
| Phone # | | Fax # | |

## ADDITIONAL ADVISORS – List by specialty

| Advisor | | Address | |
|---|---|---|---|
| Name | | City, State | |
| Specialty | | 2nd Contact | |
| Phone # | | Fax # | |

| Advisor | | Address | |
|---|---|---|---|
| Name | | City, State | |
| Specialty | | 2nd Contact | |
| Phone # | | Fax # | |

| Advisor | | Address | |
|---|---|---|---|
| Name | | City, State | |
| Specialty | | 2nd Contact | |
| Phone # | | Fax # | |

**INSURANCE INFORMATION FORM** - Individually Owned Life, Group Life, and Annuities

The characteristics for each type of policy are different and some are more complex than others. Seek needed assistance from your insurance agent.

## INDIVIDUALLY OWNED LIFE

| | |
|---|---|
| Insured Name | |
| Location of policy | |
| Policy date and number | |
| | |
| Insurance Company | |
| Insurance Agent<br>• Phone Number | |
| | |
| Policy owner | |
| Beneficiary(s)<br>• Name<br>• Phone Number<br>Contingent Beneficiary(s)<br>• Name<br>• Phone Number | |
| Date of last beneficiary review | |
| | |
| Death benefit | |
| Policy<br>• Loans: yes [ ]. no [ ]<br>  - If yes, describe<br>• Assigned as collateral: yes [ ], no [ ]<br>  - If yes, describe | |
| Type of policy (term, whole life, etc.) | |
| Policy riders<br>• Accidental death: yes [ ], no [ ]<br>  - If yes, describe<br>• Premium waiver: yes [ ], no [ ]<br>  - If yes, describe<br>• Other: yes [ ], No [ ]<br>  - If yes, describe | |
| | |
| Premiums<br>• Payment due date and amount<br>• Automatic payment: yes [ ], no [ ]<br>  - If yes, describe<br>• Third party notice: yes [ ], no [ ]<br>  - If yes, Name<br>  - Address<br>  - Phone Number | |

## GROUP LIFE

| | |
|---|---|
| Insured Name | |
| | |
| Company | |
| Company contact<br>   &bull;   Name<br>   &bull;   Phone Number | |
| Group and/or certificate number | |
| | |
| Beneficiary(s)<br>   &bull;   Name<br>   &bull;   Phone Number<br>Contingent Beneficiary(s)<br>   &bull;   Name<br>   &bull;   Phone Number | |
| Date of last beneficiary review | |
| | |
| Death benefit | |
| Policy riders<br>   &bull;   Accidental death:  yes [ ], no [ ]<br>     -   If yes, describe<br>   &bull;   Premium waiver:  yes [ ], no [ ]<br>     -   If yes, describe<br>   &bull;   Other:  yes [ ], no [ ]<br>     -   If yes, describe | |

## ANNUITIES

| | |
|---|---|
| Annuitant Name | |
| Location of policy | |
| Policy date and number | |
| | |
| Insurance Company | |
| Insurance Agent<br>  • Phone Number | |
| | |
| Policy owner | |
| Beneficiary(s)<br>  • Name<br>  • Phone Number<br>Contingent Beneficiary(s)<br>  • Name<br>  • Phone Number | |
| Date of last beneficiary review | |
| | |
| Original cash investment | |
| Tax-deferred:  yes [ ], no [ ]<br>  • If yes<br>    - Current interest rate<br>    - Term of interest rate<br>    - Surrender period | |
| Type of annuity<br>  • Fixed<br>  • Variable<br>  • Guaranteed variable | |
| | |
| Policy status<br>  • Active investment:  yes [ ], no [ ]<br>  • Income draws:  yes [ ], no [ ]<br>    - Monthly, quarterly, annual<br>    - Amount of draw<br>    - Length of payment period<br>    - Death benefits<br>  • Annuitized:  yes [ ], no [ ]<br>    - Specified number of years<br>    - Over your lifetime<br>    - Over you and your spouse lifetime<br>    - Monthly income | |

# FINAL WISHES and ARRANGEMENTS FORM

Completing this form will help to assure your final wishes are carried out and also relieve your loved ones from the burden of making difficult decisions during their time of grief.

It is important to understand that funeral homes and cemeteries typically operate on a cash basis and require immediate payment in the form of cash, check or credit card. They will accept payment via insurance, if the policy is brought in at the time of arrangements.

| | |
|---|---|
| Medical Power of Attorney<br>• Person(s) of responsibility<br>• Date of execution<br>• Location of document | |
| | |
| Durable Power of Attorney<br>• Person(s) of responsibility<br>• Date of execution<br>• Location of document | |
| | |
| Funeral Arrangements<br>• Name of Funeral Home<br>• Address<br>• Phone Number | |
| Final Arrangements:<br>• Person(s) in charge<br>  - Primary: Name<br>              Phone Number<br>  - Alternate: Name<br>              Phone Number<br>• Funeral Plan<br>  - Prepaid: yes [ ], no [ ]<br>    ✓ If yes, location of document<br>  - Budget: Dollar amount<br>• Visitation: yes [ ], no [ ]<br>• Burial, Entombment, Cremation Options<br>  - Casket<br>    ✓ Budget: Dollar amount<br>    ✓ Open Casket: yes [ ], no [ ]<br>  - Cremation Container<br>    ✓ Budget: Dollar amount<br>    ✓ Disposition to remains<br><br>***Make certain that you shared your wishes with those responsible.*** | |
| | |
| Memorial Service<br>• Location of Service<br>  - Place of Worship<br>  - Funeral Home<br>  - Graveside<br>  - Crematorium<br>  - Chapel<br>  - Other<br>• Address<br>• Phone Number | |

| | |
|---|---|
| Service Arrangements<br>• Religious Ceremony:  yes [ ], no [ ]<br>  - If yes, reference advisor contact worksheet<br>  - Preferred prayers, psalms, readings<br>  - Preferred hymns, music, vocalist<br>  - Person(s) other than clergy to speak at the service<br>  - Preference regarding pallbearers<br>  - Preference on who should attend the service | |
| | |
| Resting Place<br>• Name of Cemetery<br>• Address<br>• Phone Number | |
| Cemetery Arrangements<br>• Plot and deed number<br>  - Location of documents<br>• Headstone [ ], Ground Plaque [ ]<br>• Instructions for epitaph | |
| | |
| Obituary<br>• Have you written your obituary?<br>  - If yes, where is it located<br>  - If no, do you have preferences as to what it should say?<br>• Where would you like it posted?<br>• Do you want a photo included?<br>  - If yes, do you have a photo preference? | |
| | |
| Do you wish to have any of your organs donated?:  yes [ ], no [ ]<br>• If yes,<br>  - Which one(s)<br>  - To which organization<br>  - Who will assume the cost of removal and transferring | |
| | |
| Additional issues, comments and requests | |

## BENEFICIARY INFORMATION FORM

In the event of your death, your executor(s) or trustee(s) will need the following information concerning the person or persons you have designated eligible for a benefit.  It is important to provide information for each beneficiary.


## BENEFICIARIES

| Share % | Social Security / Tax Number | |
|---|---|---|
| Name (First) | (Middle) | (Last) |
| Home Street Address (no P.O. boxes) | | |
| City, State, Zip code | | |
| Relationship | Telephone Number | Date of Birth (mm/dd/yyyy) |

| Share % | Social Security / Tax Number | |
|---|---|---|
| Name (First) | (Middle) | (Last) |
| Home Street Address (no P.O. boxes) | | |
| City, State, Zip code | | |
| Relationship | Telephone Number | Date of Birth (mm/dd/yyyy) |

| Share % | Social Security / Tax Number | |
|---|---|---|
| Name (First) | (Middle) | (Last) |
| Home Street Address (no P.O. boxes) | | |
| City, State, Zip code | | |
| Relationship | Telephone Number | Date of Birth (mm/dd/yyyy) |

| Share % | Social Security / Tax Number | |
|---|---|---|
| Name (First) | (Middle) | (Last) |
| Home Street Address (no P.O. boxes) | | |
| City, State, Zip code | | |
| Relationship | Telephone Number | Date of Birth (mm/dd/yyyy) |

as of (date)

## CONTINGENT BENEFICIARIES

| Share % | Social Security / Tax Number | |
|---|---|---|
| Name (First) | (Middle) | (Last) |
| Home Street Address (no P.O. boxes) | | |
| City, State, Zip code | | |
| Relationship | Telephone Number | Date of Birth (mm/dd/yyyy) |

| Share % | Social Security / Tax Number | |
|---|---|---|
| Name (First) | (Middle) | (Last) |
| Home Street Address (no P.O. boxes) | | |
| City, State, Zip code | | |
| Relationship | Telephone Number | Date of Birth (mm/dd/yyyy) |

| Share % | Social Security / Tax Number | |
|---|---|---|
| Name (First) | (Middle) | (Last) |
| Home Street Address (no P.O. boxes) | | |
| City, State, Zip code | | |
| Relationship | Telephone Number | Date of Birth (mm/dd/yyyy) |

| Share % | Social Security / Tax Number | |
|---|---|---|
| Name (First) | (Middle) | (Last) |
| Home Street Address (no P.O. boxes) | | |
| City, State, Zip code | | |
| Relationship | Telephone Number | Date of Birth (mm/dd/yyyy) |

as of (date)

## GRANDCHILDREN

| Share % | Social Security / Tax Number | |
|---|---|---|
| Name (First) | (Middle) | (Last) |
| Home Street Address (no P.O. boxes) | | |
| City, State, Zip code | | |
| Relationship | Telephone Number | Date of Birth (mm/dd/yyyy) |

| Share % | Social Security / Tax Number | |
|---|---|---|
| Name (First) | (Middle) | (Last) |
| Home Street Address (no P.O. boxes) | | |
| City, State, Zip code | | |
| Relationship | Telephone Number | Date of Birth (mm/dd/yyyy) |

| Share % | Social Security / Tax Number | |
|---|---|---|
| Name (First) | (Middle) | (Last) |
| Home Street Address (no P.O. boxes) | | |
| City, State, Zip code | | |
| Relationship | Telephone Number | Date of Birth (mm/dd/yyyy) |

| Share % | Social Security / Tax Number | |
|---|---|---|
| Name (First) | (Middle) | (Last) |
| Home Street Address (no P.O. boxes) | | |
| City, State, Zip code | | |
| Relationship | Telephone Number | Date of Birth (mm/dd/yyyy) |

as of (date)

## FRIENDS / ORGANIZATIONS

| Share % | Social Security / Tax Number | |
|---|---|---|
| Name (First) | (Middle) | (Last) |
| Home Street Address (no P.O. boxes) | | |
| City, State, Zip code | | |
| Relationship | Telephone Number | Date of Birth (mm/dd/yyyy) |

| Share % | Social Security / Tax Number | |
|---|---|---|
| Name (First) | (Middle) | (Last) |
| Home Street Address (no P.O. boxes) | | |
| City, State, Zip code | | |
| Relationship | Telephone Number | Date of Birth (mm/dd/yyyy) |

| Share % | Social Security / Tax Number | |
|---|---|---|
| Name (First) | (Middle) | (Last) |
| Home Street Address (no P.O. boxes) | | |
| City, State, Zip code | | |
| Relationship | Telephone Number | Date of Birth (mm/dd/yyyy) |

| Share % | Social Security / Tax Number | |
|---|---|---|
| Name (First) | (Middle) | (Last) |
| Home Street Address (no P.O. boxes) | | |
| City, State, Zip code | | |
| Relationship | Telephone Number | Date of Birth (mm/dd/yyyy) |

as of (date)

## FINANCIAL ASSETS FORM
### Life Insurance, Bank Accounts, Invested and Deferred Savings Securities

This form, organized by type of asset, allows you to keep track of each asset's location and other relevant information.  This will also be of assistance to you as you plan for the disbursement of funds throughout your retirement.

The easiest way to keep this information updated is to include copies of your statements.  Permanente life insurance and annuity statements are typically generated only at year end.  Quarterly statements will be sufficient for all other investment categories.

While some of this information will also be recorded on other forms, this form will provide you with a summary of your financial assets.

## LIFE INSURANCE

| | |
|---|---|
| Insured Name | |
| Policy Owner | |
| Insurance Company | |
| Agent | |
| Phone Number | |
| Policy Number | |
| Premium and due date | |
| Method of payment | |
| Principal Sum | |
| Accumulated Cash Value | |
| Beneficiary(s) | |
| Location of Document | |

| | |
|---|---|
| Insured Name | |
| Policy Owner | |
| Insurance Company | |
| Agent | |
| Phone Number | |
| Policy Number | |
| Premium and due date | |
| Method of payment | |
| Principal Sum | |
| Accumulated Cash Value | |
| Beneficiary(s) | |
| Location of Document | |

| | |
|---|---|
| Credit Card Insurance <br> • List by credit card name <br> • Amount | |
| Beneficiary(s) | |
| Location of Document(s) | |

## BANK ACCOUNTS

| | |
|---|---|
| Name on Account | |
| Type of Account<br>   • Checking<br>   • Savings<br>   • Equity Line | |
| Financial Institution<br>   • Branch Address<br>   • Phone Number | |
| Agent | |
| Account Number<br>   • Checking<br>   • Savings<br>   • Equity Line | |
| Routing Number | |
| Location of Checks / Deposit Slips | |
| List others with signature authority | |
| Does bank have a copy of your Abstract of Trust: yes [ ], no [ ]<br>   • If no, get them one | |
| Beneficiary(s) | |

## SECURITIES – DEFFERED SAVINGS

### IRA – Individual Retirement Account

| | |
|---|---|
| Owner Name | |
| Holding Company | |
| Agent | |
| Phone Number | |
| Account Number | |
| Original Investment and Contributions | |
| Year End Value | |
| Beneficiary(s) | |

### TSA – Tax Sheltered Annuity

| | |
|---|---|
| Participant Name | |
| Company | |
| Plan Name | |
| Agent | |
| Phone Number | |
| Account Number | |
| Original Investment and Contributions | |
| Year End Value | |
| Beneficiary(s) | |

## Annuity

| | |
|---|---|
| Insured Name | |
| Policy Owner | |
| Insurance Company | |
| Agent | |
| Phone Number | |
| Policy Number | |
| Type of Policy | |
| Original Investment | |
| Year End Value | |
| Beneficiary(s) | |

## Retirement Plan (401(k) contributions)

| | |
|---|---|
| Participant/Owner Name | |
| Holding Company | |
| Agent | |
| Phone Number | |
| Account Number | |
| Type of Plan | |
| Original Investment and Contributions | |
| Year End Value | |
| Beneficiary(s) | |

## Pension Plan (employer paid taxable income upon receipt)

| | |
|---|---|
| Participant Name | |
| Company | |
| Plan Name | |
| Agent | |
| Phone Number | |
| Participant Number: usually employee number or social security number | |
| Type of Plan | |
| Year End Value | |
| Beneficiary(s) | |

# SECURITIES – INVESTED SAVINGS

## Managed Accounts - Spendable

| | |
|---|---|
| Owner Name | |
| Holding Company | |
| Agent | |
| Phone Number | |
| Account Number | |
| Type of Plan | |
| Original Investment and Contributions | |
| Year End Value | |
| Beneficiary(s) | |

## Managed Accounts – Short Term

| | |
|---|---|
| Owner Name | |
| Holding Company | |
| Agent | |
| Phone Number | |
| Account Number | |
| Type of Plan | |
| Original Investment and Contributions | |
| Year End Value | |
| Beneficiary(s) | |

## Managed Accounts – Long Term

| | |
|---|---|
| Owner Name | |
| Holding Company | |
| Agent | |
| Phone Number | |
| Account Number | |
| Type of Plan | |
| Original Investment and Contributions | |
| Year End Value | |
| Beneficiary(s) | |

**STOCKS** – List those stocks that are privately held or individually recorded in your financial portfolio.

| Stocks | Number of Shares | Basis Cost | Location of Certificates | Title held as: in trust, joint tenancy, individual |
|---|---|---|---|---|
| | | | | |
| | | | | |
| | | | | |
| | | | | |
| | | | | |
| | | | | |
| | | | | |
| | | | | |

**MUTUAL FUNDS** – List both the Mutual Fund Company and the specific name of the fund as recorded on you tax returns.

| Company Name Fund Name | Number of Shares | Account Number | Location of Statements | Title held as: in trust, joint tenancy, individual |
|---|---|---|---|---|
| | | | | |
| | | | | |
| | | | | |
| | | | | |
| | | | | |
| | | | | |
| | | | | |
| | | | | |

**BONDS** – List each bond, recording by type: Savings, Municipal or Corporate.

| Bond by Type | Basis Cost | Maturity Date | Maturity Value | Title held as: in trust, joint tenancy, individual |
|---|---|---|---|---|
| | | | | |
| | | | | |
| | | | | |
| | | | | |
| | | | | |
| | | | | |
| | | | | |
| | | | | |

**CDs** – List each Certificate of Deposit.

| Institution | Basis Cost | Term | Certificate Number and Location | Title held as: in trust, joint tenancy, individual |
|---|---|---|---|---|
| | | | | |
| | | | | |
| | | | | |
| | | | | |
| | | | | |
| | | | | |
| | | | | |
| | | | | |

## REAL ESTATE FORM
### Primary Residence, Vacation Home and Rental Property

Fill out a form for each property you own. Pay special attention to the original purchase price, as well as the cost of improvements you have made. Also include information concerning your wishes for each property in the event of your illness, disability, incapacity or death.

## PRIMARY RESIDENCE

| | |
|---|---|
| Address | |
| | |
| Date of purchase and purchase price | |
| Location of escrow documents | |
| Title as appears on deed | |
| Location of deed | |
| | |
| Mortgage information <br> &bull; Date of finance or refinance <br> &bull; Financial Institution <br> &bull; Address <br> &bull; Phone Number <br> &bull; Loan Number <br> &bull; Original Loan Amount <br> &bull; Payment due date and amount <br> &bull; Last payment due date <br> &bull; Terms of loan <br>   - Fixed-rate <br>   - Adjustable-rate <br>   - Interest only <br>   - Assumable <br>   - Prepayment penalty <br>   - Other | |
| Second Mortgage or Home Equity Loan information <br> &bull; Date of finance <br> &bull; Financial Institution <br> &bull; Address <br> &bull; Phone Number <br> &bull; Loan Number <br> &bull; Original Loan Amount <br> &bull; Payment due date and amount <br> &bull; Last payment due date <br> &bull; Term of loan <br>   - Fixed-rate <br>   - Adjustable-rate <br>   - Interest only <br>   - Assumable <br>   - Prepayment penalty <br>   - Other | |
| Property taxes <br> &bull; Due Date <br> &bull; Current years payment amount <br> &bull; Tax parcel number <br> &bull; Impound Account: yes [ ], no [ ] | |

| Homeowner's Insurance information<br>• Company<br>• Agent<br>• Address<br>• Phone Number<br>• Policy Number<br>• Premium due date and amount<br>• Location of policy | |
| --- | --- |
| Home warranty information<br>• Company<br>• Agent<br>• Address<br>• Contract Number<br>• Policy Number<br>• Premium due date and amount<br>• Location of contract | |
| What do you want done with the property in the event of your<br>• Disability<br>• Incapacity<br>• Death | |

**PROPERTY IMPROVEMENTS** - You should keep a file of receipts for all improvements. Receipts often fade so make photo copies and attach to the originals.

Location of file: _____

| ITEM: Description of improvement | Date of Improvement: |
| --- | --- |
| | Cost of Improvement: |

| ITEM: Description of improvement | Date of Improvement: |
| --- | --- |
| | Cost of Improvement: |

| ITEM: Description of improvement | Date of Improvement: |
| --- | --- |
| | Cost of Improvement: |

| ITEM: Description of improvement | Date of Improvement: |
| --- | --- |
| | Cost of Improvement: |

| ITEM: Description of improvement | Date of Improvement: |
| --- | --- |
| | Cost of Improvement: |

## VACATION HOME

| | |
|---|---|
| Address | |
| | |
| Property Manager:  yes [ ], no [ ]<br>    • If yes<br>      - Name<br>      - Phone Number<br>      - Fee for service<br>      - Location of service agreement | |
| | |
| Date of purchase and purchase price | |
| Location of escrow documents | |
| Title as appears on deed | |
| Location of deed | |
| | |
| Mortgage information<br>    • Date of finance or refinance<br>    • Financial Institution<br>    • Address<br>    • Phone Number<br>    • Loan  Number<br>    • Original Loan Amount<br>    • Payment due date and amount<br>    • Last payment due date<br>    • Terms of loan<br>      - Fixed-rate<br>      - Adjustable-rate<br>      - Interest only<br>      - Assumable<br>      - Prepayment penalty<br>      - Other | |
| | |
| Second Mortgage or Home Equity Loan information<br>    • Date of finance<br>    • Financial Institution<br>    • Address<br>    • Phone Number<br>    • Loan  Number<br>    • Original Loan Amount<br>    • Payment due date and amount<br>    • Last payment due date<br>    • Term of loan<br>      - Fixed-rate<br>      - Adjustable-rate<br>      - Interest only<br>      - Assumable<br>      - Prepayment penalty<br>      - Other | |
| | |
| Property taxes<br>    • Due Date<br>    • Current years payment amount<br>    • Tax parcel number<br>    • Impound Account:  yes [ ], no [ ] | |

| Homeowner's Insurance information<br>• Company<br>• Agent<br>• Address<br>• Phone Number<br>• Policy Number<br>• Premium due date and amount<br>• Location of policy | |
| --- | --- |
| Home warranty information<br>• Company<br>• Agent<br>• Address<br>• Phone Number<br>• Contract Number<br>• Premium due date and amount<br>• Location of contract | |
| What do you want done with the property in the event of your<br>• Disability<br>• Incapacity<br>• Death | |

**PROPERTY IMPROVEMENTS** - You should keep a file of receipts for all improvements. Receipts often fade so make photo copies and attach to the originals.

Location of file: _____

| ITEM: Description of improvement | Date of Improvement: |
| --- | --- |
| | Cost of Improvement: |

| ITEM: Description of improvement | Date of Improvement: |
| --- | --- |
| | Cost of Improvement: |

| ITEM: Description of improvement | Date of Improvement: |
| --- | --- |
| | Cost of Improvement: |

| ITEM: Description of improvement | Date of Improvement: |
| --- | --- |
| | Cost of Improvement: |

| ITEM: Description of improvement | Date of Improvement: |
| --- | --- |
| | Cost of Improvement: |

## RENTAL PROPERTY

| | |
|---|---|
| Address | |
| | |
| Property Manager:  yes [ ], no [ ]<br>    •   If yes<br>        -  Name<br>        -  Phone Number<br>        -  Fee for service<br>        -  Location of service agreement | |
| Renter<br>    •   Name<br>    •   Rent due date and amount<br>    •   Payment (direct deposit, mail)<br>    •   Rental period end date<br>    •   Location of rental agreement | |
| | |
| Date of purchase and purchase price | |
| Location of escrow documents | |
| Title as appears on deed | |
| Location of deed | |
| | |
| Mortgage information<br>    •   Date of finance or refinance<br>    •   Financial Institution<br>    •   Address<br>    •   Phone Number<br>    •   Loan  Number<br>    •   Original Loan Amount<br>    •   Payment due date and amount<br>    •   Last payment due date<br>    •   Terms of loan<br>        -  Fixed-rate<br>        -  Adjustable-rate<br>        -  Interest only<br>        -  Assumable<br>        -  Prepayment penalty<br>        -  Other | |
| Second Mortgage or Home Equity Loan information<br>    •   Date of finance<br>    •   Financial Institution<br>    •   Address<br>    •   Phone Number<br>    •   Loan  Number<br>    •   Original Loan Amount<br>    •   Payment due date and amount<br>    •   Last payment due date<br>    •   Term of loan<br>        -  Fixed-rate<br>        -  Adjustable-rate<br>        -  Interest only<br>        -  Assumable<br>        -  Prepayment penalty<br>        -  Other | |

| | |
|---|---|
| Property taxes<br>• Due Date<br>• Current years payment amount<br>• Tax parcel number<br>• Impound Account: yes [ ], no [ ] | |
| Homeowner's Insurance information<br>• Company<br>• Agent<br>• Address<br>• Phone Number<br>• Policy Number<br>• Premium due date and amount<br>• Location of policy | |
| Home warranty information<br>• Company<br>• Agent<br>• Address<br>• Phone Number<br>• Contract Number<br>• Premium due date and amount<br>• Location of contract | |
| What do you want done with the property in the event of your<br>• Disability<br>• Incapacity<br>• Death | |

**PROPERTY IMPROVEMENTS** - You should keep a file of receipts for all improvements. Receipts often fade so make photo copies and attach to the originals.

Location of file: _____

| ITEM: Description of improvement | Date of Improvement: |
|---|---|
| | Cost of Improvement: |

| ITEM: Description of improvement | Date of Improvement: |
|---|---|
| | Cost of Improvement: |

| ITEM: Description of improvement | Date of Improvement: |
|---|---|
| | Cost of Improvement: |

# MOTOR VEHICLES INFORMATION FORM
## Automobile, RV, Boat, and Trailer

Fill out a form for each vehicle you own. In the event of a casualty loss, should an item be damaged or stolen, the recorded information will facilitate the claims process. In the event of your illness, disability, incapacity or death, this information will be useful for your trustee(s) or executor(s), ensuring your requested disposition of the vehicle.

## AUTOMOBILE

| | |
|---|---|
| Year, Make, Model | |
| Vehicle identification number (VIN) | |
| Date of purchase and purchase price | |
| Registration or ownership as recorded on title | |
| | |
| License plate number | |
| Registration renewal date and fee | |
| Financed or leased information<br>• Financial Institution<br>• Address<br>• Phone Number<br>• Loan/Lease Number<br>• Payment due date and amount<br>• Last payment due date<br>• Location of title or certification of ownership if title is clear<br>• Location of lease agreement | |
| | |
| Warranty and special service contract information<br>• Extended service contract<br>• Road Assistance Program (On Star) (AAA)<br>• Satellite Radio<br>List for each<br>• Servicing Company<br>• Billing Address and Phone Number<br>• Contract number<br>• Location of contract<br>• Payment due date and amount | |
| | |
| Insurance information<br>• Company<br>• Agent<br>• Address<br>• Phone Number<br>• Policy Number<br>• Premium due date and amount<br>• Location of policy | |
| | |
| Disposition of vehicle upon your<br>• Disability<br>• Incapacity<br>• Death | |

## RECREATIONAL VEHICLE (RV)

| | |
|---|---|
| Year, Make, Model | |
| Vehicle identification number (VIN) | |
| Date of purchase and purchase price | |
| Registration or ownership as recorded on title | |
| | |
| License plate number | |
| Registration renewal date and fee | |
| Financed or leased information<br>&bull; Financial Institution<br>&bull; Address<br>&bull; Phone Number<br>&bull; Loan/Lease Number<br>&bull; Payment due date and amount<br>&bull; Last payment due date<br>&bull; Location of title or certification of ownership if title is clear<br>&bull; Location of lease agreement | |
| Warranty and special service contract information<br>&bull; Extended service contract<br>&bull; Road Assistance Program (On Star) (AAA)<br>&bull; Satellite Radio<br>List for each<br>&bull; Servicing Company<br>&bull; Billing Address<br>&bull; Phone Number<br>&bull; Contract number<br>&bull; Location of contract<br>&bull; Payment due date and amount | |
| Storage information<br>&bull; Storage Company<br>&bull; Location Address<br>&bull; Billing Address<br>&bull; Phone Number<br>&bull; Contract number<br>&bull; Location of contract<br>&bull; Payment due date and amount | |
| Insurance information<br>&bull; Company<br>&bull; Agent<br>&bull; Address<br>&bull; Phone Number<br>&bull; Policy Number<br>&bull; Premium due date and amount<br>&bull; Location of policy | |
| Disposition of vehicle upon your<br>&bull; Disability<br>&bull; Incapacity<br>&bull; Death | |

# BOAT

| | |
|---|---|
| Year, Make, Model | |
| Vessel Hull Number | |
| Date of purchase and purchase price | |
| Registration or ownership as recorded on title | |
| | |
| CF number | |
| Registration renewal date and fee | |
| Financed information<br>• Financial Institution<br>• Address<br>• Phone Number<br>• Loan Number<br>• Payment due date and amount<br>• Last payment due date<br>• Location of title or certification of ownership if title is clear | |
| | |
| Warranty and special service contract information<br>• Extended service contract<br>• Boaters Assistance Program<br>List for each<br>• Servicing Company<br>• Billing Address<br>• Phone Number<br>• Contract number<br>• Location of contract<br>• Payment due date and amount | |
| | |
| Storage and docking information<br>• Storage/Docking Company<br>• Location Address<br>• Billing Address<br>• Phone Number<br>• Contract number<br>• Location of contract<br>• Payment due date and amount | |
| | |
| Insurance information<br>• Company<br>• Agent<br>• Address<br>• Phone Number<br>• Policy Number<br>• Premium due date and amount<br>• Location of policy | |
| | |
| Disposition of vehicle upon your<br>• Disability<br>• Incapacity<br>• Death | |

## TRAILER

| | |
|---|---|
| Year, Make, Model | |
| Identification number | |
| Date of purchase and purchase price | |
| Registration or ownership as recorded on title | |
| | |
| License plate number | |
| Registration renewal date and fee | |
| Financed information<br>• Financial Institution<br>• Address<br>• Phone Number<br>• Loan  Number<br>• Payment due date and amount<br>• Last payment due date<br>• Location of title or certification of ownership if title is clear | |
| | |
| Warranty and special service contract information<br>• Extended service contract<br>List for each<br>• Servicing Company<br>• Billing Address<br>• Phone Number<br>• Contract number<br>• Location of contract<br>• Payment due date and amount | |
| | |
| Storage information<br>• Storage  Company<br>• Location Address<br>• Billing Address<br>• Phone Number<br>• Contract number<br>• Location of contract<br>• Payment due date and amount | |
| | |
| Insurance information<br>• Company<br>• Agent<br>• Address<br>• Phone Number<br>• Policy Number<br>• Premium  due date and amount<br>• Location of policy | |
| | |
| Disposition of vehicle upon your<br>• Disability<br>• Incapacity<br>• Death | |

## VALUABLES INVENTORY FORM

This form should include your possessions that have either financial or emotional value. It is important to provide as much information as possible for each of your possessions.

In the event of a casualty loss, should an item be damaged, lost, or stolen, the recorded information will facilitate the claims process. In the event of your death, this inventory will be useful for your executor(s) in ensuring the requested disposition of your valuables. It also will provide a baseline for pricing of items should the beneficiary choose to sell them.

You should also keep a file of receipts and appraisals.

Location of file: _____

| ITEM: Brief description and location | Purchase Date: | Appraised: YES [ ], NO [ ] | Requested Disposition: |
|---|---|---|---|
| | Purchase Price: | Appraised Value: | |

| ITEM: Brief description and location | Purchase Date: | Appraised: YES [ ], NO [ ] | Requested Disposition: |
|---|---|---|---|
| | Purchase Price: | Appraised Value: | |

| ITEM: Brief description and location | Purchase Date: | Appraised: YES [ ], NO [ ] | Requested Disposition: |
|---|---|---|---|
| | Purchase Price: | Appraised Value: | |

| ITEM: Brief description and location | Purchase Date: | Appraised: YES [ ], NO [ ] | Requested Disposition: |
|---|---|---|---|
| | Purchase Price: | Appraised Value: | |

| ITEM: Brief description and location | Purchase Date: | Appraised: YES [ ], NO [ ] | Requested Disposition: |
|---|---|---|---|
| | Purchase Price: | Appraised Value: | |

| ITEM: Brief description and location | Purchase Date: | Appraised: YES [ ], NO [ ] | Requested Disposition: |
|---|---|---|---|
| | Purchase Price: | Appraised Value: | |

| ITEM: Brief description and location | Purchase Date: | Appraised: YES [ ], NO [ ] | Requested Disposition: |
|---|---|---|---|
| | Purchase Price: | Appraised Value: | |

| ITEM: Brief description and location | Purchase Date: | Appraised: YES [ ], NO [ ] | Requested Disposition: |
|---|---|---|---|
| | Purchase Price: | Appraised Value: | |

| ITEM: Brief description and location | Purchase Date: | Appraised: YES [ ], NO [ ] | Requested Disposition: |
|---|---|---|---|
| | Purchase Price: | Appraised Value: | |

| ITEM: Brief description and location | Purchase Date: | Appraised: YES [ ], NO [ ] | Requested Disposition: |
|---|---|---|---|
| | Purchase Price: | Appraised Value: | |

| ITEM: Brief description and location | Purchase Date: | Appraised: YES [ ], NO [ ] | Requested Disposition: |
|---|---|---|---|
| | Purchase Price: | Appraised Value: | |

| ITEM: Brief description and location | Purchase Date: | Appraised: YES [ ], NO [ ] | Requested Disposition: |
|---|---|---|---|
| | Purchase Price: | Appraised Value: | |

| ITEM: Brief description and location | Purchase Date: | Appraised: YES [ ], NO [ ] | Requested Disposition: |
|---|---|---|---|
| | Purchase Price: | Appraised Value: | |

| ITEM: Brief description and location | Purchase Date: | Appraised: YES [ ], NO [ ] | Requested Disposition: |
|---|---|---|---|
| | Purchase Price: | Appraised Value: | |

| ITEM: Brief description and location | Purchase Date: | Appraised: YES [ ], NO [ ] | Requested Disposition: |
|---|---|---|---|
| | Purchase Price: | Appraised Value: | |

Once you have completed your personal information file, keep it in a safe, preferably fireproof and accessible place, because you will need to update it from time-to-time.

Here are a few access suggestions that will benefit you now, and should something happen to incapacitate you in the future, will be helpful for loved ones and your trustee(s) or executor(s).

## ACCESS SUGGESTIONS

- If you have a safe, make certain that a designated person(s) knows the combination or has access to the keys.
- If you have a safe-deposit box, make certain that all signatures are on the bank access card and a designated person(s) knows the bank location, box number, and location of keys.
- If you store information in your computer, make certain a designated person(s) knows your computer password, the file name, and the location of your documents. Keep a back-up file on a CD or flash drive and make certain that a designated person(s) knows where it is kept.
- Assemble and label a master set of keys. This should include all vehicles and properties, storage sheds, lock boxes, gates, etc. Also include off-property sites such as storage units, facility gates, and parking complexes.
- Draw up a schematic that provides the location of your most important items stored in your home, garage, and storage sites. This will help your loved ones find things much easier. I get teased about my schematic, but the fact is, John and I both use it frequently when looking for items, especially the storage cabinets in our garage.

---

*That we all must die, we always knew;*
*I just wish I had remembered it sooner.*
—Samuel Johnson

---

If you don't act on any other suggestions made in this book, please act on this one. Begin working on your personal information file as soon as possible. What used to be called getting our affairs together has become so complex, it is an absolutely essential task. It will give you great peace of mind, and your loved ones will admire you for your consideration.

# NOTES

# NOTES

# NOTES

*The world is a book and those*
*who do not travel read only one page.*
—Saint Augustine

# CHAPTER 9

# TRAVEL ADVENTURES
### By Trisha and John

One of the best things about retirement is having the time to do things you didn't have time for earlier in your life. Probably high on your list of things to do is travel. We've previously described our busy preretirement life with children and careers that didn't allow for many pleasure trips. Now, living *The Best of Our Lives*, we've begun to travel more and have learned a lot from our research and personal experiences. In this chapter, we share with you our favorite travel considerations and suggestions.

As we begin this discussion on travel, be assured we are well aware of the expense factor. We understand that most every retired person or couple has a limited amount of financial resources. We are no different, and each year we try to budget a reasonable amount for travel. Regardless of the amount set aside, our goal is to get the most for our money. For you folks with extra funds, you will find some worthwhile suggestions for your travel adventures in this chapter. For those of you with more modest funds, our goal is to provide you with information that will expand your ability to travel and experience wonderful adventures.

Let's first define what we mean by travel adventures. Our adventures range from explorations of interesting places near our home to pleasure cruises through distant seas. We have adopted the philosophy of making every trip, even the shortest and most inexpensive, a travel adventure.

As an example, we recently took a break from writing and went for a short car ride. After seeing a small plane flying low over our house, we decided to find out where it landed. It appeared to come down in the farmland a few miles away. After exploring several rural gravel roads, we discovered a landing strip, a couple of old hangars, and a few vintage aircraft. "There's the windsock," Trisha exclaimed when we finally found the target of our adventure. Along the way, we discovered numerous scenic locations. They included quaint farms, picturesque vineyards, thoroughbred horse ranches, and a beautiful lake. All of this a short distance from our home, and neither we nor our neighbors knew any of it existed. It was a fun adventure, exciting and scenic, and cost a few dollars for gas.

## WHERE DO I WANT TO GO?

Isn't that an exciting question? It's also the first one you should ask yourself, because it's time to make up your travel adventure wish list. This might seem like an obvious first step, but we know many retired people who use their time and money to visit the same place every year. We're sure these folks have chosen a nice place, but *every year*?

Of course, everyone should make their own travel decisions. Since we retired, we tend to be a bit more adventuresome. For us, few things in life are better than visiting new places, seeing different sights, and meeting interesting people. It's exciting to find someplace completely out of our everyday experience. It can be just around the corner, or on the other side of the planet, but if we've never been there before, it might make our list. So, where do you want to go? Have an open mind and start brainstorming. Write down every possible place you've dreamed of visiting. Don't yet worry about time, expense, or anything else that might interfere with your process. This is truly a wish list, so don't limit your possibilities.

Once you've made up your list, it's time to prioritize. From your brainstorming list, narrow it down to your most desired destination. We recommend couples work on their lists independently and compare notes later. If you're like us, you may not be able to narrow it down to one absolute top pick. We usually have about five adventures at the top of our wish list and are constantly adding and revising. We actually maintain two lists. One is for short-range adventures and the other is for more distant travel. Once you know where you want to go, the real planning can begin.

## CAN I AFFORD IT?

As we stated previously, given your financial resources, you should set up a reasonable travel budget. This budget will easily determine whether or not a particular travel adventure is financially advisable. If you find one is too expensive this year, take another one you can afford and start saving and planning for next year. We've had to do this on a number of occasions. Try not to be discouraged; you'll get there one day. We've known so many people that retired, traveled very little, and later regretted it when they got to an age when travel was no longer feasible. We sometimes think a better question might be, "Can you afford *not* to go?" Get your travel adventure wish lists ready, set up your budget, and remember, we are living *The Best of Our Lives*. Let's make it happen.

To help make your travel adventures more affordable, we have put together "Our Thirty Best Cost-Cutting Suggestions." These suggestions come from a variety of expert travel sources and our personal travel experiences.

### OUR THIRTY BEST TRAVEL COST-CUTTING SUGGESTIONS

*1. Limit your home expenses while traveling.* Look to see where you can cut costs. There are obvious areas, such as stopping delivery of your newspaper and cancelling routine cleaning services. There are other less obvious ones, such as suspending your cable or satellite service and shutting off your hot water heater. Savings like these may seem small, but they could add up and pay for several meals while on your adventure.

*2. Plan and make reservations according to the current economy.* In good economic times you will typically obtain the cheapest transportation and hotel rates by booking early. In a weaker economy, it is sometimes better to book later in order to get the best deals.

*3. Make your reservations online.* Most travel experts agree that making your reservations online will save you money. If you don't have or use a computer, get a family member or friend to help you; it will be worth the effort.

*4. Use coupon codes to get discounts.* Several websites provide coupon codes that will give you discounts on travel, shopping, hotels, car rentals, restaurants, etc. While we don't endorse any one site, a good example is couponcodes.com.

*5. Consider traveling during the off-season.* Keep in mind that other parts of the U.S., and certainly foreign countries, do not have the same travel seasons. While off-season usually means the climate is not the best, we have had great luck traveling during these times. As an example, when planning an off-season September trip to Alaska a couple of years back, we had some friends decline our invitation because they thought it would be too rainy and cold that time of year. The weather turned out to be perfect, and we even missed the mosquitoes that are so prevalent in-season.

*6. Find the best airport parking solution.* Of course, the best solution is to have a family member or friend drop you off and pick you up. Airport parking is the worst option for more reasons than just being too expensive. We actually know of one major U.S. airport where the local police are let in every day to check cars for violations and give out citations. If being dropped off isn't an option, compare all the different discount lots near the airport. In addition to lower rates, they often have specials such as one day free or 10 percent off on extended stays. Look for these specials.

*7. Stay at a hotel near the airport the night before departing.* When we travel for two weeks or less, we often stay at a local airport hotel. Of course we try to get the best rate, but in addition to the extra sleep in the morning, the real deal is the two weeks free parking and shuttle to the airport. Our one night in the hotel is much less than even discount parking lot charges.

*8. Rent a car for travel to the airport.* This suggestion is very practical for long distance travel to an airport where car service or other transportation is very expensive or too much trouble. We recently went on a long travel adventure that required more luggage than usual. In researching the possible modes of transportation to the airport, some one hundred miles away, a commuter train seemed least expensive. It would have cost around $20. Unfortunately, this also meant finding transportation to the train station, carrying the luggage across a bridge at the station, and then catching a bus from the destination station to the airport. We checked with a local rental car company and rented a minivan for $39. Once the luggage was packed, we drove to the airport, checked the luggage at curbside, returned the car, and had a short shuttle ride back to the airport. Since we would also have had to pay for initial transportation to the train station, this was by far our best and least expensive solution.

**9. Consider all flight times.** Leaving a bit earlier or later can often make a big difference in the cost of your flight, so consider all of your options. Always leave sufficient time between connections.

**10. Seek out alternate airports.** Sometimes departing from or arriving at smaller, less-traveled airports can save you money. Of course, you must consider the expense of transportation at both ends of your trip.

**11. When booking a hotel, always ask for a lower rate.** We know this is difficult for some people, but if a better rate exists, why shouldn't you get it? It's really a bit of a game, and the hotels know this. When you ask for a lower rate, they will often ask you if you belong to membership clubs such as AAA or Costco so they can justify giving you a discount.

**12. Consider renting a house or condo when planning to stay in one location for an extended time.** Renting a house or condo at a weekly rate is almost always much less costly than a hotel. To find a house or condo, simply type the word rental and your desired location into a search engine.

**13. Stay in hotels and motels that include breakfast.** While the cost is built into your bill, it will still save you a lot of money during your stay. Meals are one of your biggest expenses while traveling, so save where you can. On our most recent travel adventure, we stayed at a very nice hotel that not only included a wonderful buffet breakfast but also provided buffet dinners.

**14. Reserve rooms that have kitchen facilities.** Once again, you can cut down on meal expenses by cooking some meals yourself. This is especially useful if your travel adventure is a road trip.

**15. Look for hotel freebies.** In addition to a free breakfast, look for things like free transportation, newspapers, maps, health clubs, etc.

**16. Avoid room service and minibars.** Unless you have money to burn, these are not good options. If you want a good meal in your room, it's often much less expensive to have a local restaurant deliver it.

**17. Find discount coupons at your hotel.** These coupons, found at the front desk, on display racks, in your room, and in the yellow pages of the phone book, will give you discounts for restaurants, attractions, and shopping. We once found the best antipasto and pizza we've ever eaten by checking with the front desk and getting a coupon for a nearby Italian restaurant. They even delivered.

**18. Pack a lunch for driving trips.** Save money by making your own sandwiches or picking something up at a deli. It's less costly than a restaurant and so much better than fast food. You might also find a nice scenic place to have a picnic.

**19. Carry an empty plastic water bottle.** Filling up your own bottle at the hotel before you leave each day will save you money. Of course, the purity of your water while traveling should always be a consideration.

**20. Check the currency exchange rate before planning a trip to a foreign country.** Exchange rates fluctuate, so consider traveling to countries that give you the best value for your money.

**21. Find the best places to exchange your currency.** We suggest you always obtain a small amount of foreign currency to have on hand before you travel to each country on your itinerary. Airports, especially those in foreign countries, typically offer the worst exchange rates, and banks offer the best. A little research can save you a lot of money.

**22. Make special cell phone arrangements with your provider or use phone cards while traveling.** This suggestion has saved us considerable money during our travels. For a small additional fee, many cell phone providers will offer you greatly reduced rates for both domestic long-distance and foreign calls. Some phone cards also offer better rates, so compare offers and select the best deal. We suggest you never use the phone service from a hotel or phone booth, especially in a foreign country.

**23. Take necessities with you.** If you need to buy items like sunscreen, toothpaste, or any other small necessity while traveling, it will be expensive. Plan ahead and take all those items with you.

**24. Buy travel insurance.** Health care while traveling is beyond expensive. Most travel agencies can provide you with travel insurance that will cover your medical expenses or emergency cancellations. Check with your own health care organization or insurance provider and find out what they recommend.

**25. Rent a car at an off-airport location.** The taxes and fees are often much less expensive at those sites. If you must rent a car at the airport, return it the next day at an off-airport site, and re-rent it. This may seem like a lot of trouble, but we've saved a lot of money over the last few years by following this suggestion.

**26. Consider a "repositioning" cruise.** Each travel season, the cruise lines must reposition their ships to accommodate the flood of travelers to a given location. For example, they must get most of their ships in position for Caribbean cruises in the winter and Alaska each summer. When the ships are repositioned, the cruise lines offer discounts on their rates. The downside of these cruises might be some slight off-season travel or a few extra days at sea. We know many folks who have had their best travel experiences on these cruises.

**27. Be smart when paying with a credit card in a foreign country.** There are three things to be aware of when using a credit card in a foreign country. The first is to always keep your card in sight and make sure you get it returned to you. The second is to check the accuracy of your bill. Don't be afraid to ask questions. The third is the surcharge credit card companies place on foreign purchases. Some companies charge much more than others, so find and use the credit card that has the lowest foreign purchase surcharge rate.

**28. Pay for your trip using the credit card with the best rewards.** Credit card companies are constantly changing their reward programs, so do the research and read the fine print to get the best deal. As an example, some airlines offer credit card deals that give you a free flight for merely signing up. If you read the fine print on some of these "deals," you will find they obligate you to a yearly fee. Be careful, and find the card with the best rewards. By doing this, your expensive travel adventure might provide you with some great credit card benefits.

**29. Ask for senior discounts.** If you haven't gotten used to this by now, it's time to start. You will find senior discounts for transportation, lodging, and restaurants. We recently took a two-hundred-mile round trip tour of south Florida on a very nice domed commuter train for $2. The key here is you typically have to ask for these discounts. We enjoy it when someone asks us to prove we are seniors; we call it reverse carding.

**30. Look for travel agency specials or travel groups.** Each year there are a number of travel agency special tours, senior travel clubs, and even churches that offer you wonderful travel adventures at reduced prices. We travel with a group at least once per year. Not only will you save money, there is safety traveling in numbers, and you have the opportunity to make lots of new friends. We have met wonderful new friends by traveling with a group.

These cost-cutting suggestions have saved us money on every travel adventure we have taken since we retired. Try them. See if they help cut your costs, and start enjoying the travel adventures of your dreams.

Once you've decided where to go and saved enough money to make your trip afford-able, it's time to pack.

## WHAT DO I CONSIDER BEFORE PACKING?

There are three important considerations for efficient packing. They are weather, activities, and the length of your trip.

**1. Weather** – Make sure you research the weather conditions for each of your destinations on sites like worldclimate.com. We recently traveled to South America in January. It was summertime there. It was very warm, but as part of our adventure, we also sailed around Cape Horn and past the glaciers of Chile. We had to research and be prepared for a variety of weather conditions.

**2. Activities** – Carefully consider all the possible activities you may want to experience during your trip. Will you be swimming, hiking, bus touring, dancing, horseback riding, sailing, etc.? It's also important that you inquire about the style and formality of any events you may want to attend. As an example, if you are going on a cruise, will you attend the formal dining nights? How many are scheduled? Are there any special theme events, such as a Western night or a Mexican fiesta? Once again, do your research and pack accordingly.

**3. Length of trip** – Once you've taken into consideration the weather and possible activities, you must factor in the number of days you will be traveling. We actually write out each day's clothing requirements. By doing this, we come very close to packing just the right amount for each travel adventure.

## WHAT DO I PACK FOR SHORT TRIPS?

Since retiring, we've found we can be much more spontaneous in our traveling. For our short or spontaneous trips we've created individual "go bags." These bags are actually small rolling travel bags that easily meet all airline requirements for carry-on luggage and are already packed and ready to go.

In these bags we carry three basic items. First, we have a toiletry kit that contains all of our personal grooming necessities. This includes such things as shaving cream, hair spray, toothpaste, etc. Many stores now have a full line of these products in miniature versions for traveling. For those items we can't find in smaller quantities, we simply fill small plastic bottles. Second, we include a small medical kit that carries our personal medications and first aid items. Such things as cold medications, pain relievers, and band-aids are examples of the items in this kit. Finally, we include a three to five day assortment of clothing. We have found that a light sweater, a pair of nylon pants, and a nylon jacket should always be in our go bags. These items take up very little room, and they are light and extremely versatile. Always check current travel security guidelines at tsa.gov.

In addition to using our go bags for short trips, they have become our carry-on bags for longer travel adventures. The beauty of this strategy is that you already have your toiletry kit, medical/first aid kit, and a few changes of clothes available should anything happen to your checked luggage.

Over the last few years, our go bags have proved to be invaluable. We have used them on several occasions when unexpected travel adventures presented themselves. One such adventure included a daughter-in-law going into an early labor. Having a go bag saved valuable time and energy, and also allowed us to be present at the birth of our first grandson.

## HOW SHOULD I PACK FOR A TRAVEL ADVENTURE?

Packing for a travel adventure is a bit of an art form. Everyone seems to have a method that works best for them. We constantly research travel books, articles, and websites looking for new ideas on packing. Based on all the information we have collected from travel experts and our own personal experiences, we have put together "Our Twenty Best Packing Suggestions."

## OUR TWENTY BEST PACKING SUGGESTIONS

*1. Always use a packing list.* Since we now travel more frequently, we have created our own individual travel packing lists and always keep a few copies on hand. Whether it's a long travel adventure or a short weekend getaway, we simply pull out our lists and start packing. The effort you spend putting a packing list together at the front end will save you considerable time and anxiety later. There is nothing worse than realizing you left behind something important when you reach your destination. We recommend you create your own list; to give you examples, we have provided our actual packing lists at the end of this chapter. When using these lists, our packing procedure is as follows:

- Pack at least two days before departure
- Go through the packing list one item at a time
- Cross out any item/category not required for the current trip
- For each item, determine and write down the quantity required
- Check off each item as you lay it out

- Circle each item as it is actually packed

*2. Pack as lightly as possible.* In addition to the convenience of having fewer pieces of luggage to wrestle, you will also save on tip money for baggage handlers at hotels and airports. Airlines are constantly changing their policies on luggage charges, and all airlines have weight limits. Foreign airlines typically have stricter weight limits. The penalties are costly, so you will need to research these restrictions and limits for each airline in your travel plans. We use our bathroom scale every time we pack a bag. Traveling light simply makes good sense no matter where or how you travel.

*3. Take a photo of your items during the packing process.* Having a photo of your packed items could be helpful in dealing with an airline, cruise line, or insurance company should your items be lost or stolen. It is also one of the reasons we lay out our items before actually packing them into travel bags.

*4. Keep your completed packing list.* This is important, because it will become your packing list for the return trip home. It might also be helpful should your luggage get lost or stolen.

*5. When two of you are traveling together, carry a few items of clothing in each other's bag.* Once again, if your bag gets delayed or lost, one or two changes of clothing will come in very handy.

*6. Place a copy of your itinerary in your bag.* Get in the habit of doing this as a last step in packing. We assume that everyone already has their home address on an information tag on each bag. By including your itinerary, should your luggage be delayed or lost, once recovered, it can be forwarded to your current travel location.

*7. Roll or fold clothes within sheets of plastic or tissue paper.* This will prevent your clothes from getting wrinkled. The plastic from your dry cleaner will work just fine.

*8. Place small objects into shoes.* Admittedly, this works best with men's shoes, and can be a real space saver. Such things as rolled up belts and ties fit very nicely.

*9. Place shoes into plastic bags before packing.* By doing this, you will not get your other packed items soiled with dirt or shoe polish. Shoes will also be much easier to pack. We have found the plastic bag our daily newspaper comes in works perfectly.

*10. Place sheets of fabric softener within your travel bags.* This will help dry up moisture in humid climates, and will also keep items smelling nice and fresh.

*11. Use a flexible plastic cooler as a toiletry or make-up case.* This will protect the other items in your travel bag, and when you arrive at your destination and unpack, you will have a nice little beverage cooler for the beach or a road trip.

*12. When packing electronic items, reverse the batteries.* This will prevent them from accidentally being turned on. When you arrive, don't forget why your electronics don't work.

*13. Always include extra plastic bags.* These can be used for a variety of things such as extra shoe bags, storing dirty clothes, transporting damp swimsuits, etc.

*14. Readers should take old magazines and books.* By doing this, you can discard or donate your reading material as you go, and make your luggage lighter.

**15. Shoppers should fold up and pack an extra tote bag.** By doing this, you can use it as a carry-on for souvenirs, clothing, or gifts on your return trip.

**16. Take along a couple of rubber doorstops.** This will provide you with some measure of additional security in your hotel room. Simply place one of these under your door after closing and locking it.

**17. Wrap gifts or presents after you arrive at your destination.** Given the current heightened security concerns, it is unwise to wrap and pack anything. This is especially true for items you have in carry-on bags, because you may be asked to open them for security personnel.

**18. Backpacks should have most of the weight at the top.** If you travel with a backpack, place the heavier objects on top so the pack will be supported by your shoulders. Placing weight at the bottom will put too much pressure on your back. Such light items as dirty clothes work well in the bottom of your backpack.

**19. Make your travel bags distinctive.** Since most people use black travel bags that look very similar, create a way to make yours stand out. This is for your own recognition and to make sure fellow travelers don't pick up your bags by mistake. Some people put colorful ribbons around their bags, but flimsy items are easily pulled off during the loading and unloading process. We have found that colorful plastic tape wrapped around the handles of each bag does the trick.

**20. Use travel bags with rollers.** Find sturdy bags with durable rollers for your travel adventures. If you spend more than a few minutes in any airport or port terminal, the first thing you will notice is how many people still struggle with old-fashioned luggage, over-the-shoulder bags, or some top-heavy roller bag that isn't rolling properly.

Try these packing suggestions and discover which ones work for you. Do more research and come up with your own creative ways to make packing easier and more efficient. This is an essential element for a successful travel adventure.

By now, we hope you have you have planned a fantastic travel adventure, found numerous ways to cut costs, and are efficiently packed and ready to go. There are just a few more things we think you should consider before you leave. For this reason, we put together a list of "Our Twenty-Five Best Travel Tips." These tips are to make certain you have a fun, safe, and stress-free travel adventure.

## OUR TWENTY-FIVE BEST TRAVEL TIPS

*1. Pack all medications and prescription information in your carry-on bag.* You should always travel with more than enough medication in case you are somehow delayed. Keep your prescription information with your other important papers in case you lose or need to purchase additional medication.

*2. Keep your updated immunization record with you when traveling to a foreign country.* Many health care organizations now have travel offices that will do the research for you. Tell them which countries you plan to visit and they will determine the necessary immunizations. If you don't have such a service, you can go to the Centers for Disease Control website, cdc.gov, and find out for yourself what is required. In either case, be sure to give yourself enough time for this process. Many of the required immunizations must be given weeks in advance of traveling.

*3. Check your medical and insurance coverage for your destinations.* Ask your representative to go over your coverage and make sure you have the appropriate contact numbers in case of an emergency.

*4. Ask your travel agent about travel insurance.* Many agencies now require travel insurance in case you become ill during your trip or have to cancel due to illness.

*5. Make sure you have all your travel documents.* Travel documents include your itinerary, travel tickets, confirmation numbers, valid signed passport (current passport requirements can be found at travel.state.gov), updated passport emergency information card, necessary visas (some countries require them), updated immunization record, and a valid driver's license or alternative picture ID. We suggest you keep all of these documents in a large wallet-type holder designed specifically for this purpose.

*6. Leave copies of your document information with family and friends.* This will help them in case of an emergency. You should also include your personal cell phone number and any other numbers where you can be reached.

*7. Scan documents and send them to yourself in an e-mail through your secure online account.* Should any of your documents become lost or stolen, you will be able to retrieve and print copies from anywhere in the world.

*8. Consider registering with the State Department in case of an emergency.* This will make it easier for family or friends to reach you. Go to travelregistration.state.gov.

*9. Carry a list of important phone numbers.* We suggest you keep a paper list since cell phone batteries can go bad. You might also want to send this list of numbers to yourself in an e-mail.

*10. Set up direct deposit or online bill pay before you depart.* Use these options or pay all your bills in advance. Knowing your ongoing bills are being paid will give you peace of mind and allow you to better enjoy your travels.

*11. Leave a key with a trusted neighbor.* Leaving a key with a neighbor, or hiding a key and giving a neighbor the location, will make it possible for emergency personnel, such as police or fire, to enter your home if necessary. On our last trip away from home, the security alarm kept going off because of shorting in a faulty window connection. Since we really do follow these suggestions, we left our cell phone numbers and hide-a-key location with neighbors. When we were called, we asked them to go into our house and gave them instructions to shut off the system.

*12. When traveling to a foreign country, familiarize yourself with local and national customs, laws, and travel restrictions.* Some countries, for instance, have very strict regulations about what can and cannot be brought across their borders. Chile, for example, is a beautiful and exciting country. However, their travel restrictions are very strict and must be followed without exception.

*13. Don't carry large sums of cash or wear flashy jewelry.* We keep our cash in a hotel safe when on land, and in the purser's safe when at sea. The fact is, we really don't keep much cash on hand. There are so many ways to get cash, it's not necessary to carry large sums. We also wear inexpensive watches and jewelry when traveling (OK, all the time).

**14. Carry one credit card and secure the others in a safe.** This will provide you with backup should your wallet be lost or stolen.

**15. Know your credit card balance and limits before you depart.** If you have paid for expensive items such as airfare prior to leaving, you may be close to your credit limit.

**16. Keep a list of your credit card numbers and credit card company phone numbers.** Be prepared in case your card is lost or stolen, or if you encounter a problem using a credit card.

**17. Contact your credit card companies and let them know where you will be traveling.** This is the case for both foreign and domestic travel. When we first began traveling, we encountered many problems using our credit cards. Once we figured out credit card companies get suspicious when charges start being made in distant locations, we got smart and let them know in advance where we were going.

**18. Make sure you have the proper electrical converter and plugs for your electronic devices.** Keep in mind that not all countries have the same electrical systems. Traveling to a number of different countries can present a problem, so you may need to find the proper converters and plugs for your destinations. Take your list of destinations and electronic devices to an electronics specialty store for help. If you are traveling on a cruise ship, this is not a problem.

**19. Take a couple sheets of printed mailing labels.** This will come in handy for those of you who send lots of postcards to friends and family.

**20. Ask family and friends to stop e-mailing.** Politely ask all those folks who regularly send you e-mail to refrain while you are away. Not having that avalanche of e-mails when you get home will be a great relief.

**21. Know how to tip.** Tipping, even in foreign countries, is pretty much the same as in the U.S. When eating at a restaurant, the tip should be from 15 to 20%, depending on the service. Understand, it's the custom in the restaurants of many countries to include the tip on the bill. Unfortunately, many uninformed people often leave a double tip. Look at your bill to see if it already includes the tip. Bartenders typically receive a dollar or two for each order. Cab drivers expect $1 to $3 for fares under $10, and 10 to 15% for fares over $10. Baggage handlers at airports get $1 per bag, $2 if it's a heavy bag. The same goes for a hotel bellman. Hotel maids typically get $2 to $3 per day, which can be left in your room. Salon personnel receive 15 to 20% in most cases. Valets generally expect to get $2 to $3 for delivering your car. For those of you experienced travelers, you already know that in certain major cities, such as New York, the expectations for tipping are higher. For such cities, add a couple of dollars to these recommendations.

**22. Prevent jet lag.** Prior to traveling from one time zone to another, start to acclimate yourself by gradually going to bed earlier or later.

**23. Protect your health.** Few things are more disappointing than planning a travel adventure and then not being able to enjoy it. Watch what you eat and be sure to drink plenty of water to stay hydrated. In all cases, make sure the water is safe. Standing, stretching, and walking are always recommended for long flights.

**24. Find answers to many of your travel questions by visiting the website travel. state.gov.**

**25. Have fun.** This may seem like a curious travel tip, but the fact is, traveling can be stressful. Try to focus on the beauty and excitement of your travel adventure rather than the occasional frustrations. We wish you all great fun.

While writing this chapter, we could not help reminiscing about the travel adventures we've taken since retiring. It brought back wonderful memories and reinforced our love of travel. Both of us have selected a few of our favorite travel memories and shared a brief remembrance.

## TRISHA

One of my favorite travel adventures was one in which we did virtually no destination planning. At the time, our nephew and his family lived on the East Coast near Washington, D.C., so we decided that would be our first stop. Traveling from our home on the West Coast, we were able to find and purchase some bargain airline tickets. We also decided to invite John's travel-loving parents to join us.

The round trip tickets gave us just over a week to spend on our travel adventure. We got to the East Coast, visited our nephew and his family on the first day, and then asked each other, "Where should we go now?"

I don't remember who made the suggestion, but someone said they wanted to see George Washington's Mount Vernon home. That's all it took and off we went in our rental car. Mount Vernon turned out to be a fascinating historic site and we were all beaming as we left. "Where should we go next?" John asked. While we were thinking, and because he has always been a flight enthusiast, John said he would like to see Andrews Air Force Base, where the president's plane Air Force One is located. Again, off we went. Each time we finished visiting one place, we entertained suggestions for the next. After dinner each night, we would look for a reasonably priced place to spend the night. Believe it or not, this went on for the entire week.

Some of our more notable stops on this adventure included the United States Naval Academy in Annapolis, the Liberty Bell in Philadelphia, 9/11's Ground Zero in New York, Fenway Park in Boston, and Plymouth Rock in Massachusetts. As we were driving back to Baltimore to catch our plane for home the following day, we stopped for lunch in New Jersey. As we were eating and looking at our map, someone asked, "Anybody ever been to Atlantic City?" We all smiled, rushed out to the car, and headed to the coast.

While I'm not sure I would recommend this type of extemporaneous travel adventure for everyone, it's one that provides some of my fondest memories.

## JOHN

A couple of years ago, my old Air Force buddy and his wife, two of our dearest friends, invited us to come join them for an extended weekend in the beautiful coastal town of Monterrey, California. Years before, they had discovered a very inexpensive hideaway, and they try to visit there at least once a year. We had not seen our friends for some time and it was great to get together again.

On the second day, we had breakfast and then decided to explore the shops and stores in the Monterrey Pier area. As we strolled along, the ladies shopped and my buddy and I just enjoyed chatting with each other. At lunchtime, we had a leisurely meal at one of the outdoor seaside restaurants. It's such a beautiful spot in the world, and to enjoy it with good friends made it more special.

After lunch we all walked along the ocean path, taking in the extraordinary beauty of the place. What happened next might not seem too exciting or interesting to some folks. We found a bench behind a railing that overlooked the ocean. All four of us sat down, put our feet up, and just sat there quietly. I'll never forget how we all became silent and simply enjoyed the beauty and serenity of the ocean. I don't know how long we sat there, but on reflection, this is a wonderful memory. We actually wound up spending the entire day in the same general location. We ended the day with dinner at sunset on the end of the pier. It was a brief but memorable trip.

## TRISHA

One of our most interesting travel adventures was taking a trip to Alaska. We spent three days on land and then embarked on a beautiful cruise that included the scenic glaciers and several interesting Alaskan port cities.

We traveled with a group of friends, which made our adventure even more fun. Along the way, we tried to experience as much of the history and culture as we could. I joined a group of friends who ventured off to go white water rafting. Yes, this was Alaska, but we decided to go anyway. As you can guess, it was wet, cold, and extremely exhilarating.

Both John and I were overwhelmed by the grandeur and beauty of this wonderful state. I must admit, neither of us had much previous knowledge of Alaska and its people before we had this opportunity to visit. The best memory we have of Alaska is the people. They seemed to be rugged individualists and very warm and friendly. We were also privileged to meet and get acquainted with several native Alaskans from the Athabascan tribe. They turned out to be some of the most fascinating people either of us has ever met. They spoke with both great humility and wisdom. They also beamed with pride when talking about their children and the future. We will never forget them and hope to return one day to learn more about their culture and witness more of Alaska's majesty.

## JOHN

Last year, it became necessary for Trisha and me to take care of some business in Florida. It was summertime, and the weather was very hot and sticky. We decided to spend a few extra days, and the weather turned unusually hot, even by Florida standards. As is typical for us, we decided to go exploring and drove up the coast. When we got near the Kennedy Space Center, even though we had not planned on it, we decided to buy a couple of tickets, see the exhibits, and go on a tour. As luck would have it, there was a space shuttle on one of the two launch pads. I can't tell you how exciting it was to see that shuttle poised and ready to go into space. You should understand that when I was a kid, I would set my alarm on the West Coast for 2:00 or 3:00 in the morning to watch every blast off. Our next decision was obvious; we would return in two days to watch the launch.

On launch day, we packed up food, cold drinks, and a plastic tarp. We set up in a park along the banks of the Indian River. Even though the weather had reached over 100 degrees, nothing was going to spoil this adventure. We shared our location and the afternoon with some wonderful tourists from England. Finally, it was time for the launch. All of us in the park counted down, and then it happened—*blast off*. The shuttle Endeavour and its crew blasted into space atop an indescribable orange ball of flame with the roar of thunder. When it reached a certain altitude and jettisoned the main fuel tank, all of us felt our natural tension release, and the entire park full of people began to applaud. Even strangers were high-fiving and hugging. It was truly amazing.

When we returned home to California, I was having breakfast with my father who is now 90% blind. He was enthralled by our story and told us he had always wanted to see a launch. Trisha and I looked at each other, went to the computer where she worked her magic, and found a good deal on some airline tickets. I went to the Kennedy Space Center website and was able to reserve four of the last tickets for viewing the next launch at the center.

Without going into the other details of the trip, I will never forget my mother's face, with tears of pride and amazement rolling down, as she watched the shuttle Discovery climb into the blue Florida sky. My father could not help but smile as he made out the orange glow and felt the rumbling vibrations. My mother said, "I've never seen anything like that in my life." Trisha and I smile every time we think about those two trips.

## TRISHA

Earlier this year, we went on an adventure we had been planning for some time. We traveled to several wonderful places in South America. We have family and friends, by way of marriage, in Buenos Aires, Argentina. One of our sons is married to a young lady who lived there briefly when she was a teenager and still has family there. After our son and his wife vacationed there, they encouraged us to go. It was an easy sell.

Our adventures in South America could fill an entire book, but let me share just a few. Our extended family member Jackie picked us up at the airport and spent several days and evenings entertaining us, along with other friends and family, and shared the warmth, history, hospitality, and good food of Buenos Aires.

We were then joined by some friends in our travel group and took a side trip to Iguassu Falls, which is on the border of Argentina and Brazil. This place is truly the greatest natural wonder we have ever seen. Imagine 275 falls that are twice as high as Niagara Falls over a one-and-one-half mile stretch. We spent nearly three days hiking above, around, and below the falls. Then we did something we will never forget. We took a ride through the rainforest on a large truck, hiked down to the bottom of the canyon, got on a zodiac-type boat, and headed back up the river through the rapids. Not only did we get close to the falls, our captain took us under several of them. Yes, under them. Imagine looking up as the falls pour down on you. It sounds crazy, but it was truly one of the most exciting things we have ever experienced.

Back in Buenos Aires, we joined the rest of our travel group and headed off on an exciting cruise. We stopped in Montevideo, Uruguay, where we toured the city and visited the Palacio Legislativo, the extraordinary building that houses their Declaration of Independence and where the government convenes. We then sailed on to the Falkland Islands, where we saw the penguins and avoided stepping on land mines left over from the war between England and Argentina. Another thrill was sailing around Cape Horn. I don't think John or I ever thought we would see such a place on this earth. We turned north, through the Straits of Magellan, and saw the glaciers of Chile. During stops at several cities in Chile, we visited sites such as the Volcano Osorno, rode a tram in the hills of Valparaiso, and explored the famous castle at Cerro Santa Lucia in the capital of Santiago. It was the adventure of a lifetime.

## JOHN

Not long after we retired, we took a cruise down the Mexican Riviera. This cruise offered a number of different price options and was quite reasonable. We were just getting used to being retired and learning to relax, and there were several things I fondly remember about our adventure.

One of the first things that comes to mind is having breakfast on our stateroom balcony while docked in Acapulco Bay. It was as if Steven Spielberg had designed the backdrop for us. The sky was lit up with orange and pink clouds high above us as we sipped our coffee and juice. The colors reflected in the water, creating a scene the likes of which we had never experienced.

Another fun memory is taking a walk around a hotel along the Pacific coast south of Acapulco. Of course, taking a walk may not seem memorable, but in this case, we were walking in a four-foot-deep walking pool. The pool extended around the hotel for one full mile past waterfalls and a lake, and, of course, overlooking the Pacific Ocean. It was quite memorable.

My best memory of this trip, however, is not a specific location or excursion. It actually took place one night while we were at sea. I can't remember where we were geographically, but it's not really important. What I do remember, and will always remember, is a smile on Trisha's face. As I said, we had recently retired, and were just getting used to these wonderful travel activities. The ship's crew was putting on a Mexican fiesta night, with all the appropriate food, drinks, decorations, and music. There we were, cruising along out in the Pacific on a dark moonless night, with the ship lit up in all its glory. As the music played, Trisha jumped into a conga line, which proceeded to snake its way around the pool on the lido deck. The look of relaxation and enjoyment on her face was simply amazing. After years of dedication and hard work given to her family and career, she was now taking some time for herself. It's something I will always remember.

In concluding this chapter, we want to wish you all exciting and safe travel adventures. As for us, we actually feel fortunate we didn't get to travel as much during our working years. There are still so many wonderful places left for us to discover as we live *The Best of Our Lives*. Hopefully, we will see you along the way. *Bon voyage!*

## *Trisha's Travel Checklist*

|  |  |  |
|---|---|---|
| # | # | # |
| [ ] ___ Go Bag | [ ] ___ Tops (long-sleeved) | [ ] ___ Dresses (cocktail) |
| [ ] ___ Med/First Aid Kit | [ ] ___ Shorts (sport) | [ ] ___ Jackets (casual) |
| [ ] ___ Underwear | [ ] ___ Shorts (casual) | [ ] ___ Jackets (dress) |
| [ ] ___ Bras | [ ] ___ Shorts (dress) | [ ] ___ Coats |
| [ ] ___ Slips | [ ] ___ Pants (casual) | [ ] ___ Hat/visors |
| [ ] ___ Sleepwear | [ ] ___ Pants (dress) | [ ] ___ Glasses |
| [ ] ___ Stockings | [ ] ___ Pants (fancy) | [ ] ___ Sunglasses |
| [ ] ___ Socks | [ ] ___ Belts | [ ] ___ Swimsuits |
| [ ] ___ Shoes (casual/sport) | [ ] ___ Jewelry | [ ] ___ Cover-ups |
| [ ] ___ Shoes (surf/boots) | [ ] ___ Sweater | [ ] ___ Umbrella |
| [ ] ___ Shoes (dress) | [ ] ___ Sweats (tops/pants) | [ ] ___ Music player |
| [ ] ___ T-shirts | [ ] ___ Workout clothes | [ ] ___ Cell phone |
| [ ] ___ Tops (sleeveless) | [ ] ___ Dresses (casual/sun) | [ ] ___ Wallet/ID |
| [ ] ___ Tops (short sleeve) | [ ] ___ Dresses (formal) | |

**Documents**:
[ ] Itinerary   [ ] Driver's license
[ ] Tickets     [ ] Immunization
[ ] Passports      record
[ ] Visas       [ ] Emergency Info.
[ ] Coupons

### *John's Travel Checklist*

| # | # | # |
|---|---|---|
| [ ] ___ Go Bag | [ ] ___ Shorts (sport) | [ ] ___ Swimsuits |
| [ ] ___ Med/First Aid Kit | [ ] ___ Shorts (casual) | [ ] ___ Glasses |
| [ ] ___ Underwear (shorts) | [ ] ___ Belts | [ ] ___ Sunglasses |
| [ ] ___ Underwear (shirts) | [ ] ___ Pants (casual) | [ ] ___ Sports gear |
| [ ] ___ Socks (sport) | [ ] ___ Dress slacks | [ ] ___ Umbrella |
| [ ] ___ Socks (dress) | [ ] ___ Sport coats | [ ] ___ Cameras (still/video) |
| [ ] ___ Thermal underwear | [ ] ___ Suits/tuxedo | [ ] ___ Music/video players |
| [ ] ___ Shoes (casual) | [ ] ___ Ties | [ ] ___ Cell Phone |
| [ ] ___ Shoes (dress) | [ ] ___ Gloves | [ ] ___ Reading materials |
| [ ] ___ Shoes (sandals/surf) | [ ] ___ Suspenders | [ ] ___ Maps/travel info. |
| [ ] ___ T-shirts | [ ] ___ Handkerchiefs | [ ] ___ Wallet/ID |
| [ ] ___ Tank tops | [ ] ___ Sweaters | [ ] ___ Money |
| [ ] ___ Polo shirts | [ ] ___ Sweatshirts | |
| [ ] ___ Sport shirts | [ ] ___ Jackets | |
| [ ] ___ Dress shirts | [ ] ___ Hats/visors | |

**Documents:**
[ ]    Contact number
[ ]    Itinerary
[ ]    Tickets
[ ]    Passports/visas
[ ]    Driver's license
[ ]    Immunization record

**BUENOS AIRES, ARGENTINA**

**CAPE HORN**

**LAKE LLANQUIHUE, CHILE**

**FALKLAND ISLANDS**

**GLACIER BAY, ALASKA**

**GOLDEN GATE**

**KAUAI, HAWAII**

**HILTON HEAD ISLAND**

**IGUAZU FALLS, ARGENTINA**

**KENNEDY SPACE CENTER**

**KEY WEST, FLORIDA**

**SHUTTLE LAUNCH**

**St. Lucia**

**Montevideo, Uruguay**

**Volcano Orsono, Chile**

**Whitewater Rafting, Alaska**

*Don't simply retire from something;*
*have something to retire to.*
—Harry Emerson Fosdick

# CHAPTER 10

# WHAT NOW?

*By Trisha and John*

If not before, at some point after retiring, we all must answer the question, "What do I want to do now?" We can almost hear the humorous responses to that question. And yes, sleeping or fishing all day is a perfectly acceptable answer. After our working years, most of us choose a much less strenuous schedule, spending more time with loved ones, friends, and recreation. As much as we both love to travel, we certainly wouldn't want to do it all the time, even if we had the resources. But given reasonably good health and a positive outlook, all of us are capable of doing great things after we've retired.

Before retirement, the responsibilities of family and career determined how most of us spent our time. Now, we have the opportunity to start anew and set meaningful goals. For those not yet ready to stop working completely, this might mean an interesting second career, even starting a new business. For others, the opportunity for philanthropy and working in the service of others may be the answer. We can all probably agree that one of our goals should be to set aside more time to enjoy our established relationships, make new friends, and reconnect with those from our past. Regardless of how you decide to spend your time, seize the opportunity and follow your passion. It's all part of living *The Best of Our Lives.*

*Taking care of business every day,*
*taking care of business every way.*
—Bachman-Turner Overdrive

## SECOND CAREERS

Hopefully, you have spent most of your life raising a family or working in a career that you enjoyed. Whether you still need a paycheck or simply enjoy the challenge of working, a second career should be something you find interesting and rewarding. The National Council on Aging reports that one out of three retired persons sixty-five or over has a retirement job. These jobs include both part-time and full-time employment. Of course, we understand that financial necessity is often the major factor in the decision to continue working. Whether it's working for someone else or starting your own business, we hope you make every effort to find something you enjoy.

Since retiring, we have met a number of people who have turned a hobby or other passion into a second career. Here are some of their stories:

- While traveling in Florida, we met a man who retired after serving in the United States Merchant Marine. After retiring, and still having a passion for the water, he bought a large pontoon boat and now takes tourists on a two-hour excursion each day. He told us he enjoys meeting a new group of people every day, and he seems to relish displaying his knowledge of the area, telling jokes, and sharing stories. His boat holds thirty people, and at $35 each, he does pretty well financially.

- Each year, a gentleman we know used to purchase a number of tickets to watch his favorite major league team play baseball. After he retired, he landed a job at the stadium as an usher during the season. Now he gets to see every game.

- While waiting for a recent flight, we met a woman at an airport who had retired and began making beautiful handcrafted jewelry. She said she loves what she is doing, enjoys traveling to the many shows and exhibitions, and also has her own website where she sells her creations.

- A local man we recently met used to spend a lot of his free time away from work perusing the local hardware store. It was a bit of a hobby, and every chance he got, he loved to explore the store with all its gadgets and tools. He reminded us of Tim the Tool Man from the TV show *Home Improvement*. Well, he's retired now and you guessed it, he works part-time helping people locate items at the very same store. He told us he loves it and said, "They actually pay me."

- A few years back, we became acquainted with a couple who had spent most of their lives running a small furniture store in the north. When it was time to retire, they still needed an income, so they reinvented their business. They decided to specialize by selling only two types of computer desks online. They hired a couple of people to handle and ship the desks, and moved to a condo in Florida. Since then, they check their site each day and send in the orders to be shipped. Of course, they do this after they return from fishing or golfing.

- We have a relative who worked most of his life as a mechanic. When he got near retirement age, he sold his business and, with his wife, bought a new home in a beautiful retirement community. After moving, he didn't feel ready to stop working, so he found a job at one of the local golf and tennis clubs maintaining golf carts. Of course, he was overqualified, but to this day he continues to enjoy everything about his second career, especially the lack of pressure. He also helps out in the tennis shop, and frequently gets paid to be a tennis partner for some of the members and guests.

We've shared these examples to illustrate our point that a second career should be something you enjoy. For those of you who do not have an entrepreneurial spirit, or must continue working due to financial necessity, we still encourage you to seek something you find fulfilling. The possibilities are endless. The fact is, there is an emerging market for older workers in the job force. Companies have discovered that older workers typically have a good work ethic, show up on time, tend to be more honest, and can be relied upon to get the job done. There are several websites that specialize in assisting older workers such as seniorjobbank.com and seniors4hire.org.

Recently, Merrill Lynch conducted a survey that asked baby boomers what types of jobs they looked forward to after retiring. These are the jobs they selected, in order of preference:

- Consultant (27%)
- Teacher or professor (20%)
- Customer greeter (15%)
- Tour guide (13%)
- Retail sales clerk (13%)
- Bookkeeper or auditing clerk (10%)
- Home handyman (10%)
- Bed and breakfast owner or manager (9%)
- Security screener (8%)
- Real estate agent (7%)

Based on our review of expert advice and our own personal experience, here is our compilation of "Second Career Suggestions" for those of you who decide to work for someone other than yourself:

## SECOND CAREER SUGGESTIONS

*1. Evaluate your personal financial situation and determine if a desired career is financially feasible.* You need to figure out exactly how much money you will make, how much you will require, and any possible transition costs you might encounter, such as moving, housing, cost of living, insurance, etc.

*2. Assess your personality, interests, skills, and likes and dislikes to determine if you and your new career will be a good fit.* It's one thing to want a particular career, and another to actually be right for it. Both careerpath.com and Monster.com offer assessment tests online in their career advice section.

*3. Do your research on both the career and the company.* You should have enough experience to know that not all companies operate or treat their employees in the same manner. Check them out carefully and find the one that best suits your needs and desires.

*4. Network to make valuable contacts.* At this point in your life, you probably have made more career contacts than you realize. Once you've determined your goals, make a list of potential contacts and seek them out. Just the term "network" brings back memories of just starting out, but in this case, you should be more comfortable with the process.

**5. Obtain the necessary skill upgrades or education for your new career.** In most cases, this probably won't be too extensive. However, if you find the right situation, and the training is something you find interesting, we say go for it.

We wish those of you seeking a second career good fortune. We also trust that if not before, this time around you will measure your career success primarily by your personal enjoyment and fulfillment.

For those of you who plan to start a new business as a second career, it's even more important that you select something you truly enjoy. Starting and running a business requires a lot of time and energy. By following your passion, you will find it easier to reach your goals.

As an example, not long ago we learned that two of our retired friends, both physical fitness enthusiasts, completed the required training to become certified water aerobics instructors. They both now work as private contractors teaching water aerobics at senior centers and health clubs.

Brad Sugars, the author of fourteen books on business, including *The Business Coach*, has recently written an article in which he provided several guidelines for starting a postretirement business. Here are his guidelines:

- **Find the market gap in the business you know.** Find a need that isn't being served by the business you came from and start a business that will fill it.
- **Turn your hobby into a business.** What could be better than making money doing something you love? (We have a friend who spends his winters in Florida fishing. He spends his summers in New England working as a fishing guide.)
- **Use your connections.** At your current age, you may find you know people who can help you with every phase of your business venture.
- **Investigate franchising.** The benefits are a low start-up cost and prebuilt systems and support materials.
- **Keep upfront expenses to a minimum.** Start small and keep your debt low.
- **Avoid a forty-hour work week to start.** While you might initially enjoy your new business, overdoing could burn you out.

Additionally, there are many websites that provide checklists and suggestions to help seniors start their own businesses. Two of the best websites we've found are provided by the U.S. Government. They are sba.com and irs.com.

If you decide to launch a postretirement career, we wish you much success. We're sure you all remember the story of Colonel Harland David Sanders, who used his first Social Security check of $105 to launch his fried chicken franchises at the youthful age of sixty-five. While none of us realistically expect that kind of success, we must first have a dream before it can come true. We wish you great fortune.

*It is one of the most beautiful compensations of life, that no man can sincerely try to help another without helping himself.*
—Ralph Waldo Emerson

## IN SERVICE OF OTHERS

Try to remember a time when you didn't have a personal care in the world, you felt great about yourself, and you had a sense of pride in what you were doing. We'll wager it was a time when you were working in the service of another person. There are numerous reported cases of people who have worked in very stressful situations, and despite the difficulty or danger, said they never felt more alive and fulfilled than when working in the service of others. Such accounts have come from military doctors in the field, police and fire personnel, and other persons engaged in similar activities. While most of us are not currently engaged in such extreme activities, the principle is the same. When working in the service of others, we tend to focus less on our own circumstances and come away with a great sense of pride and accomplishment.

At this time of life, you may be better able to share your good fortune with others. Whether it's your monetary wealth, possessions, time, or expertise, there is someone out there that can use your help. One of the ways to work in the service of others is to become a volunteer. There are numerous organizations throughout the country that provide wonderful opportunities to help others. There are national organizations such as the National Senior Service Corps, the Foster Grandparent Program, and the Senior Companion Program. All of these organizations have local chapters in which you could provide service.

Of course, every community has local volunteer programs that would love to have your help. Check with your state and local governments, charities, religious organizations, and philanthropic service clubs. The fact is, many of us boomers have been able to prepare adequately for our retirement. Good planning and good fortune have provided us with a comfortable lifestyle. We believe that as retired persons, we should spend at least some of our time working in the service of others. The White House Conference on Aging Policy Recommendations have revealed some interesting facts about retired persons and volunteerism. One of these facts, reported in April of 2009 by the National Association of Retired Senior Volunteer Program Directors, revealed that even though sixteen million people will live through retirement at a "very low level of income," these folks are just as inclined to volunteer as the more well off among us.

If you don't become part of an organization, there are always opportunities to help others. Similar to so many people our age, we have acquired lots of stuff over the years. In addition to regular gifting to our church and selected charities, when we hear of an individual that might benefit from any of these items, we make them available.

As an example, a short time back, we heard of a young man who had just separated from his wife. He was going through a difficult time, which was exacerbated by the fact he was making very little money. Having moved into a new apartment, he was not able to furnish it adequately for his child to visit. As luck would have it, we had recently stored several furniture items in our storage space. We immediately contacted the young man and met him the next day, and he soon had a nice place for his child to stay. We felt very blessed for the opportunity to help out. The following Christmas we received a card and note from that young man that brought tears to our eyes. We were embarrassed because we had done so little. But at that time for him, it had made a big difference in his life.

We try to share as much of our time and good fortune as we can, but we also know our service to others pales in comparison to the compassionate acts of so many other retired folks. If working in the service of others is something you do on a regular basis, bless you. If not, we suggest you find a way to get started. There is no greater way to spend your time, and there is no greater reward in life.

---

*Let us be grateful to people who make us happy, they are*
*the charming gardeners who make our souls blossom.*
—Marcel Proust

---

## RELATIONSHIPS

Two weeks after he retired, Dad (John's father) got a call from an old friend. It was a man he had served with in the Naval Air Corps during World War II. The man explained he had been trying to track thirteen men, all of whom had been assigned to the same unit on the island of Guadalcanal during the war. Dad was the last man to be found, and this gentleman actually cried as they spoke for the first time in over forty years. The following week, all of the men and their wives got together at the Lake of the Ozarks for a reunion. They had all recently retired and were in their midsixties. In an interesting side-note, they were all still with the women they married when they returned from the war.

As the years have passed, these men have gotten together as a group almost every year. They speak on the phone regularly, visit each other's homes, and have developed a great support system. At eighty-seven, Dad has survived most of his friends. He does, however, still have a number of what he calls his brothers from the war. He is forever grateful his friend was able to locate him so many years later.

As we get older, we need to tend our relationships with great care. If not now, at some point in the future we will realize they not only make up our support system, but actually define us.

## PARTNERS

If you are fortunate to have a loving partner with whom you share your life, let that person know every day how much they mean to you. We all know of people who appear to take their loved ones for granted. Some constantly criticize or bicker with their partners. These actions are often just behavioral habits, and the person may not realize that potential damage is being done. After retiring, most of us will probably spend more time with our partners. It's a great time to assess our relationships and ask what can be done to make them better. Minor behavior changes can often be made easily. If you encounter more serious issues, seek out the professional guidance your relationship deserves.

Based upon our research, we have created the following summary of issue-based questions that many professionals suggest you use as a starting point in assessing your relationship:

- Are you both part of decision-making?
- Do you both feel supported by one another?
- Do you both listen to each other?
- Do you both give each other positive feedback?
- Do you both enjoy spending time with each other?
- Are you both attracted to each other?
- Do you both demonstrate your affection?
- Do you both enjoy your love life?

As you can see, these are very direct and personal questions. If you are honest in your answers, they may begin to provide you with key insights for assessing your relationship. Once again, don't be afraid to seek professional assistance if you consider it necessary.

If you are now retired, and you and your partner have a sound and loving relationship, make it even better. We've previously shared the fact that we are treating this time of life as a second honeymoon. If you think we are exaggerating, we're not. We really try to do everything we can to make our relationship the best it can be. Our affection for each other is demonstrated in a variety of ways, both in words and actions. While this sometimes embarrasses our sons, they are always quick to tell us how pleased they are that we show our love for each other.

## WHAT WE DO

We want to say up front that neither of us is a marriage counselor, couples counselor, life coach, dating coach, or therapist. In other words, we're still married. Of course, we're joking. The fact is, we've been married nearly forty years, and continue to have a very loving and enduring relationship. As with all couples, we've hit a few bumps along the way, but nothing we couldn't get through. Over the years, young friends about to get married have asked us countless times to share our "secrets" for a successful marriage. Now, for the first time, we have formally tried to answer the question, "Why has our relationship worked so well for so long?"

Before sharing our answers to this question, we want to make sure everyone understands two very important points. First, we do not consider our experience to be a formula or recipe for anyone else's relationship. Each one is unique and should be considered as such. Secondly, we are also aware of the countless other successful relationships in the world. Many of our friends share wonderful relationships and have been together for many years. We undertook this exercise in the hope that something in our answers might be of benefit for other retired couples. Are we perfect? No, but we truly love each other and can't imagine living any other way.

Our process was simply to ask ourselves the question, "What are the reasons our relationship has worked so well for so long?" We wrote out our answers independently prior to sharing and discussing them with each other. Not surprisingly, our answers were almost identical. We did not disagree on any single answer, and it was only our wording that sometimes differed. Following are the reasons we believe our relationship has worked so well:

- **We like each other.** While that might seem a bit obvious, we really do like who the other person is and has become. We sometimes get the feeling some people claim to be in love, but don't even really like their partner.
- **We are both self-confident.** Before and after we married, we have always maintained our individual identities and senses of confidence. We believe in the axiom that most interpersonal problems stem from insecurity and a lack of self-confidence. That can be the case in one or both partners in a relationship, and is a sure recipe for problems.
- **We have common interests.** Both of us had this high on our respective lists, and in our discussion, we agreed this has been a key reason for our relationship working so well. Now retired, in looking at how we spend our time, we realize that neither of us is ever left out. Sure, there are times when we each do things independently, but never at the other's expense.
- **We have common values.** We share a common faith, and those values have an impact on everything we do in our lives. In our discussion, we agreed it would be nearly impossible for any relationship to thrive or even survive in which the two people involved had different values.
- **We have developed a good balance.** Over time, we have determined which of us does certain things better than the other. This has evolved into established roles, and provides for a very harmonious relationship. We also understand these roles do not stem from expectations or stereotypes.
- **We are flexible.** This reason has a number of different explanations. It actually works as part of good balance, since there have been a number of times we have had to change roles in our relationship. While one of us is clearly the best chef in the kitchen, for a number of years we had to switch that primary role. Flexibility has also been important in the everyday tedium of life. We don't argue over who takes out the trash, or who does the dishes, or who does this or that. If there is trash to take out, one of us does it. In other words, we don't sweat the small stuff.
- **We trust and respect each other.** Each of us knows that the other one can always be counted upon in any situation. While we might disagree occasionally, we never discount one another or intentionally try to hurt the other one's feelings. Should we ever have a serious disagreement, we would never do so in front of others.

When we witness couples arguing in public, we find it embarrassing, degrading, and downright tacky.

- **We've been lucky to have very good role models.** Our parents and friends have always provided us with positive examples.
- **We appreciate humor.** Interestingly, we have very different senses of humor. But there is never a day without laughter, and we feel it's a surprisingly important aspect of our relationship.
- **We continue to be attracted to each other.** This is based mostly on natural chemistry, but we've never taken it for granted and have always tried to act, dress, and groom ourselves in a way that pleases the other. It could also be that love really is blind.
- **We share an enthusiastic love life.** Being retired has given us more time to be with each other, and we have definitely taken advantage of that time.
- **We have been lucky.** We were fortunate to find each other and fortunate to have a wonderful family. These are among our many blessings and we acknowledge and give thanks for them every day.
- **We make our relationship a priority.** While we really don't like the term work when it comes to our relationship, we do put ours at the center of our universe. Since we have both evolved and changed over the years, we try very hard to make sure our relationship has also evolved.

Well, there you have it. Probably no big surprises or mystical secrets revealed, but we have reported our reasoning in a very straightforward and honest assessment. While we found this to be a very interesting exercise, decide for yourself if you and your partner would benefit from a similar process. If you find the results reaffirming, that's wonderful. If you find some areas that need to be addressed, that could also be beneficial. We wish you all the best.

## Family

As with most people, in addition to our personal relationship as a couple, we have many other types of family relationships. As mentioned previously, we try to be respectful of everyone, but the truth is, these relationships can be as difficult as any others, if not more so.

As we all know, no one gets to choose his or her relatives. This is especially true for folks our age. If you are like us, your children are probably married, and you now have new members of your extended family. We have been very fortunate and get along well with all of our new family members.

If you do have married children, you probably also have grandchildren by now. It's the best, isn't it? Beautiful little wonders who love to see you, and you don't have all the responsibilities. What could be better? We are absolutely crazy about our grandkids, and miss them terribly between visits.

The closeness of family relationships depends on several factors. For instance, it may be more difficult to have a close relationship with a family member who lives a long distance away. At one time you may have been very close, but it's very difficult now. Try as you may, it might not be the same as before. On the other hand, we have family who live across country, and we have remained as close as ever. It just takes a little more effort.

In other family situations, some people will develop closer relationships with certain relatives simply because they naturally like and get along with them better than others. That doesn't make anyone a bad person; it's just natural human behavior. There is also the possibility of having a family member who exhibits behaviors that create problems whenever he or she is present. While we believe in family unity as much as anyone else, we also believe that being part of a family comes with a certain degree of responsibility. It does not give anyone a free pass in terms of his or her behavior. Common sense tells us more problems are probably created when people try to force close family relationships, when the fact is, they simply won't work. While it's certainly a natural goal to want all family members to get along, some never will.

We suggest you value all your family members, spend the majority of time with those you enjoy most, and respect the others. It's what you would ask of them, and really all you can do.

## FRIENDSHIPS

As the saying goes, "You can never have too many friends." Well, it's true. And one of the best things about retirement is having the time to enjoy your friendships, make new ones, and reconnect with those friends from your past.

Nothing gives us more pleasure than spending time with our friends. A quiet afternoon chatting on the back deck, a golf outing, a holiday celebration, or a travel adventure, are all made more enjoyable when shared with good friends. Sharing any time in the company of good friends is one of the true gifts of life.

It's likely that as the years have passed, somewhere along the line you've lost track of valued friends. Now that you've retired, the chances are quite good you will be able to reconnect with many of these folks through the use of internet searches.

Since we retired, we've been able to get in touch with several of our old friends, both from school and military service. In just the last six months, we have reunited with two of John's Air Force buddies that we had not seen in over thirty-five years. We met one man and his wife in Las Vegas, and the other man and his wife in San Francisco. In both situations, we could not have had a better time. There was constant laughter and numerous "war stories" recounted. Now we have re-established our relationships with these old friends, and added their wives to our list of new friends.

Both of us have also made an effort to seek out old friends from our school days, and the result has been fantastic. Just recently, we spent the afternoon and evening with friends we have known since we were kids. This last year, we even spent time on a travel adventure through the Florida Keys with dear friends from school. We feel badly that during our working years we did not keep in close touch, but better late than never.

We have also found that retirement presents many opportunities to make new friends. Since we retired, we have made several. It seems as though we have known them forever. If you haven't already done so, open yourself up to the opportunities to meet new people. One thing is certain, old or new, as some now say, "It's all good."

So, what will it be? How are you going to spend your time? Will it be a second career, working in the service of others, or spending time with your loved ones and friends? We suspect that if you are like us, it will be a blend of all these things. Regardless of how you spend your time, we wish you all the very best retired life can provide. Hopefully, someday soon, you and your partner or you and your friends will say, "We are living *The Best of Our Lives.*"

# GLOSSARY OF FINANCIAL TERMS

**401(k) plan** An employer-sponsored defined contribution plan that allows you to contribute pretax earnings through payroll deductions. The annual limits for contributions are determined each year and taxes on contributions are deferred to a later date.

**403(b)(7) plan** A defined contribution plan that is sponsored by the government or nonprofit organizations. Annual contribution limits and tax-deferred payments apply.

**After-tax contribution** The portion of your salary that you have contributed to your retirement plan. This is often called a voluntary contribution. The earnings on after-tax contributions are tax-deferred.

**Annuity** A contract that offers periodic payments. These payments can either be of a fixed or variable amount provided over your lifetime or for a defined period of time.

**Asset** Anything you own that has monetary value. Assets can be financial or personal. Financial assets include savings and investments. Personal assets include your house, motorized vehicles, jewelry, art, etc.

**Asset class** An investment category in which your financial assets are typically allocated. The most common of these categories are stocks, bonds, and cash reserves.

**Beneficiary** The person or persons that you have designated to be eligible for a benefit when you die.

**Bond** A type of investment in which you are the lender of money, typically to the government, a government agency, or a corporation. Then, in the form of a bond, they agree to pay you back the loan amount plus interest by a certain date. Bonds generally are considered moderate risk.

**Capital gain and capital loss** The difference between the purchase price and the sale price of the asset. A capital gain is realized if the sale price is more than the purchase price. A capital loss is realized if the sale price is less than the purchase price.

**Cash reserves** A category of available monetary assets typically used to purchase contracts, CDs, U.S. Treasury bills, and annuities. The bank, government, or company then agrees to pay you interest over the period of time they have use of your money. This type of investment enables you to stage the terms of contract, interest rate, and time frame to fit your financial funding schedule. Cash reserves are considered low risk because they protect your initial investment while providing you with an income. The risk is the impact of inflation on the income received because of low rates of return.

**Cash value of life insurance** The money accumulated within a life insurance policy. The cash value includes the death benefit plus any tax-deferred accumulation.

**Certificate of Deposit (CD)** A money-market bond of a preset face value that is purchased at a bank and pays interest of a specified amount over a defined period of time. A short-term certificate of deposit matures in twelve months or less and a long-term certificate of deposit matures in twelve months or more.

**Compounding** When you increase your investment year after year by reinvesting the amount of capital gain realized.

**Death benefit** The amount of money that an insurance company is required to pay upon the death of the insured.

**Deferred savings** Earnings that have been deposited into a deferred account 401(k), IRA, or annuity. These earnings and the realized gain from these investments are not subject to taxes until the money is withdrawn. Usually these funds will be available to you without penalty when you reach the age of 59 1/2.

**Diversification** The strategy by which you spread your financial assets over a variety of asset classes. Ideally, this approach not only reduces your risk but also provides flexibility to manage your money for the greatest yield.

**Dividend** The distribution, usually quarterly, of earnings from those companies or funds that you have a right to share in the profit of. You will benefit by compounding dividends if they are reinvested in the fund or used to purchase more shares of stock.

**Durable power of attorney** A legally executed durable power of attorney enables the person or persons you have stated with the authority to act on your behalf. You need to have a durable power of attorney for both personal property and health care. A durable power of attorney for personal property ensures that your financial affairs and assets can be attended to if your capacity is limited. A durable power of attorney for medical care ensures that decisions related to life-sustaining treatment can be made on your behalf based upon your stated directions in the event you become incapacitated.

**Executor** The person or persons that you have named in your will to oversee the management and distribution of your estate.

**Heir** The beneficiary and/or person you intend to receive proceeds or property from your estate.

**IRA** An individual retirement account is a tax-deferred retirement savings account for those individuals who are working but are not active participants in an employer-sponsored plan.

**Inflation** The cost-of-living increase is expressed as the annual rate of inflation. The general increase to the prices of goods and services determines the increase to the cost of living. While you cannot control inflation, you need to understand the impact of inflation on your investment's returns.

**In-service distribution** Allows you to transfer 401(k) assets into an IRA while you are still employed. If available, this is a good option if you plan to work after you leave your employer.

**Invested savings** Financial products you have purchased with earnings that have already been taxed or were not subject to being taxed; for example, last year's bonus that you used to purchase some stock or a CD, or the nontaxable realized capital gain from the sale of a primary residence that you put into an investment fund. Make certain that you understand the tax liability before you sell or liquidate investments.

**Joint tenancy with rights of survivorship** Joint tenancy is when two or more persons hold ownership of property. Upon the death of one, the remaining survivor(s) becomes the sole owner(s).

**Long-term care insurance** An assisted-care insurance policy that pays for and covers both medical and nonmedical care at the time of disability or chronic medical condition.

**Pension** An employer-sponsored defined benefit plan; the benefit is predetermined based on your average salary over a period of time and your length of employment. You are entitled to the benefit once you meet the retirement eligibility rules.

**Permanent life insurance** An insurance policy that covers your lifetime. This type of policy can accumulate a cash value that can be withdrawn. You can also borrow against or add to your death benefit.

**Portfolio** All of your financial assets. Your portfolio is diversified if assets are spread over a variety of classes.

**Pretax contribution** The portion of your salary that you have contributed to your retirement plan, which has decreased your federal taxable income. The contributions and earnings on pretax contributions are tax-deferred.

**Principal** The original amount of your investments.

**Rate of return** The amount of your return, plus additional interest or dividends received, divided by your original investment. The change in value of your investment over a period of time is your amount of return. A rate of return is expressed in a percentage.

**Retiree distributions** A withdrawal from an employer retirement plan. As a retiree, you can take distributions from your account without penalty beginning at age fifty-five. This means that if you retire from your employer and leave your money in their plan, you would be able to take distributions at any time, without penalty, once you reach age fifty-five. If you were to transfer the funds out of your employer plan into an IRA, distributions prior to age 59 1/2 would be subject to a 10 percent federal tax penalty.

**Risk** The likelihood that your investment will not keep pace with the rate of inflation or will decline in value. Both of these events will result in the decrease in the value of your investment.

**Spendable income** The amount of money you have or will have at your disposal to fund your daily living expenses now and in the future. A pension, rental property income, or social security benefits are examples of spendable income.

**Spendable savings** Money that is easily accessible for monthly draws to supplement your spendable income or fund your monthly budget or special events such as vacations.

**Stock** A type of investment where you purchase ownership in a company. As a stock-holder, you share in the company's profit. These earnings are distributed in the form of dividends. Additional capital gain or loss will be realized over time based on the company's market value. Stocks generally are considered high risk.

**Tax-deferred** An investment for which payment of taxes on income and earnings is delayed.

**Term life insurance** An insurance policy for a specified period of time. The policy can be renewed at the conclusion of the contract period, assuming qualifications are met. A death benefit is provided. There is no money accumulation with this type of policy.

**Trust** A trust is established by transferring the ownership of your property and financial assets to a trustee. While capable, you are the trustee. The trustee is responsible for the management of the property and financial assets as set forth in a legal document. A trust provides benefits to you, your spouse, and your family, both during and after your lifetime.

**Trustee** The individual or individuals that hold legal title to property or financial assets for their own use and benefit or for the use and benefit of others. The state in which the trust was entered sets forth the fiduciary regulations from which the trustee is governed.

**Will** The document that governs the management and distribution of your estate by your executor. A will becomes effective only upon death and has no benefit in the event of mental or physical incapacity. A will should be legally executed.

**Yield** An amount of gain or income, usually expressed as a percent of your original investment. The amount of cash you receive from your investments.

# REFERENCES

American Medical Association. (2006). AMA resolutions for a happy new year. Retrieved from www.ama-assn.org.

American Psychological Association. (1998). *What practitioners should know about working with older adults.* [Brochure]. Washington, DC: APA.

Atchley, R. (1999). *Continuity and adaptation in aging: Creating positive experiences.* Baltimore: Johns Hopkins University Press.

Beckman, N., Waern, M., Gustafson, D., & Skoog, I. (2008). Secular trends in self-reported sexual activity and satisfaction in Swedish 70 year olds: Cross sectional survey of four populations, 1971-2001. *British Medical Journal, 337,* a279.

Buscaglia, L. (1992). *Born for love: Reflections on loving.* Thorofare, NJ: Slack.

Buscaglia, L. (1982). *Living, loving and learning.* New York: Ballentine.

Cousins, N. (1979). *Anatomy of an illness as perceived by the patient.* New York: Norton.

Glass, L. (1995). *Toxic people: 10 ways of dealing with people who make your life miserable.* New York: Simon & Schuster.

Greider, K. & Neimark, J. (2008). Making our minds last a lifetime. *Psychology Today.* Retrieved from http://www.psychologytoday.com/articles/pto-19961201-000028.html.

Groneck, S. & Patterson, R. (1971). Human aging II: An eleven-year biomedical and behavioral study. *U. S. Public Health Service Monograph.* Washington, DC: Governmental Printing Office.

Hess, T.M. (2005). Memory and aging in context. *Psychological Bulletin, 131*(3), 383-406.

Human Nutrition Research Center on Aging, Agricultural Research Service. (2008). High-ORAC food may slow aging. Retrieved from www.ars.usda.gov.

Khaw, K.-T., Wareham, N., Bingham, S., Welch, A., Luben, R., & Day, N. (2008). Combined impact of health behaviours and mortality in men and women: The EPIC-Norfolk Prospective Population Study. Retrieved from http://www.medscape. com/viewarticle/571492.

LePoncin, M. (1990). *Brain fitness: A proven program to improve your memory, logic, attention span, organizational ability, and more.* New York: Ballantine Books.

Levy, B.R., Slade, M.D., Kunkel, S.R., & Kasl, S.V. (2002). Longevity increased by positive self-perceptions of aging. *Journal of Personality and Social Psychology, 83*(2), 261-270.

Lindau, S.T., Schumm, L.P., Laumann, E.O., Levinson, W., O'Muircheartaigh, C.A., & Waite, L.J. (2007). A study of sexuality and health among older adults in the United States. *The New England Journal of Medicine, 357*(8), 762-774.

Mayo Clinic. (2008). 10 tips for better sleep. Retrieved from http://www.mayoclinic.com/health/sleep/HQ01387.

Merrill Lynch. (2006). The 2006 Merrill Lynch New Retirement Study: A perspective from individuals and employers. Retrieved from http://www.ml.com/media/66482. pdf.

National Association of RSVP Directors. (2009). White House Conference on Aging Policy Recommendations. Retrieved from http://www.whcoa.gov/about/policy/ meeting/summary/INDIANAMoorman.pdf

National Cancer Institute. (2007). Report on initial screening for colon cancer. Retrieved from http://www.faqs.org/health/topics/72/Health-screening.html.

National Council on Aging. (2005). *RespectAbility web survey executive summary.* Washington, DC: National Council on Aging.

National Institute on Aging. (2007). *Growing older in America: The health and retirement study.* NIH Publication No. 07-5757. Washington, DC: National Institutes of Health.

National Institute on Aging. (2006). Falls and older adults: About falls. Retrieved from http://nihseniorhealth.gov/falls/aboutfalls/01.html.

National Institute on Aging. (2005). Sleep and aging. Retrieved from http://nihseniorhealth.gov/sleepandaging/toc.html.

Nelson, M., & Wernick, S. (2000). *Strong women stay young.* New York: Bantam Books.

Ostir, G., Ottenbacher, K., and Markides, K. (2004). Onset of frailty in older adults and the protective role of positive effect. *Pscychology and Aging, 19*(3), 402-408.

Parker, J., & Weathers, J. (1990). *The student success workbook* (3rd ed.). Los Angeles: Student Success Publishing.

Selye, H. (1975). *Stress without distress.* New York: New American Library.

Seniors-Site.com. (2005). Physical fitness and senior citizens. Retrieved from http://seniors-site.com/sports/fitness.html.

Stewart, M. (2006). Duke University study finds hearing aids are underused. Retrieved from www.InHealth.org.

Sugars, B. (2007, November). Bored with retirement? Start a business. Retrieved from www.Entrepreneur.com.

Tannen, S. (2007) Mental fitness-exercises for the brain. Retrieved from www.bellydoc.com.

University of Warwick (2007). Lack of sleep doubles risk of death, but so can too much sleep. *ScienceDaily.* Retrieved from http://www.sciencedaily.com/releases/2007/09/070924092553.htm.

# ABOUT THE AUTHORS

## Trisha Parker

Trisha began her professional life working as a teen model in southern California and was a finalist in the Miss Teen USA contest. After working in both print ads and television, she moved to New York and worked as a flight attendant. During this time she became engaged to John Parker, a young man she had first met in high school, who was serving in the United States Air Force. After their wedding, Trisha and John began married life in San Antonio, Texas, where she got her first taste of finance while working at a local bank. When John was deployed to Italy, she soon joined him and landed a job managing the base Officer's Club. After two years in Italy, they returned to southern California and settled down to start a family. They were blessed when Trisha gave birth to their three sons, Michael, David, and Daniel.

As her family grew, so did her business career. Working her way up the ranks, she became one of the top compensation and benefits professionals in the country. She went on to hold executive positions, including vice president of compensation, benefits, and relocation, for two major corporations. In addition, she was elected president of her regional professional association and named to the board of directors of her national association.

Married for thirty-nine years, Trisha is an accomplished chef, seamstress, home decorator, and fitness enthusiast. She is most proud of her three sons, three daughters-in-law, and four grandchildren. She loves spending time with her family and is an avid travel adventurer, shopper, and bargain hunter. She is also a spiritual person and enjoys working on a variety of charitable projects. Most of all, Trisha is bright, beautiful, cheerful, and fun loving.

## John Parker

As a young man, John was an aspiring athlete and played winter baseball with the Los Angeles Angels before an arm injury ended that dream. In his early twenties, he attended college and pursued many diverse interests such as playing guitar in a band and becoming a licensed pilot. During the Vietnam War, John joined the United States Air Force and served as an intelligence analyst. While in the military, he married his long-time girlfriend Trisha Nystrom.

After John completed his tour of duty, he and Trisha returned to southern California where they settled down and raised their three sons. After finishing his B.A., he went on to complete his master's and doctorate degrees in organizational communication. Over the course of his career, John served on the faculties of several major institutions, including Pepperdine University, California State University in Los Angeles, the University of Southern California, and St. Mary's College of California. He also spent considerable time in the business world and was a founding partner in a successful management consulting firm that continues to operate to this day. As a management consultant and personal advisor, John has worked for numerous legal, corporate, and governmental organizations. As an author, John co-wrote the popular study skills text, *The Student Success Workbook*. He has also been a featured speaker for numerous organizations and a guest on several radio and television programs.

John is a devoted family man and enjoys sports, traveling, music, and photography.